THE COVENANT SEALED:
THE DEVELOPMENT OF PURITAN
SACRAMENTAL THEOLOGY
IN OLD AND NEW ENGLAND,
1570-1720

THE COVENANT SEALED:
THE DEVELOPMENT OF PURITAN
SACRAMENTAL THEOLOGY
IN OLD AND NEW ENGLAND,
1570-1720

E. BROOKS HOLIFIELD

NEW HAVEN AND LONDON, YALE UNIVERSITY PRESS, 1974

Copyright © 1974 by Yale University.
All rights reserved. This book may not be
reproduced, in whole or in part, in any form
(except by reveiwers for the public press),
without written permission from the publishers.
Library of Congress catalog card number: 73-92695
International standard book number: 0-300-01733-2(cloth)

Designed by Sally Sullivan
and set in Baskerville type.
Printed in the United States of America by
Vail-Ballou Press, Inc., Binghamton, N.Y.

Published in Great Britain, Europe, and Africa by
Yale University Press, Ltd., London.
Distributed in Latin America by Kaiman & Polon,
Inc., New York City; in Australasia and Southeast
Asia by John Wiley & Sons Australasia Pty. Ltd.,
Sydney; in India by UBS Publishers' Distributors Pvt.,
Ltd., Delhi; in Japan by John Weatherhill, Inc., Tokyo.

FOR IRENE AND ELMER HOLIFIELD

CONTENTS

PREFACE

In 1647 the English Independent Thomas Goodwin insisted that no one with "insight into the Controversies of these times" could overlook the "very high importance" of the many sacramental debates in England and New England.[1] Goodwin might well have added that no group exhibited greater concern about the sacraments than the Puritans, who wrote literally hundreds of sermons, meditations, and polemical treatises on baptism and the Lord's Supper. Yet there has been no attempt to describe and interpret the development of Puritan sacramental theory and practice throughout the seventeenth century.[2] It has been widely recognized that many Puritans became increasingly indifferent and hostile to sacraments. Geoffrey Nuttall has described the transformation of one stream of Puritanism into a Quaker movement that discarded both baptism and the Lord's Supper, and the Baptists obviously represented another serious challenge to traditional sacramental doctrine and practice.[3] But there was a momentous reaction within the Puritan tradition against the antisacramental mood. I attempt to trace the emergence during the seventeenth century of a Puritan "sacramentalism," a term to which I ascribe four specific meanings. It can refer to: (1) the efforts of Puritan theologians to use covenantal themes as a defense against Baptist attacks on infant baptism; (2) the attempts of a small group of Puritan intellectuals to reevaluate conventional Reformed doctrines of sacramental efficacy either by affirming baptismal regeneration or by otherwise stressing the importance of baptism for salvation, or by ascribing converting

1. Thomas Goodwin, "To the Reader," in John Cotton, *The Grounds and Ends of the Baptisme of the Children of the Faithfull* (London, 1647).

2. Horton Davies, *The Worship of the English Puritans* (London, 1948), has examined Puritan concerns about the sacramental liturgy.

3. Geoffrey Nuttall, *The Holy Spirit in Puritan Faith and Experience* (Oxford, 1946).

efficacy to the Lord's Supper; (3) the reaffirmation of a distinctively Calvinist doctrine of the Lord's Supper within Puritanism; (4) and finally, the growing inclination among a significant number of Puritan ministers to encourage a widespread sacramental piety through baptismal sermons and eucharistic meditations. The term "sacramentalism" should not be confused with the epithet "sacramentarian," which Lutherans invented to rebuke continental Reformed theologians for their allegedly low symbolic conception of sacraments. It should also be distinguished from Roman Catholic and Lutheran doctrine and piety, and from efforts within the Church of England to retain traditional sacramental rituals and ceremonies, which Puritans of every variety opposed. Moreover, the term does not designate a homogeneous, self-conscious movement: a Puritan minister who zealously opposed the denigration of sacraments by Baptists and Quakers might just as zealously attack other Puritan clergymen for stating too strongly the doctrine of sacramental efficacy. Though I define Puritanism broadly and include Baptists and Quakers within the Puritan spectrum, I say little about the Baptists and nothing about the Quakers, who repudiated sacramentalism in any form. I concentrate instead on the debates about baptism and the Lord's Supper, and the devotional writings, that illuminate the variety of efforts in the large central stream of seventeenth-century Puritanism to combine Reformed theology and a vital sacramental piety.[4]

In its initial form, my study traced a doctrinal development. In the process of revising the manuscript for publication, I became increasingly aware that sacramental discussions revealed some of the enduring and fundamental presuppositions of Puritan thought. Implicit in the debates and the devotional manuals were crucial assumptions about finitude and infinity, spirit and flesh, reason and the senses. With each revision, my doctrinal history gradually transformed itself into an expanded discourse on Puritan piety and intellect, though the sacramental focus remains.

The Puritans sometimes withheld the Lord's Supper from those who lacked the gratitude deemed fitting for a meal of thanksgiving. Having benefitted from the gracious encouragement and assistance of many friends, I can understand that particular expression of Puritan rigor. I am especially grateful to Edmund Morgan, Trygve Skarsten, David Hall, William Mallard, Manfred Hoffmann, and Paul Laughlin for critical comments and constructive suggestions. Mr. Jim Heaney of

4. My main accent falls on intellectual developments within the Puritan tradition that produced the Westminster and Savoy Confessions and that dominated the four commonwealths in Massachusetts and Connecticut.

Yale Press was extraordinarily helpful. I owe a special debt to Sydney Ahlstrom for his continuing criticism and support and for his willingness to share his many insights into the intricacies of Puritan theology. Dean James Laney of Candler has helped to provide research grants to facilitate the writing, as has the University Research Committee at Emory. And my wife, Vicky, has been a perceptive critic of style and content, as well as a patient and understanding companion. For my errors, of course, I alone must assume the responsiblty; that, too, I have learned from the Puritans.

Several libraries have provided invaluable assistance: the Yale Beinecke Library, Yale Divinity School, Union Theological Seminary in New York, the Presbyterian Historical Association, the New York Public Library, the Boston Public Library, the American Antiquarian Association, the libraries of Harvard University, the Emory University Woodruff Research Library, and the library of Emory's Candler School of Theology.

Brief portions of chapters four and seven appeared in *The New England Quarterly* [45 (1972)] and *The William and Mary Quarterly* [3rd series, 29 (1972)]. I am grateful for permission to use material published in those journals. I note also that several titles have been abbreviated throughout the footnotes: the *Transactions* of the Congregational Historical Society as *CHST;* the *Dictionary of National Biography* as *DNB;* the Massachusetts Historical Society *Collections* as *MHSC;* the Massachusetts Historical Society *Proceedings* as MHSP; and the *Publications* of the Colonial Society of Massachusetts as *PCSM*.

1

THE CONTINENTAL BACKGROUND

In 1520 Martin Luther sharply challenged the entire sacramental system of medieval Christendom, but within five years he was struggling to save the sacraments themselves from radical reformers who wished to push beyond externals into a realm of pure spirit. The change reflected the momentum of the Reformation and illustrated the centrality of the sacraments in sixteenth-century worship and theology. The three great divisions of Protestantism during the century were inextricably entangled with sacramental issues. After the Marburg Colloquy of 1529 failed to resolve disagreements over the Lord's Supper, distinctive Lutheran and Reformed traditions slowly developed. The two groups soon discovered other points of tension, but the Eucharist was the prime symbol of their disunity. After 1525 there appeared a third vital movement: the Anabaptists. Though preoccupied mainly with the purity of the Church as a spiritual fellowship of believers, they were appropriately identified by their sacramental practice. They and their adversaries recognized that baptismal and eucharistic theologies were a clue to and a central element in a wide range of theological and political convictions. Shifts in sacramental theory and practice were invariably related to broader intellectual changes which no sixteenth-century churchman could ignore.

The English Puritans were heirs of the Reformed tradition, and their sacramental theology was essentially an adaptation of earlier Reformed doctrine. Ulrich Zwingli and Heinrich Bullinger in Zurich, John Calvin and Theodore Beza in Geneva, John Oecolampadius in Basel, and Martin Bucer in Strassburg—these men laid the foundation for Puritan doctrine. The Puritans admired them for both their theological precision and their piety. There were two convictions underlying Reformed piety that would persistently inform Puritan sacramental thought: first, that Christian life was an affair of the spirit; and second, that the finite could not coerce, comprehend, or contain the infinite.

The Swiss reformers were deeply offended at the sensual corporeality of a medieval Catholic liturgy that was resplendent with elaborate ceremonial, sacred statuary, rich painting, and colorful images of the saints. For such external splendor, so alluring to man's carnal nature, the Reformed theologians proposed to substitute spiritual worship. It was only fitting that God, who was Spirit, be worshipped solely in spirit and truth, and Calvin contrasted the "spiritual truth" of the Reformed liturgy to the "splendid show" of Rome, tainted by "corporeal figures." [1] Calvin clearly assumed that religion, properly understood, was an affair of mind and spirit, an assumption reflecting the humanist heritage that he shared with the other prominent Reformed leaders. As humanists, the Swiss reformers affirmed a metaphysical contrast between spirit and flesh. Reformed sacramental doctrine thus rested on the supposition that matter and spirit were fundamentally antithetical, a conviction that rendered problematic any profoundly sacramental understanding of Christian religion. How after all could corporeal elements and visible actions convey spiritual life and grace?

The Puritans shared also the second conviction underlying Reformed piety: that the finite could not contain the infinite. The phrase *finitum non capax infiniti* eventually became a commonplace in orthodox Reformed dogmatics. Historians of doctrine have debated about its importance in Calvin's theology, and their recent research suggests that we must not transform the phrase into a philosophical axiom determining the character of early Reformed theological formulations. It was, rather, an expression of piety: the Swiss theologians believed it irreverent to ignore the infinite distance between the Creator and the creature. Reverence for a holy God and his utterly incomparable nature entailed the sharpest possible distinction between God and man. Reformed theologians recoiled from any suggestion that finitude embodied infinity, as the Lutherans affirmed, or that finite man could advance any claim limiting an infinite God, as Catholics were alleged to believe. That kind of piety was not without consequence; it affected epistemology, soteriology, and Christology all in ways that were relevant to sacramental doctrine. The finite mind, which required the special assistance of the Holy Spirit even to grasp God's partial self–revelation in Scripture, could never penetrate the

1. John Calvin, *The Necessity of Reforming the Church*, in *Calvin: Theological Treatises*, ed. J. K. S. Reid, vol. 22, *Library of Christian Classics*, ed. John Baillie, John McNeill, and Henry P. Van Dusen (Philadelphia, 1954), pp. 191–93.

divine essence. The finite volition could never influence the divine will. And finite human nature, even the human nature of Christ, could not, despite Lutheran claims to the contrary, embody the infinite divine nature. Wary, then, of presuming to limit an illimitable deity, Calvin and Zwingli and their successors were inclined to devaluate tangible and visible sacraments, whether considered as instruments of grace or as means of comprehending the divine purpose and will.[2]

Yet Reformed theologians were by no means of one mind. Some would say that sacraments might in modest and appropriate ways reduce the distance between God and man and that physical sacramental elements were in fact instrumental means of spiritual communion with Christ. In contrast to the early views of Zwingli, for instance, Calvin defined baptism as a seal of a divine promise and thus a clue to the mysterious purposes of God. Unlike Zwingli again, he affirmed a real spiritual presence of the substance of Christ's body and blood in the Lord's Supper. So the Reformed tradition offered alternative accounts of the sacraments, though Calvin and Bullinger produced in 1549 a formula of consensus for uniting the Reformed churches. That formula provided an important guide for Puritan teaching and practice, but basic issues remained unresolved. Matter and spirit, finite and infinite—these dichotomies would persist in Reformed and Puritan sacramental discussion.

The shifts and transformations of Puritan sacramental thought and practice cannot, however, be divorced from other characteristically Puritan preoccupations, or, for that matter, from the social and political experiences of pastors and congregations. Attitudes toward sacraments varied according to differences of opinion about Church and Scripture, or eschatology and election. In addition, some Puritans formulated their baptismal doctrine not only in terms of their longing for a heavenly kingdom but also with an eye to the realities of daily

2. For recent discussion of this issue, see E. David Willis, *Calvin's Catholic Christology* (Leiden, 1966), pp. 3–7; Willis demonstrates that the *finitum non capax infiniti* is not a philosophical principle determining Calvin's Christology. See also G. C. Berkouwer, *The Person of Christ* (Grand Rapids, Mich., 1954), p. 282; Werner Elert, "Über die Herkunft des Satzes *Finitum infiniti non capax,*" *Zeitschrift für Systematische Theologie* 16 (1939) : 500–04; Friedrich Loofs, "Christologie," *Realencyklopädie für protestantische Theologie und Kirche* (Leipzig, 1898), 4 : 54. For my own broader use of the phrase as an expression of Reformed piety I am indebted to two books by I. A. Dorner—*History of Protestant Theology,* trans. George Bobson (Edinburg, 1871), 1 : 324–38; and *History of the Development of the Doctrine of the Person of Christ,* trans. D. W. Simon (Edinburg, 1866), 2.2 : 136–37, 407. For the use of the phrase in later Reformed dogmatics, see Heinrich Heppe, *Reformed Dogmatics Set Out and Illustrated from the Sources,* ed. Ernst Bizer, trans. G. T. Thomson (London, 1950), pp. 432 ff.

political life in England and New England. And their celebration of
the Lord's Supper often reflected not only their need for inward spiritual assurance but also their desire for a moral order in the social
relationships among their countrymen. Nevertheless, they never ceased
to remember the doctrinal controversies among their continental predecessors, and they consistently declared their allegiance to the Reformed consensus.

Lutheran and Reformed

Sacraments had provoked controversy among Christians ever since
Paul rebuked the church at Corinth for irregularities at the Lord's
Supper (1 Cor. 11 : 20–34). The rudiments of medieval baptismal doctrine emerged in the course of contention between Augustine and the
Donatists in the early fifth century.[3] Roman eucharistic dòctrine was
shaped by ninth-century debates that erupted when Radbertus of Cor-
bie in France affirmed a sacramental transmutation producing the
natural body and blood of Christ in the Lord's Supper. In the Fourth
Lateran Council of 1215 the Church decided officially that the substance of the bread and wine was transmuted into the body and blood
of Christ, but neither this definition of transubstantiation nor later
explanations of the seven sacraments at the Council of Florence in
1439 could put an end to controversy. Fifteenth-century theologians
continued earlier disputes between the Dominicans, who argued that
the sacraments themselves contained and conveyed grace, and the
Franciscans, who said that God conferred grace directly whenever the
sacraments were administered. Sacramental controversy was no innovation of sixteenth-century reformers.

To many men, however, it seemed that the sacraments could not
survive the comprehensive Protestant attack on traditional doctrine.
As early as 1518, Martin Luther denied the Catholic belief that sacraments conveyed grace by their own inherent power, and in *The Babylonian Captivity of the Church* in 1520 he revealed the revolutionary
sacramental implications of his new understanding of the gospel.
He asserted that Scripture knew only one sacrament, the Word of
Christ communicated through external signs, though he was willing to
define a sacrament more narrowly as a promise with a sign attached.
Such a definition was hardly comforting to his Roman opponents, for
Luther proceeded to deprive confirmation, ordination, marriage, and

3. Augustine rejected the Donatist claim that sacraments administered by sinful
clergy were invalid.

extreme unction of their sacramental character, and he cast doubt on penance, the fifth of the traditional seven sacraments. That left only baptism and the Lord's Supper, both of which Luther redefined.

Baptism, he said, did not impart its grace *ex opere operato,* that is, by the power of its own operation. The substance of baptism was the divine promise: "He who believes and is baptized will be saved." The benefit of the baptismal washing depended on faith in that word of promise. To seek the efficacy of the sacrament "apart from the promise and apart from faith" was to labor in vain.[4] To his opponents it seemed that Luther was sacrificing the objective sacrament to the subjective experience of faith, but in 1528, after Anabaptists proposed radical alterations in baptismal doctrine, he reaffirmed that baptism as a Word and Work of God was a true sacrament even in the absence of faith.[5] Luther now criticized any separation of the divine promise from its external sign. He insisted that God was active in and through the tangible and visible element and could even speak of the Word of God as being "in and with" the water of baptism, blessing and sanctifying it as a means of grace and the bearer of God's own glory.[6] The Lutheran Augsburg Confession (1530) therefore claimed that baptism was necessary to salvation, and it condemned the Anabaptists for saying that children were saved without the sacrament.[7]

In Zurich, however, Ulrich Zwingli, pastor of the Great Minster since 1519, met the Anabaptist challenge in quite another way. Trained as a humanist, Zwingli leaned toward a highly spiritualistic understanding of the gospel. In 1523 he was prepared to accept a radical devaluation of external sacraments: himself "deceived" for a time by Anabaptist doctrine, he "thought it better not to baptize children until they came to years of discretion." [8] He changed his mind in 1524,

4. Martin Luther, *The Babylonian Captivity of the Church,* in *Word and Sacrament II,* ed. A. R. Wentz, vol. 36, *Luther's Works* (American Edition), ed. Jaroslav Pelikan and Helmut T. Lehmann (Philadelphia, 1959), pp. 58, 66–67.

5. Martin Luther, *Concerning Rebaptism,* in *Church and Ministry II,* ed. Conrad Bergendoff, vol. 40, *Luther's Works,* p. 246.

6. Martin Luther, *Large Catechism,* in *Luther's Catechetical Writings,* ed. John Lenker (Minneapolis, 1907), p. 160. See also Martin Luther, *Small Catechism,* in *Luther's Catechetical Writings,* p. 28.

7. In Philip Schaff, ed., *The Creeds of Christendom,* (Grand Rapids, Mich., 1966), 3 : 13. See the discussions of Luther's doctrine of baptism in Paul Althaus, *Die Theologie Martin Luthers* (Gütersloh, 1962), pp. 297–318; Jaroslav Pelikan, *Spirit Versus Structure: Luther and the Institutions of the Church* (New York, 1968), pp. 76–97; Harald Diem, "Zum Verständnis der Taufe bei Luther," *Evangelische Theologie* 2 (1935) : 403–20.

8. Ulrich Zwingli, *Of Baptism,* in *Zwingli and Bullinger,* ed. G. W. Bromiley, vol. 24, *The Library of Christian Classics* (Philadelphia, 1953), p. 139.

whereupon he began planning a treatise to confute the Swiss Anabaptists, but his defense of infant baptism revealed a continuing suspicion of tangible means of grace.

The key to Zwingli's defense of the sacrament was a definition of baptism as a covenantal sign or seal (for all practical purposes, the two terms were synonymous in Zwingli's theology, the word *seal* coming from Romans 4 : 11, where Paul called circumcision "a seal of the righteousness of faith"). According to Genesis 17 : 1–14, God had entered into covenant with Abraham and his seed and thus with the whole people of Israel. The sign of the covenant was circumcision, which signified Abraham's duty to lead his offspring to God, and Zwingli saw in that sign a proleptic demand and justification for infant baptism. Christians, he said, were also under covenant with God, and their new covenant was in substance continuous with the covenant of Abraham, since both pointed in different ways to the same Christ. Baptism, in turn, according to Colossians 2 : 11–12, was the Christian analogue of circumcision. Therefore God's command that Abraham's children be circumcised was sufficient reason for Christians to baptize their children. And since children were included in the covenant with their parents, there was no reason to deprive them of the sign of that which they already possessed.[9]

Zwingli strongly emphasized the communal character of sacraments, being careful to point out that the faith sealed by circumcision (Rom. 4 : 11) was not the "trust and faith that every individual has in his heart," but rather the faith of the church.[10] He did not expound, in other words, an individualistic or entirely subjective doctrine of baptism, but he failed to develop the sacramental implications latent in the covenant motif. When Luther called the sacrament a covenantal seal, he meant that baptism visibly ratified and guaranteed God's promises, as a royal seal authenticated a government document on which it was inscribed. Only secondarily was baptism a pledge of obedience by men. For Zwingli, however, the sacrament was primarily "a covenant sign which indicates that all those who receive it are willing to amend their lives and to follow Christ." The anthropocentric character of his baptismal doctrine was clearly expressed in Zwingli's definition of the word *sacramentum* as a military oath:

> As used in this context the word sacrament means a covenant sign or pledge. If a man sews on a white cross, he proclaims that he is a Confederate. . . . Similarly the man who receives the mark of

9. Ulrich Zwingli, *Huldreich Zwinglis Sämtliche Werke IV*, ed. Emil Egli et al., vol. 91, *Corpus Reformatorum* (Leipzig, 1927), pp. 292–95.
10. Ibid., p. 621.

baptism is the one who is resolved to hear what God says to him, to learn the divine precepts and to live his life in accordance with them.

The recipients of baptism, both infants and adults, were pledged and dedicated to God by the Church. It made no difference if they were unable to offer a conscious pledge, for baptism was only an initiatory sign, like a cowl for initiates into a monastic order. "They do not know the rules and statutes when the cowls are made, but they learn them in their cowls." [11] So also, the baptizand would eventually understand his baptismal obligations.

There were two reasons for Zwingli's reluctance to speak of baptism as more than a sign of obligation. First, awed by the mystery of election, he refused to bind God to external means of grace: "For we give outward teaching and the baptism of water. But God moves inwardly according to his own sovereign choice." No creaturely activity could sway the decision of a majestically transcendent Creator. No mere sacrament could in any degree overcome the distance between God and man. Second, Zwingli believed that the Spirit acted directly on the souls of men without the mediation of material instruments. Implicit in that belief was a devaluation of external means, which, he said, could "never cleanse the soul." In effect, Zwingli divided the world into material and spiritual spheres which could never intersect, and then he located Christian existence solely in the realm of spirit. Consequently, internal spiritual baptism, constituted by an immediate relation between the Spirit of God and the spirit of man, was not necessarily related to the external water baptism. Zwingli's presuppositions left little room for baptismal efficacy. In 1525 he even denied that the sacrament could strengthen faith: "It does not justify the one who is baptized, nor does it confirm his faith, for it is not possible for an external thing to confirm faith." [12] By 1531, the year of his death, Zwingli acknowledged that sacraments could augment faith, but even then he held a baptismal doctrine far different from Luther's.[13]

By 1531, in fact, their differing sacramental views had temporarily shattered hopes for consensus and political union between the followers of Luther and Zwingli. The divisive issue, however, was not baptism but the Lord's Supper. Both Luther and Zwingli reacted against the traditional Roman Catholic doctrine of the mass, but their dissent led them to dissimilar conclusions. The ensuing controversies

11. Zwingli, *Of Baptism*, pp. 141, 131, 141.
12. Ibid., pp. 163, 153–54, 138.
13. Ulrich Zwingli, *An Exposition of the Faith*, in *Zwingli and Bullinger*, p. 264.

underlined the importance of sacramental theology as a clue to the distinguishing characteristics of Reformed doctrine, as debate over the Eucharist uncovered conflicting views on a variety of topics, including sacramental grace, Christology, and biblical hermeneutics.

When Luther set out in 1520 to rescue the sacraments from their "captivity" at the hands of the Roman curia, he criticized the Catholic conception of the mass as a meritorious sacrifice, the withholding of wine from lay communicants, and the doctrine of transubstantiation. But he still affirmed that the sacrament contained a real bodily presence of Christ and conveyed an objective gift of divine forgiveness. After 1521 he placed increasing emphasis on the real presence. Bohemian theologians raised the issue, and a Dutchman named Cornelius Hoen attracted a following by arguing that in the words of institution—"This is my body"—is (est) should be interpreted as signifies (significat).[14] Luther's long-time friend Andreas Carlstadt, pastor at Orlamunde near Wittenberg, advanced another symbolic interpretation of the sacrament in 1524 and, after being expelled from Saxony, expounded his views in Strassburg. Some of the preachers there were sympathetic, and the city council requested a judgment from both Luther and Zwingli, thus inaugurating a long and acrimonious debate.

As early as 1523 Zwingli had begun to move away from Roman doctrine, first by denouncing transubstantiation as logically inconsistent and by rejecting a sacrificial interpretation of the mass, then by stressing with Erasmus of Rotterdam the spirituality of Christ's presence, and finally, after reading Hoen's letter, by coming to regard the sacrament as a memorial, an occasion for remembering the mediatorial activity of Christ. Before the end of 1525 he published his reply to the Strassburg council, along with an earlier letter to a German Lutheran pastor in which he had directly attacked Luther's doctrine. In the following year, Luther labeled Zwingli and Carlstadt as heads of a new pernicious sect. The sacrament of Christian unity had split the Reformation.[15]

Protestant princes viewed the disarray with foreboding, and Philip of Hesse sought a united front against papal and imperial forces, though initially without success. In 1528, however, Martin Bucer, the Strassburg reformer, urged Philip to try again, and the result was a colloquy between Lutheran and Zwinglian theologians at Marburg in

---

14. Cornelisz Hoen, "A Most Christian Letter," in Forerunners of the Reformation, ed. Heiko A. Oberman (New York, 1966), p. 296. See also Hans Grass, Die Abendmahlslehre bei Luther und Calvin (Gütersloh, 1954), pp. 29 ff.

15. Walther Koehler, Zwingli und Luther. Ihr Streit über das Abendmahl nach seinen politischen und religiösen Beziehungen, 2 vols. (Gütersloh, 1924–53), 1 : 22–75, 304 ff.

1529. After three days of debate, they completed a statement of agreement on fourteen doctrines. But article fifteen acknowledged their inability to agree "as to whether the true body and blood are bodily present in the bread and wine." [16] There would be other attempts at union, but after Marburg the lines began to harden between Lutherans and the "Reformed" churches rooted in Zurich, Strassburg, and Geneva.

Lutherans designated the Reformed theologians as "sacramentarians," thus intending to rebuke them for their low doctrine of the Lord's Supper. Behind the rebuke were several unresolved issues, the first being a disagreement over the nature of divine grace and its conveyance to sinful men. Luther believed that the Lord's Supper was "a treasure through and in which we obtain the forgiveness of sins," [17] and he feared that Zwingli had robbed it of its objectively gracious character, turning it instead into an occasion for a subjective exercise in human cognition. Luther felt no incongruity in linking corporeality with spiritual grace. For him, forgiveness of sins was bound up with the doctrine of physical presence: "Without the body and blood of Christ, the new testament would not be there. Without the new testament, forgiveness of sins would not be there." [18] The central sacramental reality was the Word offering forgiveness, and not the mere bodily presence. But as Luther saw it, to deny the presence was in fact to repudiate the Word, which proclaimed explicitly that the body and blood were present.[19]

His concern for sacramental grace thus led Luther into an intricate discussion of the physical realities in the Eucharist, and three of his conclusions especially offended Zwingli. First, there was, according to Luther, a real union between the physical body and blood of Christ and the external elements of bread and wine. Christ was present not simply in the celebration but also in the elements themselves. Luther was willing to dispense with such terms as "in," "with," and "under," but not the mystical union they expressed. This entailed the further conclusion that the body and blood of Christ were received through the mouth, though this *manducatio oralis* did not preclude a spiritual eating: "The mouth eats the body of Christ physically. . . . But the

16. Hermann Sasse, *This is My Body: Luther's Contention for the Real Presence in the Sacrament of the Altar* (Minneapolis, 1959), p. 272.

17. Luther, *Large Catechism*, p. 177.

18. Martin Luther, *Confession Concerning Christ's Supper*, in *Word and Sacrament III*, ed. Robert H. Fischer, vol. 37, *Luther's Works*, p. 338. See also Koehler, *Zwingli und Luther*, 1 : 638 ff; and Pelikan, *Spirit and Structure*, p. 122.

19. Martin Luther, *Against the Heavenly Prophets in the Matter of Images and Sacraments*, in *Church and Ministry II*, pp. 210, 214.

heart grasps the words in faith and eats spiritually precisely the same body as the mouth eats physically." [20] And this, in turn, meant that everyone who received the bread and wine, be he saint or sinner, received the body and blood. Christ's flesh was "of no avail to the godless"; it was, as Paul said, "poison and death" when eaten without faith.[21] But the presence of Christ was not contingent on the worthiness of either the communicant or the administrator; the Word and power of God were not subject to the wavering uncertainties of human holiness.

To Zwingli such affirmations were both false and irrelevant to salvation. He believed that the true Christian lived in the realm of the spirit, exalted above the material and fleshly. Spiritual grace had no connection with corporeal realities. "For how could the physical flesh either nourish or give life to the soul?" The Spirit alone awakened and sustained the soul's vitality. Had not Christ taught that the flesh profited nothing? Certainly it was fair to conclude that "to eat the flesh profiteth nothing." [22] That entailed not only the denial of a physical presence but also the repudiation of any suggestion that material elements of bread and wine could themselves transmit spiritual grace.

The sacrament, then, did not convey forgiveness of sins; it rather offered an occasion for joyful remembrance and thanksgiving by the faithful community. The bread and wine constituted "a figure, a memorial" of Christ's death and "of the blood of the new testament which was shed for us."

[We speak of the bread and wine as a] representation and memorial of his body and blood, just as a faithful wife, whose husband has left her a ring as a keepsake, frequently refers to the ring as her husband, saying: This is my late husband, although what she means is that it recalls her husband.[23]

Zwingli did sometimes talk of a spiritual presence of Christ in the sacrament, and in the course of his long controversy with Luther, he acknowledged that the faithful communicant might "spiritually" eat Christ's body.[24] But he retained a highly subjective notion of sacra-

20. Martin Luther, *That These Words of Christ, "This is my Body," Etc., Still Stand Firm Against the Fanatics,* in *Word and Sacrament III,* p. 93.
21. Luther, *Confession Concerning Christ's Supper,* p. 238.
22. Ulrich Zwingli, *On the Lord's Supper,* in *Zwingli and Bullinger,* pp. 206, 210.
23. Ibid., pp. 229, 234.
24. Zwingli, *An Exposition of the Faith,* p. 254. See also Koehler, *Zwingli und Luther,* 1 : 483, 489, 671, 826; 2 : 117, 136; and Ernst Bizer, *Studien zur Geschichte des Abendmahlsstreits im 16. Jahrhundert* (Gütersloh, 1940), pp. 41 ff.

mental eating, equating it simply with faith. To feed on Christ's body, he said in 1526, was "to believe in him who was given up to death on our behalf." [25] In 1531, two years after the Marburg Colloquy, Zwingli still used the same language: "To eat the body of Christ spiritually is equivalent to trusting with heart and soul upon the mercy and goodness of God through Christ." [26]

The Lord's Supper was more for Zwingli than a bare memorial, but his characteristic tense was the past. And when he spoke of the present, he was inclined toward a subjectivism that was balanced only by his vivid sense of the corporate nature of eucharistic celebration.[27] He did finally grant that the sacraments could augment faith,[28] a power he had earlier denied them, but he continued to reject the "delusion that the bread is flesh and the wine blood, and that we partake of the flesh and blood really or essentially." Such a "delusion," said Zwingli, was incompatible with the nature of Christ himself, a claim that angered Luther and illuminated the distinctive Christology of the Reformed tradition. Zwingli claimed that the real presence was impossible in view of the creedal affirmation that Christ ascended to the right hand of God in heaven. His divine nature was omnipresent, but Christ's human nature, which comprehended his physical body, was subject to the natural limitations of the flesh, including its restriction to a circumscribed locality.[29] Humanity could not embody the properties of divinity; finitude could not embody infinity.

Luther thought that Zwingli's objection resulted from a faulty Christology. Since humanity and divinity were perfectly united in the Person of Christ, Luther said, "Christ must also be a man wherever he is God." [30] A mutual interchange of properties, a *communicatio idiomatum,* between the divine and human natures gave to Christ's humanity the divine property of ubiquity. Luther affirmed the Ascension, but he would not define heaven or God's right hand as "a particular place where Christ's body is seated," preferring to speak of it as "the almighty power of God, which at one and the same time can be nowhere and yet must be everywhere." [31] A proper Christology,

25. Zwingli, *On the Lord's Supper,* p. 198. See also Koehler, *Zwingli und Luther,* 1 : 671; 2 : 136.
26. Zwingli, *An Exposition of the Faith,* p. 258.
27. The corporate character of Zwingli's sacramental doctrine is discussed in Jacques Courvoisier, *Zwingli: A Reformed Theologian* (Richmond, 1963), pp. 76–77; and Julius Schweizer, *Reformierte Abendmahlsgestaltung in der Schau Zwinglis* (Basel, 1954), pp. 84 ff., 91 ff.
28. Zwingli, *An Exposition of the Faith,* p. 263.
29. Zwingli, *On the Lord's Supper,* pp. 186, 214.
30. Luther, *Confession Concerning Christ's Supper,* p. 229.
31. Luther, *That These Words,* pp. 57, 63.

then, was entirely consistent with the real presence. Zwingli responded that Luther confused the two natures of Christ, thus falling prey to the ancient Monophysite heresy. The *communicatio idiomatum,* he said, was simply an *alloiosis,* a figure of speech attributing to one nature the qualities of the other for rhetorical effect. An adequate Christology would ensure that "the proper character of each nature must be left intact, and we ought to refer to it only those things which are proper to it." Luther charged that this was a heretical Nestorian doctrine, the separation of the two natures of Christ.[32]

But if the body of Christ were present everywhere, Zwingli asked, why not seek him in stones? Would this not be a perfectly logical, albeit irreverent, conclusion from Luther's premises? In reply Luther pointed to the Word, thereby uncovering still another point of contention. "He is present everywhere," Luther said, "but he does not wish that you grope for him everywhere. Grope rather where the Word is, and there you will lay hold of him in the right way." [33] For both reformers, of course, Scripture was the last recourse, yet exegesis failed to produce a consensus because Luther and Zwingli held opposing hermeneutical principles. Luther thought that the Spirit revealed itself in and through the external words of the Scripture. A Biblical text such as "This is my body" was, therefore, to be taken literally unless the text itself or another clear and compelling passage indicated otherwise, or unless it contradicted an article of faith. In the end all rested on "the natural words and meanings of the Scriptures." For Zwingli, on the other hand, the Spirit acted directly upon the minds of men, enabling them properly to interpret each verse of Scripture in the light of other passages. He distinguished the Letter from the Spirit and insisted that it was inadvisable to adhere so closely to the literal sense. Zwingli explained the words of institution on the basis of John 6 : 63, which taught that the flesh profited nothing and that the Spirit gave life. The spirit of the Scriptures, he concluded, supported Hoen's figurative interpretation.[34]

In view of these differences over sacramental grace, Christology,

32. Zwingli, *On the Lord's Supper,* p. 213; see also Koehler, *Zwingli und Luther,* 1 : 479; and Luther, *Confession Concerning Christ's Supper,* p. 216.

33. Martin Luther, *The Sacrament of the Body and Blood of Christ—Against the Fanatics,* in *Word and Sacrament II,* p. 342.

34. Luther, *That These Words,* p. 32. For Luther's hermeneutical principles, see Jaroslav Pelikan, *Luther the Expositor: Introduction to the Reformer's Exegetical Writings* (St. Louis, 1959). See also Zwingli, *On the Lord's Supper,* p. 225; Sasse, *This Is My Body,* pp. 144 ff.; and Helmut Gollwitzer, "Zur Auslegung von Joh. 6 Bei Luther und Zwingli," in *In Memoriam Ernst Lohmeyer,* ed. Werner Schmauch (Stuttgart, 1951), pp. 143–68.

and hermeneutics, both Luther and Zwingli recognized the unlikelihood of a reconciliation. In the Lutheran Augsburg Confession, prepared by Philip Melanchthon in 1530, there was no trace of a concession to the Swiss viewpoint. Nevertheless, some of the Reformers refused to abandon hope for agreement. At Marburg Zwingli's chief supporter, John Oecolampadius, argued that the figure, or trope, in the words of institution belonged to the predicate, "body," rather than to the copula, "is," but both Luther and Zwingli agreed that the result was essentially Zwinglian. At Strassburg, meanwhile, Martin Bucer sought a basis for union in the statement that the outward reception of bread and wine was accompanied by an inward spiritual reception of the body and blood of Christ through faith. Bucer's proposals invariably lacked clarity, but he did say that the body and blood were "exhibited" with, though not in, the bread and wine, and he affirmed a spiritual eating that was not simply identical with faith.[35]

At Zurich in 1536, Heinrich Bullinger, along with other Swiss divines, drew up an authoritative Helvetic Confession which went beyond Zwingli in its emphasis on the "true communication" of Christ's body and blood.[36] Partly on the basis of this document, Bucer and other South German ministers worked out an agreement with Luther known as the Wittenberg Concord (1536). The Concord was a fragile instrument, for Luther and Bucer interpreted its terminology differently, Bucer still believing that the faithless received only bread and wine.[37] Nevertheless, there were other indicators that the gap could be bridged. In 1540 Melanchthon prepared an edition of the Augsburg Confession in which he removed one explicit reference to the presence and changed the remainder of the text to teach that the body and blood of Christ were "exhibited" (rather than "distributed") to communicants, "with" (instead of "under") the bread and wine—a statement acceptable to many Reformed theologians.[38] Thus, when John Calvin began reflecting seriously on sacramental doctrine, agreement between Lutheran and Reformed theologians was not considered impossible.

35. Koehler, *Zwingli und Luther,* 1 : 122–23, 318–19, 540–41; 2 : 205, 211.

36. In Schaff, *Creeds of Christendom* 3 : 225.

37. Bizer, *Studien,* pp. 106. 118–19, 127, Claimed that they were aware of their differences. Koehler felt that they were not. See *Zwingli und Luther,* 2 : 449; and Sasse, *This is My Body,* p. 310.

38. See J. Muller, ed., *Die symbolischen Bücher der evangelischlutherischen Kirche, deutsch und lateinisch* (Gütersloh, 1907), p. 41; and Robert Stupperich, ed., *Melanchthons Werke* (Gütersloh, 1955), 6 : 19.

John Calvin

Although in the 1536 edition of his *Institutes* Calvin rejected the doctrine of ubiquity, he was sympathetic to Luther's early doctrine. In a letter to his friend Guillaume Farel in 1540 he exalted Luther above Zwingli, and on the basis of Luther's testimony he refused for a time to read Zwingli and Oecolampadius. He probably remained unaware of Zwingli's later and stronger statements about the sacraments. Calvin's conceptions of the debate, and of the sacrament, were formed during a sojourn with Bucer at Strassburg between 1539 and 1541.[39] He accepted the Wittenberg Concord, but reluctantly, since it did not clearly preclude a *manducatio oralis*. He also accepted the Augsburg Confession, but only as modified by Melanchthon. Luther was expressly critical of Calvin's doctrine by 1540,[40] for it clearly presented an alternative both to Lutheran and to Zwinglian views of baptism and the Lord's Supper.

Calvin defined a sacrament as "a testimony of divine grace toward us, confirmed by an outward sign, with mutual attestation of our piety" toward God. Like Luther, he thought that the power of the sacrament came from the Word of promise which alone was a sufficient instrument of salvation; a sacrament was merely "a sort of appendix." Being adapted to human finitude, though, it provided a means of grasping the promise more firmly. Calvin therefore described sacraments as "seals," analogous to the seals authenticating "government documents and other public acts," and as "signs," graphically portraying God's "covenants" or promises.[41]

A product of humanist education, Calvin could appreciate and affirm Zwingli's elevation of the spirit over the flesh. He shared also

39. See Wilhelm Niesel, *Calvins Lehre vom Abendmahl* (München, 1935), pp. 30–39; Grass, *Die Abendmahlslehre*, p. 203; and François Wendel, *Calvin: The Origins and Development of his Religious Thought*, trans. Philip Mairet (London, 1963), pp. 329–34.

40. Grass, *Die Abendmahlslehre*, pp. 194–95. Luther and Calvin agreed that the Word and sacraments were the true marks of the Church, though some later Reformed theologians would modify or deny this. They also agreed that ordination was no sacrament, but they both retained the laying on of hands. See Althaus, *Die Theologie*, p. 286. Calvin felt that ordination was no "empty sign" when practiced with primitive purity. See John Calvin, *Institutes of the Christian Religion*, ed. John McNeill and trans. Ford Lewis Battles, vol. 21, *The Library of Christian Classics*, 2 vols. (Philadelphia, 1960), 4. 3. 16.

41. Calvin, *Institutes* 4. 13. 3–4; 4. 14. 1–4, 5–6. For a discussion of Calvin's terminology, see John Calvin, *Instruction in Faith*, ed. Paul Fuhrmann (London, 1949), p. 93, n. 223. See also John Calvin, *The Catechism of the Church of Geneva*, in *Calvin: Theological Treatises*, p. 131.

Zwingli's sense of the infinite distance between God and man. But his description of the baptismal seal indicated far greater sensitivity to sacramental worship: Calvin's doctrine of baptism differed from Zwingli's in three important ways. First, for Calvin God's promise of salvation rather than man's pledge of obedience was the substance of baptism, and he criticized Zwingli for suggesting that the sacrament was "nothing but a token and mark by which we confess our religion before men." [42] Baptism was primarily a divine gift designed to incorporate men into the Church and to reveal God's merciful intentions toward them; only secondarily was it a sign of confession before men. The initial movement was from God to man, and baptism confirmed the graciousness of the divine initiative. The visible sacrament could provide a modest clue to God's mysterious purposes.

Calvin taught, further, that baptism strengthened faith and "engrafted" the believer into the death of Christ as part of the process of sanctification. He disapproved of Zwingli's statement that "faith cannot be made better if it is already good" and told his readers that baptism offered an "increase of assurance": "As to the confirmation and increase of faith . . . I should . . . like my readers to be reminded that I assign this particular ministry to the sacraments." Sanctification, of course, was more than growth in faith; the process encompassed the Christian's gradual victory over all the vestiges of sin. Baptism, in turn, was more than a source of confirmation. Since God truly executed what he represented in the sacramental sign, it was one of the "instruments of the Spirit" with which God sanctified every area of a man's life. Calvin taught that faithful believers who held fast to the promise given in baptism could escape the dominion of sin.[43]

In calling a sacrament an instrument, Calvin moved even further away from Zwinglian doctrine. In baptism, he said, God does not "feed our eyes with a mere appearance only, but leads us to the present reality and effectively performs what it symbolizes." [44] Faith was the precondition of benefit from baptism, but faithlessness did not nullify the sacrament. Its truth was not dependent on the momentary subjective state of the recipient. "Although by Baptism wicked men are neither washed nor renewed, yet it retains that power so far as it is related to God, because although they reject the grace of God,

42. Calvin, *Institutes* 4. 15. 1.

43. Ibid., 4. 15. 15; 4. 14. 7, 9; 4. 15. 11. For the strong connection between the sacraments and sanctification in Calvin's doctrine see Alting von Geusau, *Die Lehre von der Kindertaufe bei Calvin* (Bilthoven, 1963), pp. 94, 129; and Joachim Beckmann, *Vom Sakrament bei Calvin* (Tubingen, 1926), p. 92.

44. Calvin, *Institutes* 4. 15. 14; 4. 14. 12.

still it is offered to them." [45] Defining the sacraments as instruments
was a way of emphasizing the reality and objectivity of baptism's
power.

Nevertheless, Calvin had difficulty integrating baptism into his
theology. He did not join Luther in seeking the Word "in" the water
and instructed his readers to look beyond "the visible element." He
repeatedly cautioned that baptism was of benefit only to the elect;
he repudiated emergency baptism; and he denied that the sacrament
was necessary for salvation. In fact, Calvin emphasized so strongly the
freedom of God in election that secondary means of salvation were
superfluous. The ground of election was hidden in the Divine Will:
we must "always at last return to the sole decision of God's will, the
cause of which is hidden in him." [46] Calvin frequently wrote as though
that detracted in no way from the sacrament, but elsewhere he acknowledged that he was not prepared to "bind the grace of God, or
the power of the Spirit, to external symbols." [47] Many received the
sign, but the Spirit was bestowed on none but the elect. Since the
sacrament had no efficacy without the Spirit, the reality of baptism,
Calvin acknowledged, would be "found only in a few." [48]

The tension emerged clearly in Calvin's doctrine of infant baptism.
Since faith was necessary for the perfection of baptism, and since infants could not demonstrate faith—only the elect among them would
ever persevere in it—why baptize infants at all? In the 1536 edition
of the *Institutes* Calvin joined Luther in attributing some kind of
faith to infants, but he dropped that idea after 1539.[49] He supported
infant baptism by various appeals to Scripture, noting the apostolic
practice of baptizing families and Jesus' command that infants be
brought to him. But Calvin's main argument for infant baptism was
based on the covenant motif, which first became prominent in his
sacramental theology in the 1538 edition of the *Geneva Catechism*.

> Indeed, it is most evident that the covenant which the Lord once
> made with Abraham [cf. Gen. 17 : 14] is no less in force today

45. John Calvin, *Commentaries on the Epistles to Timothy, Titus, and Philemon*,
ed. William Pringle (Grand Rapids, Mich, 1948), p. 333.
46. Calvin, *Institutes* 4. 14. 2; 4. 15. 20; 3. 23. 4.
47. John Calvin, *The Gospel According to St. John 1–10*, ed. D. W. Torrance and
T. F. Torrance, and trans. T. H. L. Parker (Edinburgh, 1959), P. 64; Calvin, *Commentaries on the First Book of Moses called Genesis*, trans. John King (Grand
Rapids, Mich, 1948), 1 : 458; Calvin, *Commentaries on the Epistles of Paul to the
Galatians and Ephesians*, trans. William Pringle (Grand Rapids, 1948), p. 320.
48. John Calvin, *Commentaries on the Catholic Epistles*, trans. John Owen (Grand
Rapids, Mich., 1948), p. 118.
49. von Geusau, *Die Lehre von der Kindertaufe*, p. 142.

for Christians than it was of old for the Jewish people. . . . Now
seeing that the Lord, immediately after making the covenant with
Abraham, commanded it to be sealed in infants by an outward
sacrament [Gen. 17 : 12], what excuse will Christians give for not
testifying and sealing it in their children today?

But though baptism "engrafted" children into the visible church, it
did not actually place them within the covenant. It simply testified
that they had been "born directly into the inheritance of the covenant." [50] Since the inheritance was ultimately destined only for the
elect, how could one say the testimony was reliable? Calvin confessed
that many children of faithful Christians would "thrust themselves
out of the holy progeny through their unbelief." [51] So even if infants
were, as Calvin often argued, baptized for future repentance and faith,
the sacrament itself offered no assurance that a child would in fact
believe.[52] Some subsequent Reformed theologians would find no justification for infant baptism outside of God's positive command; baptism would become an "ordinance" performed simply in obedience to
Christ. Others in the Reformed tradition would become Baptists.

Despite his difficulties with infant baptism, however, Calvin deplored the extreme antisacramental mood. His concern to maintain a
sensitivity to sacramental worship was manifest especially in his doctrine of the Lord's Supper, which exhibited a close affinity with Lutheran views. But Calvin shared the prevailing Reformed convictions
about flesh and spirit, finite and infinite. At three crucial points, therefore, he felt compelled to qualify his approval of Luther's doctrine.
He agreed with Zwingli, for instance, that the body of Christ "from
the time of his resurrection was finite, and is contained in heaven even
to the Last Day."

But what is the manner of the ascension itself? Is he not lifted up
on high before his disciples' very eyes? Do not the Evangelists
clearly relate that he was received into heaven? . . . But when he
is borne high into the air, and by the cloud beneath him teaches
us that he is no longer to be sought on earth, we safely infer that
his abode is now in heaven. . . .

After the ascension the body of Christ retained its human properties,
and Calvin would "let nothing inappropriate to human nature be

50. Calvin, *Institutes* 4. 16. 7, 6, 24. See von Geusau, *Die Lehre von der Kindertaufe*, p. 69.

51. John Calvin, *Commentary upon the Acts of the Apostles*, ed. Henry Beveridge
and trans. Christopher Fetherstone (Grand Rapids, Mich., 1949), 1 : 159.

52. Calvin, *Institutes* 4. 16. 20.

ascribed to his body, as happens when it is said either to be infinite
or to be put in a number of places at once." There was in a sense a
"communication of properties" between the divine and human natures of Christ, since both were united in Christ's Person; yet each
nature also maintained "unimpaired its own distinctive character."
Luther's Christology and his sacramental doctrine presupposed of
Christ's body "a ubiquity contrary to its nature." [53] The body of
Christ could not be physically present in the Lord's Supper.

As he accented in his Christology the distinction between the two
natures, one infinite, the other finite, so Calvin also, in contrast to
Luther, emphasized the distinction between the material sacramental
signs and the spiritual reality that they signified. He therefore differed
with Luther both about sacramental efficacy and about the presence
of Christ in the Lord's Supper. To connect the efficacy of the sacrament too intimately with the outward administration of bread and
wine was to limit the freedom of the Spirit. External elements were
instruments of grace only "wherever and whenever it pleases God,"
and to talk as if the sacramental presence bound Christ to earthly
things was to detract from his glory: "Let nothing be withdrawn from
Christ's heavenly glory—as happens when he is brought under the
corruptible elements of this world, or bound to any earthly creatures." [54] Calvin concluded that the Lutherans fell into a "delerious
fancy" when they said that the body of Christ was "not received unless it is introduced into the carnal mouth." [55] The spiritual presence
was not essentially related to the bread and wine, and therefore sacramental communion could not be the effect of a *manducatio oralis*.

A third characteristic of Calvin's polemic against the Lutherans was
his belief that fellowship with the Spirit was the precondition for receiving Christ in the sacrament. Christ could not "enter" into a faithless reprobate who was "devoid of his Spirit." Calvin was therefore
critical of Luther's claim that the wicked received the body and blood.
In the sacrament, he said, Christ offers his body and blood "to all in
general," but "because unbelievers bar the door to his liberality, they
do not receive what is offered." The doctrine of election prompted
this unequivocal rejection of the *manducatio impiorum*. The wicked
could not eat the flesh of Christ when it was not crucified for them,

53. Ibid., 4. 17. 26–27, 16–30. Niesel, *Calvins Lehre vom Abendmahl*, p. 77, argued
that Calvin did not conceive of heaven in spatial terms. But see Grass, *Die
Abendmahlslehre*, p. 233.

54. Calvin, *Institutes* 4. 14. 7; 4. 17. 19.

55. John Calvin, *The clear explanation of sound doctrine concerning the true
partaking of the flesh and blood of Christ in the Holy Supper*, in *Calvin: Theological Treatises*, p. 276.

or drink his blood when it was not shed to expiate their sins. Spiritual food was intended for spiritual men.[56]

By emphasizing the spirituality of communion, Calvin helped to lay the foundation for a markedly introspective sacramental piety. A rigorous insistence on preparation, including meticulous and careful self-examination, became characteristic of Reformed sacramental devotion. Calvin thought it mandatory that a communicant "examine himself" [57] to discover whether he possessed "a true repentance" and "a true faith in our Lord Jesus Christ," accompanied by a disposition of charity toward his neighbor.[58] Latent in this requirement was the possibility of a morbid introspection, and Lutherans charged that "timid consciences" were "murdered and driven to despair" by Calvin's teaching. Calvin pointed out that he did not require "perfection".[59] He admitted to communion candidates with imperfect faith and uneasy consciences, provided that they felt a "hope for salvation in Christ" and a desire to live according to "the rule of the gospel." [60] But though Calvin was no assassin of the tender conscience, he helped to establish an atmosphere that eventually caused many Reformed Christians to look upon the Lord's Supper with a sense of fear and foreboding.

Calvin stood in opposition to the Lutherans, then, in his insistence on the distance between Christ and the world, the distinction between the elements and the reality that they signified, and the "spirituality" of communion. But he did not think he had thus minimized the objective reality of Christ's presence and grace. The vanity of the reprobate, after all, did not nullify the effect of the sacrament. "It must not . . . be inferred . . . that when they reject what is given, they either make void the grace of Christ or detract at all from the efficacy of the Sacrament." [61] Against Zwingli's early doctrines, Calvin argued that communication rather than commemoration was the central feature of the Lord's Supper; he affirmed a substantial, though spiritual, presence of the whole Christ, both the divine and human natures; he accented the objective sacramental activity of the Holy Spirit as the medium of communion; and he attributed a genuine efficacy to the use of the sacrament.

For Calvin, as for Zwingli, the elements were signs reminding the

56. Ibid., pp. 285, 330.
57. Calvin, *Geneva Catechism*, p. 138.
58. John Calvin, *Short Treatise on the Holy Supper of our Lord and only Saviour Jesus Christ*, in *Calvin: Theological Treatises*, pp. 149–51.
59. Calvin, *The clear explanation*, p. 284.
60. Calvin, *Short Treatise*, p. 152.
61. Calvin, *The clear explanation*, p. 330.

communicant of God's redemptive activity, but he also believed that
they were "instruments," with which Christ truly presented to all and
effectually distributed to the faithful his body and blood. Zwingli and
Oecolampadius had failed to understand that sacramental elements
were "such signs that the reality is joined to them." They did not,
therefore, accurately perceive "the true communion which our Lord
gives us in his body and blood by the sacrament." [62] Calvin did not
believe that Christ was present in or under the bread and wine; he
espoused rather a subtle sacramental instrumentalism. At the same
time that the believer received the elements, he received the body
and blood, and—this was the crucial point—he received Christ precisely because the external signs were "testimonies and seals" that God
would inwardly perform "what the sacraments figure to the eyes." [63]

> If God cannot deceive or lie, it follows that he performs all that it
> signifies. We must then really receive in the Supper the body and
> blood of Jesus Christ, since the Lord there represents to us the
> communion of both. . . . We have then to confess that if the
> representation which God grants in the Supper is veracious, the
> internal substance of the sacrament is joined with the visible
> signs; and as the bread is distributed by hand, so the body of
> Christ is communicated to us, so that we are made partakers of
> it.[64]

Simply because God was trustworthy, the distribution of bread and
wine was invariably a communication to the faithful of the body and
blood, and in this sense the elements were efficacious instruments.
Calvin thought that the Lutherans obliterated the distinction between
sign and reality, but he did not wish to "divorce" the signs from
"their mysteries, to which they are so to speak attached," and he
feared that Zwingli had done just that.[65]

Moreover, Calvin refused to accept the suggestion in Zwingli's early
sacramental language that Christ was present only according to his
divine nature, or that the faithful were "partakers of the Spirit only."
In his 1537 *Confession of Faith concerning the Eucharist* the main
stress fell on Calvin's belief that the faithful received "the substance
of the body and blood of the Lord to everlasting life." [66]

> I do not restrict this union to the divine essence, but affirm that
> it belongs to the flesh and blood, inasmuch as it was not simply

62. Calvin, *Short Treatise,* pp. 147, 166.
63. Calvin, *The clear explanation,* p. 316.
64. Calvin, *Short Treatise,* p. 148.
65. Calvin, *Institutes* 4. 17. 5.
66. John Calvin, *Confession of Faith concerning the Eucharist,* in *Calvin: Theological Treatises,* p. 168.

said: My Spirit, but: My flesh is meat indeed; nor was it simply
said: My Divinity, but: My blood is drink indeed.[67]

It was not enough to receive Christ's divine Spirit; it was necessary
also "to partake of his humanity, in which he rendered complete
obedience to God his Father, to satisfy our debts." [68] The communication of Christ in the sacrament was a spiritual transaction, but the
faithful communicant received "the substance" of Christ and not his
"benefits" alone. "True and substantial eating of the flesh and drinking of the blood of Christ" was not equivalent simply to receiving the
"merit, fruit, efficacy, virtue, and power" of Christ's death and resurrection. Calvin used substantialist terminology loosely, and his opponents charged that his distinction between substance and benefit
was illusory. But certainly he wanted to say that believers received
Christ's benefits as a consequence of their "having been made partakers of his substance." [69]

In order to make his position comprehensible, Calvin had to explain how the believer could possibly participate in the substance of a
Christ who himself remained in heaven. He found an explanation in
his doctrine of the Holy Spirit, who became the "bond of participation" between Christ and the believer.[70] With this notion Calvin combined a theme from the liturgy, the *sursum corda,* the directive to
worshippers to "lift up their hearts." The faithful participated in the
body and blood of Christ, he said, because Christ, by the secret and
mysterious working of the Holy Spirit, lifted the soul of the communicant to himself.

> Even though it seems unbelievable that Christ's flesh, separated
> from us by such great distance, penetrates to us, so that it becomes
> our food, let us remember how far the secret power of the Holy
> Spirit towers above all our senses, and how foolish it is to wish
> to measure his immeasurableness by our measure. What, then, our
> mind does not comprehend let faith conceive: that the Spirit truly
> unites things separated in space.[71]

Calvin called sacramental communion "spiritual" partly because it
was accomplished by the Holy Spirit.[72]

Calvin's strong emphasis on the sacramental activity of the Holy
Spirit also provided a rationale for repudiating Zwingli's notion that

67. Calvin, *The clear explanation,* p. 268.
68. Calvin, *Short Treatise,* p. 146.
69. Calvin, *Institutes* 4. 17. 11; Calvin, *The clear explanation,* p. 278.
70. Calvin, *Short Treatise,* p. 166.
71. Calvin, *Institutes* 4. 17. 31–36, 10.
72. Calvin, *Short Treatise,* p. 166. See Grass, *Die Abendmahlslehre* p. 228; and
Wendel, *Calvin,* pp. 352 ff.

sacramental eating was synonymous with faith. For Calvin faith was the necessary precondition of sacramental communion, but reception of Christ was the fruit and effect of faith and the Spirit, "and therefore different from faith." [73]

> We admit indeed, meanwhile, that this is no other eating than that of faith, as no other can be imagined. But here is the difference between my words and theirs: for them to eat is only to believe; I say that we eat Christ's flesh in believing, because it is made ours by faith, and that this eating is the result and effect of faith. Or if you want it said more clearly, for them eating is faith; for me it seems rather to follow from faith. This is a small difference indeed in words, but no slight one in the matter itself.

Moreover, Calvin regarded neither faith itself nor the communion resulting from faith merely as mental events, impressions stamped on the understanding. The Lord's Supper was not simply a spectacle that enlightened the understanding and moved the emotions of the communicant. "I leave no place," he said, "for the sophistry that what I mean when I say Christ is received by faith is that he is received only by understanding and imagination." [74] A purely cognitive explanation overlooked God's promise that the believer would enjoy true participation in Christ. Through his doctrine of the Spirit, Calvin established a foundation for sacramental communion.

Finally, Calvin differed from Zwingli in his doctrine of sacramental efficacy. He designated as the "effect" of the Lord's Supper "redemption, righteousness, sanctification, and eternal life, and all the other benefits Christ gives to us," and he stressed especially the contribution of the sacrament to the process of sanctification. Since the Supper was instituted as a witness of "our growth into one body with Christ," the believer could find in it an assuring testimony that "eternal life, of which he is the heir, is ours." In this way the Lord's Supper, like baptism, established, strengthened, and increased Christian faith. Far more than a mere "mark of outward profession," it nourished the elect saint and facilitated his progress along the road of sanctification.[75]

Calvin sought a spiritual religion that could still retain a proper appreciation for the tangible and visible. His difficulty with sacraments was part of a broader problem: could one grasp the sacred through visible symbols and signs? His response was ambivalent: Cal-

73. Calvin, *The clear explanation*, p. 291.
74. Calvin, *Institutes* 4. 17. 5, 11.
75. Ibid., 4. 17. 5, 2, 6.

vin believed that human sinfulness perverted every perception of
God's self-revelation in the visible world; only the regenerated Christian, aided by Scripture and the Spirit, could glimpse the "sparks of
glory shining in every created thing." And, of course, God would
never "subject his infinite glory to visible signs." [76] But when properly
accompanied by the Word, visible realities—ranging from stars and
rainbows to the altars of Israel—could become symbols directing the
mind to God. The created order therefore possessed something of a
sacramental character, however imperceptible its significance to sinful
men.[77]

The most prominent examples of revelatory carnal forms were the
prefigurations of Christ in the Old Testament. Following the ancient
Christian tradition of Biblical interpretation by means of typology,
Calvin discovered throughout the Old Testament a variety of events,
ceremonies, and individuals ordained by God to foreshadow the Incarnation. The priests, kings, rites, and laws of the Jews in some sense
prefigured Christ's earthly appearance and revealed him to Israel.
Typology represented a conviction that spiritual truth was accessible
in and through the visible, the corporeal, the historical, and thus Calvin spoke of the Old Testament types as sacraments intended to "direct and almost lead men by the hand to Christ." [78] He based much
of his sacramental theology on this typological exegesis, thereby establishing securely an association between types and sacraments that later
Reformed theologians would enthusiastically develop.

The Later Reformed Impulse

By 1541 Zwingli's successors, especially Heinrich Bullinger, seemed
to be attuned to the positive implications of his later doctrine. Calvin,
sensing a possibility of agreement, made overtures toward Bullinger,
and in 1545 the two men began an exchange of letters on sacramental
issues. Union was not easy, since Bullinger still held a highly subjective doctrine: the idea of remembrance dominated his view of the
Lord's Supper and the image of the Roman military *sacramentum* informed his position on baptism. And he was still inclined to identify
faith and sacramental eating. Calvin insisted, though, that remembrance was not, as Bullinger seemed to think, opposed to an objectively real spiritual presence; he reaffirmed his conviction that the

76. Quoted in Edward A. Dowey, Jr., *The Knowledge of God in Calvin's Theology*
(New York, 1952), pp. 13, 136.
77. See Benjamin C. Milner, Jr., *Calvin's Doctrine of the Church* (Leiden, 1970),
pp. 110–26.
78. Calvin, *Institutes* 4. 14. 20.

sacraments increased and nourished faith; and he labeled as inadequate a definition of the sacraments as badges of human commitment and profession.

Bullinger was disturbed when Calvin seemed to suggest that God communicated grace through (*per*) the elements and that, in baptism, the subject of the sacrament immediately (*simul*) received its benefit. He thought that the Spirit offered grace to communicants, but not through the elements. And he cautioned against the implication that the benefit of baptism was immediate; he who received baptism "likewise" (*similiter*) obtained the benefit, though not always at the time of the sacrament's administration. Bullinger was closer to Calvin than he had at first thought, however, and Calvin accepted the alterations in his terminology as consistent with his conviction that sacraments were instruments of grace. To this Bullinger finally gave assent.[79]

The exchange of letters led to a meeting between Calvin and Bullinger in 1549, the result of which was the Zurich Consensus Formula (*Consensus Tigurinus*). They agreed that the sacraments were marks and badges of Christian profession and incitements to gratitude, but also that their principal end was to serve as "means" by which God might "attest, represent, and seal His grace in us." In the Lord's Supper, Christ was offered even to the faithless, and all who faithfully embraced the promises there offered actually received "Christ and his spiritual gifts." In either case, there was an objective sacramental reality, a spiritual presence of Christ that could not be overthrown by human faithlessness. God truly performed inwardly by his Spirit that which the elements symbolized. The external elements effected nothing by themselves, but they were instruments (*organa*) of the Spirit.[80] Though based largely on the Bern articles that Calvin himself wrote earlier in 1549, the Consensus did not embody the fullness of Calvin's doctrine. Nevertheless, he was satisfied and publicly defended the formula, which became a source of unity for the developing Reformed tradition. After 1549 the low sacramental doctrine of the early Zwingli ceased to be a real option for most, though not all, Reformed theologians. But as a document of compromise, the formula left considerable room for varying emphases, and several issues continued to be problematic in Reformed confessions on the continent, in England, and in America.

79. See Bizer, *Studien*, pp. 234–70, where the correspondence between Calvin and Bullinger is summarized. See also Grass, *Die Abendmahlslehre*, pp. 208 ff.

80. John Calvin, Heinrich Bullinger, et al., *Consensio Mutua in Re Sacramentaria*, in *Joannis Calvini Opera Quae Supersunt Omnia VII*, ed. G. Baum, E. Cunitz, and E. Reuss (Brunsvigae, 1868), pp. 738–40.

One was the problem of defining the sacramental presence. When, in the Gallican Confession of 1559, Calvin asserted that Christ "by the secret and incomprehensible power of his Spirit . . . feeds and strengthens us with the substance of his body and of his blood," it was clear, in the light of his earlier statements, that he meant to exclude the belief that only the benefits of Christ were received. Most of the early Reformed confessions taught that Christ communicated both his Person and his benefits in the Supper, though they rarely used Calvin's substantialist terminology.[81] Theodore Beza, Calvin's successor at Geneva, repeated in 1566 what came to be a common Reformed clarification.

> For the Lord did not say, "this is my death," or "this is the virtue of my death," or "this is the monument of my body," but: "This is my body, which is given for you, and this is my blood, poured out for you." The apostle did not write: "the bread which we break is the communion of the efficacy of Christ," and "the cup which we bless, is the virtue of his blood," but rather: "the communion of the body and blood of the Lord." [82]

But in Bullinger's 1566 Second Helvetic Confession this ambiguity pervaded the sacramental doctrine. Bullinger said, on the one hand, that communicants actually received "the flesh and blood of the Lord," but then he described the spiritual presence in terms not of "substance" but of "lively operation." [83] At the very least, he was not so concerned as Calvin to show that the substance, and not merely the efficacy, of Christ was present to the faithful. The difference of emphasis was visible in their dissimilar use of solar metaphors. For Calvin the sun illustrated the possibility of participation in the substance of Christ.

> For if we see that the sun, shedding its beams upon the earth, casts its substance in some measure upon it in order to beget, nourish, and give growth to its offspring—why should the radiance of Christ's Spirit be less in order to impart to us the communion of his flesh and blood.[84]

Bullinger, however, used the same metaphor to point out that "the sun, being absent from us in the heavens, is yet, notwithstanding,

81. In Schaff, *Creeds of Christendom*, 3 : 380, 430, 468–69.
82. Theodore Beza, *Epistolarum Theologicarum Theodori Bezae I* (Geneva, 1575), n.p.
83. In Schaff, *Creeds of Christendom*, 3 : 895.
84. Calvin, *Institutes* 4. 17. 12.

present among us effectually." [85] His use of the image suggested that the believer experienced the efficacy of a body that was itself absent and in the heavens. Among later Reformed theologians, including English Puritans, some ministers were always tempted to describe the sacrament simply in terms of its efficacy.

A second unresolved issue was an ambiguity in the definition of sacraments as covenantal seals. The Reformed confessions indicated a slowly developing emphasis on the covenant motif in sacramental theology. The early Gallican and Scotch Confessions never alluded to the covenant in defining the sacraments; subsequent confessions invariably used it to defend infant baptism, and in general revealed a greater interest in covenantal imagery. By 1647 the Westminster Confession began its seventeenth chapter by defining sacraments generally as "holy signs and seals of the covenant of grace." [86] It was not always clear, however, what was meant by calling a sacrament a covenant seal. Early Christian references to baptismal sealing, usually based on Romans 4 : 11, suggested connotations ranging from the branding of slaves to the ratification of public documents with an official stamp.[87] In the Reformation the notion of a sacramental seal proved susceptible to various interpretations. Calvin defined it as analogous to the seal authenticating "government documents" [88] and concluded that baptism was a divine guarantee, or certification, of God's promises of salvation; Zwingli, however, spoke of the baptismal "seal" as simply a testimony of faith and obedience by the baptizand and the Church. This ambiguity pervaded the concept of the "covenant seal." Did sacraments seal by certifying God's covenant promise? Or did they testify to the faith and covenant membership of the baptized? By the middle of the seventeenth century, some English Puritans agreed that the question was crucial—and disagreed about its answer.

85. In Schaff, *Creeds of Christendom,* 3 : 895. This difference is discussed by Cyril C. Richardson, *Zwingli and Cranmer on the Eucharist* (Evanston, 1949), pp. 23, 26.
86. Ibid., p. 660.
87. G. W. H. Lampe, *The Seal of the Spirit* (London, 1951), pp. 59–60, 169, 245.
88. Calvin, *Institutes* 4. 14. 5.

2

THE SACRAMENTAL DOCTRINE OF
THE EARLY PURITANS

Despite their enormous concern for the principles of admission to the sacraments, Puritans have never been celebrated for their sacramental theology. Early Puritan doctrine, derived from continental Reformed theology, offered no new insights into the spiritual presence or the signification of baptism. The Puritans were selective in their adaptation of the Reformed tradition, and the process of selection had nothing to do with the subtleties that divided Calvin and Zwingli. Though aware of the earlier Reformed alternatives, they overlooked controversial distinctions, often combining, with no sense of incongruity, characteristic Calvinist and Zwinglian themes. By selective quotation one could depict most of them as heirs either of Zurich or of Geneva. In part their imprecision reflected the almost universal tendency of second generation Reformed divines to minimize earlier disagreements. Even Calvin and Bullinger found it possible to blur distinctions in 1549 when they signed the *Tigurinus Consensus*. Equally important, though, was Puritan indifference to the issues that once divided their predecessors. Early Puritan sacramental thought represented the practical and pastoral application of a broad Reformed consensus.

The outlines of their sacramental doctrine varied according to the distinctive interests of various Puritan groups. The call for communal reformation created the peculiar contours of much Puritan teaching, especially for the radical reformers who left the Church of England to establish Separatist churches. For other Puritans ecclesiastical controversy had little influence on baptismal and eucharistic doctrine. Scores of ministers avoided agitation for reform and rejected separation, preferring to exploit the pastoral implications of the sacraments.

But whether a Puritan was a reformer or a shepherd of souls, or a bit of both, his doctrine displayed several persistent characteristics. It was Reformed in tone and substance, though without perpetuating Zwingli's early denigration of the sacraments or maintaining Calvin's stronger feeling for them and his appreciation of doctrinal niceties. It evinced a fondness for covenantal imagery; one reason for the popularity of the covenant doctrine in England was its usefulness as a foundation for the sacraments. And it mirrored, even magnified, the earlier Reformed ambivalence about the sacraments. The Puritan's desire to escape Roman "superstition," his fascination with his own internal spiritual life, and his rigorous insistence on the holiness of the communicant undercut a sacramental view of Christianity. Some Puritans wished to discard the word "sacrament," preferring to designate baptism and the Lord's Supper as "ordinances," retained simply because Christ had commanded their use. Other groups within the Puritan spectrum, like the Quakers, repudiated sacraments altogether. But the study of the Puritans is also a story of their resistance to their own antisacramental impulse, a resistance that grew increasingly outspoken as the seventeenth century progressed.

The English Background

For his defense of traditional sacramental doctrine against Luther in 1521, King Henry VIII of England earned from Pope Leo X the title "defender of the faith." Despite the royal defense of tradition, however, Protestant sacramental thought attracted proponents in England as early as 1530, when Robert Barnes, prior of the Augustinian friars in Cambridge, publicly expounded a doctrine of the real presence strikingly Lutheran in tone. The book foreshadowed a spirited discussion. While imprisoned in the Tower in 1533, John Frith, an erstwhile canon of Cardinal College, Oxford, wrote a treatise on the Lord's Supper that was indebted to Oecolampadius, and one on baptism that also moved in a Reformed direction. In the same year, George Joye, a Cambridge graduate and former fellow of Peterhouse, attacked the mass in a book subsequently described as little more than a restatement of Zwingli's 1526 essay *On the Lord's Supper*. By 1533 William Tyndale was fearful that English Protestants were destined to repeat among themselves the sacramental quarrels that divided Protestants on the continent.[1]

1. William A. Clebsch, *England's Earliest Protestants 1520–1535* (New Haven, 1964), pp. 19–20, 113, 170–219. For a different interpretation see C. W. Dugmore, *The Mass and the English Reformers* (London, 1958), pp. 96–102.

For a time Henry himself seemed open to Protestant views. His Ten Articles Act in 1536 mentioned only three sacraments—baptism, the Eucharist, and penance—and contained descriptions of both baptism and the Lord's Supper that were perfectly amenable to Lutheran interpretation. By 1539, though, Henry changed his mind about the Protestants; the Six Articles Act of that year declared the rejection of transubstantiation to be a capital offense. The following year he assigned to eight bishops and twelve theologians the responsibility for preparing a new book of doctrine, which they presented to Convocation in 1543. Known popularly as *The King's Book,* it taught that "the creatures" of bread and wine were "by the virtue of Christ's word in the consecration . . . changed and turned to the very substance of the body and blood of our Saviour Jesus Christ." The book contained also a straightforward doctrine of justification through baptism.[2]

The death of Henry in 1547 and the accession of his young son, Edward VI, prepared the way for a steady influx of Protestant ideas into the doctrinal and liturgical standards of the Church of England. Both of Edward's protectors, Northumberland and Somerset, were receptive to ecclesiastical changes, and the highly influential Archbishop of Canterbury, Thomas Cranmer, began in 1546 to move away from Roman doctrine. By 1548 he publicly abandoned the doctrine of transubstantiation, and he no longer believed the Eucharist to be a propitiatory sacrifice. The precise character of his transformation has long been debated, but by 1549 he was clearly looking to the Reformed tradition. Cranmer asserted that the faithful communicant "spiritually" ate and drank "the very flesh and blood of Christ, which is in heaven and sitteth on the right hand of his Father."[3]

Cranmer's change of mind was important, for he was the chief author of the first Edwardian Prayer Book of 1549. The book was based mainly on a rite that originated at Salisbury in the thirteenth century, but by excision, rearrangement, and modest addition, Cranmer diminished the sacrificial overtones of the older missal, forbade the elevation of the Host, and modified allusions to transubstantiation. The innovations were modest. The service still proclaimed that infants were

2. Charles Lloyd, ed., *Formularies of Faith Put Forth by Authority During the Reign of King Henry VIII* (Oxford, 1825), pp. xxiii, xix, xxv, 263, 336. *The King's Book* also taught that ordination was a special "gift of grace," pp. 277–78. See also E. C. S. Gibson, *The Thirty-Nine Articles of the Church of England* (London, 1902), p. 640.

3. Thomas Cranmer, *A Defence of the True and Catholic Doctrine of the Sacrament of the Body and Blood of our Saviour Christ,* in *The Work of Thomas Cranmer,* ed. G. E. Duffield (Appleford, Berkshire, 1964), p. 65. See Peter Brooks, *Thomas Cranmer's Doctrine of the Eucharist: An Essay in Historical Development* (New York, 1965).

"saved from perishing" by baptism, and Stephen Gardiner, the conservative Bishop of Winchester, argued that the Prayer Book was consistent throughout with traditional Catholic belief, though Cranmer replied that Gardiner failed to understand the book.[4] Despite his protests and clarifications, however, Cranmer met opposition from two sides. While Gardiner was ingenious in finding ways to affix a traditional interpretation to his language, the extreme proponents of the Reformed tradition thought that Cranmer betrayed the faith by his timidity. In a letter to Bullinger in December, 1549, John Hooper, Bishop of Gloucester, objected that the "public celebration of the Lord's supper is very far from the order and institution of our Lord." Hooper did not object to Cranmer's doctrine. He informed Bullinger that the "archbishop of Canterbury entertains right views as to the nature of Christ's presence in the supper . . . his sentiments respecting the eucharist are pure, and religious, and similar to yours in Switzerland." Hooper's objections were directed against such liturgical practices as kneeling, which implied transubstantiation, or the retention of altars, which suggested that the Supper was a sacrifice, or the continued use of Roman ceremonial in place of apostolic simplicity. Hooper was so offended that he threatened to abstain from the Lord's Supper altogether.[5]

Hooper has been called a Zwinglian, but his ideas were similar to the *Tigurinus Consensus,* and like the later Puritans, he was far more interested in the sacrament's effect on "the private and particular conscience afflicted" and its pure administration than in the subtleties of the sacramental presence.[6] At any rate, the more influential critics of the Prayer Book, the continental theologians Peter Martyr and Martin Bucer, were by no means disciples of the early Zwingli. At Cranmer's invitation, Bucer proposed alterations in ceremonies that still implied transubstantiation or sacrificial motifs, and he urged more diligent

4. F. E. Brightman, *The English Rite: Being a Synopsis of the Sources and Revisions of the Book of Common Prayer* (London, 1921), pp. xvi, xcviii; William Keeling, ed., *Liturgiae Britannicae, Or the Several Editions of the Book of Common Prayer of the Church of England, From Its Compilation to the Last Revision* (London, 1842), pp. 165–235, 239; E. C. Ratcliff, *The booke of common prayer of the Churche of England* (London, 1949), pp. 45–60; E. P. Echlin, *The Anglican Eucharist in Historical Perspective* (New York, 1968), pp. 9 ff.

5. Hooper to Bullinger, "Letter XXXVI, Dec. 27, 1549," in Hastings Robinson, ed., *Original Letters Relative to the English Reformation* (Cambridge, 1846), 1 : 71–72. See also John Hooper, "The Sixth Sermon Upon Jonas," in *Early Writings of John Hooper* (Cambridge, 1843), pp. 528–45, and Hooper to Bullinger, "Letter XXXVIII, March 27, 1550," in *Original Letters,* 1 : 79.

6. Hooper, "Sixth Sermon," pp. 530–31. For an argument against Hooper's alleged Zwinglianism, see August Lang, *Puritanismus und Pietismus* (Buchhandlung des Erziehungsvereins Neukirchen Kreis Moers, 1941), pp. 42–45.

exclusion of the sinful, but he did not want the Anglican liturgy to suggest that there was "nothing in the Lord's Supper except mere signs of Christ, through which a recording of the absent Christ should be somehow aroused." [7]

Moved by such criticisms, Cranmer helped prepare a second Prayer Book, which appeared in 1552. If Bucer and his friend Paul Fagius were correct, the first book was intended only as a temporary concession to "the infirmity of the age." [8] In the 1552 revision, Reformed motifs abounded. Cranmer simplified the service by omitting ceremonies, and in place of traditional vestments he authorized only a surplice for priests and deacons. He removed the remaining allusions to sacrifice, prescribing a "table" in place of the "altar," and eliminated or modified rubrics that could suggest transubstantiation. He also removed or rearranged the prayers between the Consecration and the Communion, lest there be any occasion for adoration of the elements, and for the same reason he excised the *Agnus Dei*, the traditional petition to "the Lamb of God" in the Mass. And Cranmer drastically altered the formula of distribution: in place of "the body of our Lorde Jesus Christ" he inserted "Take and eate this, in remembrance that Christ dyed for thee, and feede on him in thy heart by faythe, with Thankes gevinge." "The bloud of our Lord Jesus Christ" was changed to "Drinke this in remembraunce that Christes blood was shed for thee, and be thankefnl." John Knox, the Scottish Reformer, secured the addition of the "Black Rubric," which explained that kneeling did not imply transubstantiation but only gratitude for "the benefites of Christe, geven unto the woorthye receyver." Cranmer also changed the rubric on baptism, omitting the claim of the 1549 Prayer Book that infants were baptized "and so saved from perishing." There was little if anything in the Prayer Book to displease even a Zwinglian.[9]

The increasingly Reformed tenor of Anglican sacramental doctrine was visible also in the Forty-two Articles of Faith published in 1553. Cranmer inserted a clause denying that sacraments conveyed grace *ex opere operato*, and in the twenty-ninth article he spoke out against "the real and bodily presence (as they term it) of Christ's flesh and

7. Bucer to Peter Martyr, in Martin Bucer, *Scripta Anglicana*, ed. Conrad Hubert (Basle, 1577), p. 549, cited in Echlin *Anglican Eucharist*, p. 62. For a study of Martyr's doctrine, see Joseph McLelland, *The Visible Words of God: An Exposition of the Sacramental Theology of Peter Martyr Vermigli A. D. 1500–1562* (London, 1957).

8. Bucer and Fagius to the Ministers at Strassburg, "Letter CCXLVIII, April 26, 1549," in *Original Letters*, 2 : 535.

9. *Liturgiae Britannicae*, pp. 165–235, 239. See also Echlin, *Anglican Eucharist*, pp. 65 ff.

blood in the sacrament," on the ground that Christ's body had been taken up into heaven. In true Reformed fashion, the Articles limited effective communion to worthy receivers and repeated earlier admonitions against adoration of the Host and reservation of the elements.[10]

The accession of the Catholic Mary Tudor in 1553 halted such innovations. In her first Act of Repeal, Mary abolished the second Prayer Book, and thereafter she struggled to return England to Rome. Zealously Protestant churchmen migrated in large numbers to the continent, where many of them were enchanted by the simplicity of Reformed doctrine and worship. When Elizabeth succeeded Mary in 1558, ardent Protestants, whether they had remained in England or fled to the continent, entertained hopes for the elimination of all remaining vestiges of "popery" from the Church of England.

Elizabeth was not amenable to their demands for drastic change. The Elizabethan Prayer Book of 1559, which replaced the Edwardian liturgy, contained only three major changes; none was designed to please advocates of further reform. The ornaments rubric made mandatory the sacramental vestments prescribed by the Prayer Book of 1549; the Black Rubric disappeared; and the words of institution underwent a dramatic change. The Elizabethan liturgy juxtaposed the language of the 1549 book, suggesting the presence in the elements of the body and blood of Christ, with the words of the 1552 Prayer Book, which merely exhorted communicants to "remembrance" of Christ's death. The 1559 liturgy thereby permitted interpretations of the presence that the 1552 book had ruled out.[11]

The publication of the Thirty-nine Articles in 1563 compounded the disappointment of the reformers. The Articles did make clear that "only such as duly received" the sacraments had from them "a wholesome effect of operation." But in place of the clause in the older Articles that denied the "real and bodily presence," Elizabeth's clergy inserted a statement, written by Bishop Edmund Guest of Rochester, explaining that the body of Christ was given, taken, and eaten in a heavenly and spiritual manner. Guest later said that he intended his clause to affirm the presence while rejecting gross corporeal conceptions of it, so the article was still Reformed. But some reformers viewed with alarm the removal of the one clause that positively rejected a bodily presence. It also appeared as though some Reformed

10. John Lamb, *An Historical Account of the Thirty-Nine Articles From the First Promulgation of them in M.D.LIII to their Final Establishment in M.D.LXXI With Exact Copies of the Latin and English Manuscripts, and Facsimiles of the Signatures of the Archbishops and Bishops* (Oxford, 1829), pp. 9–10.

11. *Liturgiae Britannicae,* pp. 166–235.

teachings were being deliberately excluded. Matthew Parker, Elizabeth's first Archbishop of Canterbury, prepared an article explaining that the impious did not receive the body and blood of Christ, and the bishops in Convocation affirmed the article with their signatures. For some mysterious reason, however, perhaps because of Elizabeth's disinclination to offend the conservatives, Parker's article did not appear in the 1563 edition of the Articles. Only in 1571 did the Queen ratify it as article twenty-nine.[12]

The fact remained that the Thirty-nine Articles were open to a Reformed interpretation. The Church of England appropriated the main insights of the Reformed tradition. Only a committed disciple of the early Zwingli could have complained that the Articles, taken as a whole, spoke too highly of the sacraments, and the Puritans were not Zwinglians. It was rather their anxiety about practical sacramental issues, matters of admission and ceremonial, that brought them into conflict with civil and ecclesiastical authorities.

The Sacraments and Radical Puritan Reform

Puritanism began as a movement of "divers Godly and Learned . . . which stand for and desire the Reformation of our Church in Discipline and Ceremonies according to the pure Word of God and the law of the land." [13] The earliest Puritans were reformers—first of the Church, but of themselves as well, and of their fellow men. Their criterion of reform was the Scripture, in which they found explicit and indispensable directives for the structuring of the Church and its worship. They would retain only the practices that Scripture positively affirmed and denounce practices about which Scripture was silent. They were thus "precisianists." Puritans united in a sense of disquiet about Elizabeth's refusal to sweep away ceremonial accretions and traditional practices that corrupted the purity of the sacraments.

In 1572 two radical Puritans, Thomas Field and John Wilcox, who were organizing a drive to reorganize the Church of England along Presbyterian lines, published an *Admonition to Parliament* outlining objections to current practices. They and their allies disliked kneeling at communion, the use of wafer cakes, the repetition of the Nicene Creed, the reading of disconnected fragments from Scripture, the sing-

---

12. Gibson, *Thirty-Nine Articles*, pp. 668 ff.
13. This was the heading to *A Parte of a Register*, a manuscript collection described in Albert Peel, ed., *The Second Parte of a Register: Being a Calendar of Manuscripts Under that title intended for Publication by the Puritans about 1593, and now in Dr. Williams's Library, London*, 2 vols. (Cambridge, 1915), 1 : 12, 30–33.

ing of the Gloria, and the pomposity of "singing, pyping, surplesse and cope wearyng." Such practices they viewed as unedifying human inventions with no Scriptural justification. They demanded ministerial examination of communicants, the exclusion of the sinful, and the preaching of the Word before every administration of the Supper. The Puritans also faulted the baptismal liturgy. They disliked private baptism, the surplice worn by the minister, interrogatories addressed to the infant, the participation of godparents in the service, the sign of the cross in the ceremony, and special holy fonts for sacramental purposes. Such practices, they charged, were reminiscent of the papist Babylon.[14]

Puritans were ever fearful that their opponents compromised with Rome; historians have often been convinced that the Puritans were consorting with Zwinglians.[15] Neither conclusion can withstand close scrutiny. In the controversy over the *Admonition,* disagreements about practice rather than doctrine occupied both parties. John Whitgift, the vice-chancellor of Cambridge, wrote the main response to the *Admonition.* His major opponent, Thomas Cartwright, Lady Margaret Professor of Divinity at Cambridge from 1569 to 1571 and the theoretician of the early Puritan movement, found that Whitgift refused to take issue with him on doctrinal matters. Cartwright charged that kneeling at the sacrament misled the common people into over-valuing the communion elements. Whitgift defended kneeling, however, only because it expressed the gratitude appropriate for the Eucharist. He did not suggest that Cartwright's doctrine differed from his own. When Cartwright, along with the authors of the *Admonition,* opposed private, emergency baptism because it implied the necessity of baptism for salvation, Whitgift defended the practice while agreeing entirely with the rejection of baptismal regeneration. "I do mislike as much as you," he said, "the opinion of those that think infants to be condemned which are not baptized." [16] On such issues the Puritans were defending the prevailing opinion. They were angry only because the official spokesmen seemed insufficiently sensitive to the implications of their practices.

Dudley Fenner (d. 1587) outlined the radical Puritan doctrine of the sacraments during a period of exile on the continent after the *Admonition* controversy. A friend of Cartwright and a meticulous systematic

14. W. H. Frere and C. E. Douglas, eds., *Puritan Manifestoes* (London, 1907), pp. 11–14. For a discussion of the ceremonial and liturgical issues, see Horton Davies, *The Worship of the English Puritans* (Westminster, 1948).

15. E. C. E. Bourne, *The Anglicanism of William Laud* (London, 1947), p. 68.

16. John Whitgift, *The Works of John Whitgift,* ed. John Ayre (Cambridge, 1851), 3 : 90; 2 : 522.

theologian, Fenner wrote a treatise on *The Whole Doctrine of the Sacraments* that repeated one Calvinist doctrine after another. Baptism was an instrument sealing God's covenant promises, engrafting the infant into Christ, and augmenting the process of Christian growth. In the Lord's Supper the faithful Christian received spiritually not only the benefits of Christ, but also Christ himself, both as God and as man, through the activity of the Holy Spirit. Both sacraments strengthened and increased faith and assisted the Christian to mortify his sinful nature and to advance into new life; they also sealed God's covenant of grace with his faithful elect. Fenner may have lacked Calvin's sense of sacramental mystery, but by no stretch of the imagination could he be called a Zwinglian.[17] Even Richard Hooker, the ablest defender of the Anglican establishment, acknowledged that he could see "on all sides" a "general agreement" about participation in Christ through the Lord's Supper, though he did think that the Puritans erred in failing to recognize that baptism "maketh us Christians," rather than simply confirming and declaring discipleship. But on that issue Hooker would have had difficulty with Calvin himself.[18]

There were, however, doctrinal dimensions, usually implicit, though sometimes explicit, in the arguments between the early Puritans and their opponents. For one thing, the Puritan reformers were more zealous to rule out any overemphasis on the material sacramental elements. Field and Wilcox complained in 1572 about the addition of the phrase, "The body of our Lorde Jesus Chryst which was geven for thee," to the Elizabethan Prayer Book.[19] In 1573 Robert Johnson, a Puritan preacher at Northampton, was indicted for refusing to repeat the words of institution each time he brought new bread and wine to the table while administering the Lord's Supper. Dean Goodman of Westminster told him that the words of institution were words of consecration spoken for the elements as well as the communicants. Johnson said that they were spoken for the communicants alone. In so saying he was following Calvin but also manifesting a tendency to deprecate external, physical aids to sacramental communion.[20]

Corresponding to suspicion of the outward and material was a con-

17. Dudley Fenner, *The Whole Doctrine of the Sacramentes, plainlie and fullie set downe and declared out of the word of God* (Middelburg, 1588), n.p. See also Dudley Fenner, *The Groundes of Religion Necessarie to be knowen of every one that may be admitted to the Supper of the Lord* (Middelburg, 1587), n.p.

18. Richard Hooker, *The Works of that Learned and Judicious Divine Mr. Richard Hooker, Containing Eight Books of the Laws of Ecclesiastical Polity*, ed. Isaac Walton, 3 vols. (Oxford, 1807), 2 : 248, 327.

19. *Puritan Manifestoes*, p. 13.

20. E. C. Ratcliff, "The English Usage of Eucharistic Consecration 1548–1622," *Theology* 60 (July, 1957) : 276 ff.; Calvin, *Institutes* 4. 7. 39.

viction that conceptual understanding was essential to sacramental worship. The radical reformers carried to its logical conclusion the Reformed belief that sacraments were appendages of the Word. Since the Word was addressed to the understanding, so also must be the sacraments. It was of course through the senses that baptism and the Lord's Supper "lively set forth to the understanding" their inward spiritual matter, but the final purpose was still knowledge, not sensual delight or imaginative mystery. Thus in the Lord's Supper the Puritan reformers insisted that every outward action of the ceremony ought to produce an inward comprehension of doctrinal truths.[21] A certain rationalism also prompted Puritan objections to the interrogatories addressed to infants during baptism. They considered it both unbiblical and irrational to direct questions to uncomprehending children. Richard Hooker insisted that baptized infants were Christians despite their intellectual incapacities. He found it offensive "that some, when they labour to show the use of the holy Sacraments, assign unto them no end but only to teach the mind, by other senses, that which the Word doth teach by hearing," [22] which was not precisely descriptive of the Puritan view, though it did uncover a distinct Puritan inclination.

Since sacraments were visible words addressed to the understanding, early Puritan reformers asserted that a valid sacrament presupposed a minister capable of preaching the Word. Not only did Cartwright desire a sermon before every sacrament, but he also told Whitgift that it was improper for a mere "reader," an ecclesiastical functionary who read specified homilies, to baptize or to administer the Lord's Supper.

> Indeed, upon this point, whether he be good or evil minister it dependeth not, but on this point, whether he be a minister or no, dependeth not only the dignity but also the being of the sacrament.

Whitgift challenged this claim. So long as an infant was baptized in the name of the Trinity, he said, "the sacrament remaineth in full force and strength, of whomsoever it be ministered." Cartwright said later that he did not actually presume the minister to be necessary to the substance of a sacrament, but his friend Dudley Fenner was less circumspect.[23] The sacraments had no natural property to represent and apply Jesus to the faithful, he said; they received this property from the Word of God. And who but the minister was the spokesman and interpreter of the Word? His verbal participation in the service,

21. Fenner, *Groundes of Religion*, n.p.
22. Hooker, *Works*, 2 : 237.
23. Whitgift, *Works*, 2 : 525, 528–29, 532.

therefore, was "of such necessitie, as if it be omitted, it destroyeth the Sacrament." [24] Hooker ridiculed the "fumbling shifts" of these attempts to make a preaching ministry essential to a proper sacrament and thus to prohibit women and laymen from baptizing, and "dumb readers" from celebrating communion.[25] But the Puritan reformers believed this necessary in order to prevent "mystical" superstition.[26] Words, even divine sacramental words, were intended to enlighten, not to mystify, the mind.

A further characteristic of the Puritan reformers was an accent on the communal dimensions of the sacraments. Prominent in their denunciations of private sacraments, this concern was also visible in their repeated insistence that the plural, collective form of administration, "take ye," should replace the singular, "take thou," in the liturgy for the Lord's Supper.[27] Fenner believed that this reform was needful for two reasons: it signified "the fellowship and communion of the Churche" in sacramental worship, and it succored the faithful whenever they could consciously join "together with one harte" in meditation on the sacramental Word. Fenner made communal participation as essential to a sacrament as preaching:

> Not the Ministers alone must worke here, but the Church with him, in witnessing his work, in approving the same by one consent of the spirit of grace, by consenting in prayer and thankes-giving, for which they are saide to doe the workes of the Sacraments.[28]

Implicit in that definition was a notion of the Church itself as a society characterized by voluntary, communal consent among its members. The authority even of sacraments rested upon obedient consent and participation.[29]

Such a Church, and such a sacrament, required a pure and faithful membership. The Puritans wanted communicants knowledgeable in the faith and willing to examine themselves rigorously; Fenner had written an entire treatise on *The Groundes of Religion Necessarie to be knowen of every one that may be admitted to the Supper of the Lord.* They also wanted the right to examine and excommunicate the notoriously scandalous, and for Cartwright this meant, among other things, that Roman Catholics should be forbidden access to a sacra-

24. Fenner, *Whole Doctrine*, n.p.
25. Hooker, *Works*, 2 : 273.
26. Fenner, *Whole Doctrine*, n.p.
27. *Puritan Manifestoes*, p. 13; Whitgift, *Works*, 3 : 97.
28. Fenner, *Whole Doctrine*, n.p.
29. See David Little, *Religion, Order, and Law: A Study in Pre–Revolutionary England* (New York, 1969).

ment that signified God's favor. For him it meant also that discipline, the admonition and correction of sin, was an essential mark of the Church, a claim that Calvin refused to make.[30]

Before the end of the century, radical Puritan reformers had thus raised two sets of related but distinguishable sacramental issues. One was created by their predisposition to exalt abstract mentality and inward subjectivity over physical concreteness and the sensuous imagination. A second focused on the disciplined and communal character of the Christian life. The doctrinal implications were not immediately clear to everyone, but Elizabeth, along with Whitgift, who became Archbishop in 1583, sensed some disturbing political implications. Whitgift believed that if the reformers acquired the right of sacramental discipline and achieved their other goals, every minister would become "king and pope in his own parish." The pulpit would threaten even the throne, for within his domain the minister, chosen by the congregation, would be elevated over every other man "in that parish, yea, the prince herself." [31] Elizabeth would relinquish to no man or congregation authority over the regulations and ceremonies of sacramental worship, and with Whitgift's assistance she thwarted the Puritan reforms. Her success helped to divide the reformers and, incidentally, to inform the new directions of Puritan sacramental thought. Increasing numbers of Separatists illegally formed their own churches, apart from the Anglican establishment, where they were compelled to consider the meaning of sacraments within pure communities of the faithful. Conforming Puritans acknowledged their losses in Parliament, Convocation, and the court, but still argued that fundamental reformation within the Church of England was imminent so long as they retained access to the pulpit. Their activities represented a retreat from direct structural reform, a move toward an inward, introspective piety that temporarily bypassed institutional restructuring. The first step, as they now saw it, had to be the inculcation of piety, not dramatic innovations in polity. They spoke of the sacraments, therefore, primarily as aids in the pastoral task of recreating the English laity, though in so doing they also reconsidered Reformed sacramental doctrine, particularly in relation to the subjective introspection of the pure in heart.

The Conforming Puritan Ministers

William Perkins, a fellow of Christ's College and for years the lecturer at Great St. Andrews in Cambridge, was one of the most cele-

30. Hooker, *Works*, 2 : 349; Whitgift, *Works*, 1 : 201, 290.
31. Whitgift, *Works*, 3 : 9; 1 : 121–22.

brated spokesmen of the Puritan ministers who remained within the establishment. In 1587, when he was twenty-eight, Perkins clashed with authorities after his criticisms of sacramental practices, and four years later he was implicated in the Classis movement, a final unsuccessful effort by Elizabethan Puritans to propagate Presbyterian notions within the Church of England. His experiences helped to convince him that Puritan pastors must imitate the apostles, who "yielded to bear with the use of Circumcision for a time, when they would not otherwise utterly cut it off," and he began to concentrate on innovative pastoral methods and pulpit oratory that "left a doleful echo in his auditors ears a good while after." [32] Perkins' ministry was not unique, but his proposals and activities brought approval even from Puritans who refused to yield to circumcision. After leaving England over the surplice issue, William Ames acknowledged by 1630 that the single-minded effort "to purge the floore of the Church" had allowed "a grievous spiritual plague" to decimate English congregations.[33] By the time that Ames wrote, scores of Puritan ministers were laboring to rectify the imbalance. Without entirely abandoning their aspirations to become architects of a new ecclesiastical order, they were laboring increasingly as physicians of the soul.

Their pastoral labors were legion: they prepared catechisms, devotional manuals, casuistical handbooks, and, above all else, sermons. Perkins was famed for his capacity to "speake a word in due season to him that is weary." Through the "godly sermons" of his successors, pastoral concern began to "encrease, and be glorified throughout England." [34] Puritans became increasingly adept at diagnosing spiritual pride and fleshly temptation. They also discovered, however, that their theology could itself intensify pastoral problems. When Calvin claimed that God, through his eternal decree, foreordained eternal life for some

32. William Perkins, *The Whole Treatise of the Cases of Conscience*, in *The Works of that famous and worthy Minister of Christ, William Perkins*, (London, 1617), 2 : 11; Thomas Fuller, "The Life of Mr. Perkins," *The Holy State* (Cambridge, 1648), pp. 81–82. William Ames attested to Perkins' pastoral originality in *Conscience with the Power and Cases Thereof, divided into Five Books*, in *The Workes of the Reverend and Faithful Minister of Christ William Ames* (London, 1643), p. 2. Perkins was not indifferent to questions of administration. He preferred that ordained, preaching ministers administer sacraments and considered baptism by laymen a "mere nullitie." Unlike the early Separatists, however, he accepted as valid sacraments administered by unworthy ministers, even by heretics and idolaters, or by Roman Catholic priests. So long as a sacrament was dispensed by a minister "in the name and power of Christ," it was valid. Perkins, *Cases of Conscience, The Workes of that Famous and Worthie Minister of Christ in the Universitie of Cambridge*, 3 vols. (London, 1608–1631), 1 : 71–73. This edition cited hereafter as *Works*.

33. Ames, "To the Reader," *Works*, n.p.

34. Ibid.

men and eternal damnation for others, he felt himself to be propounding a comforting doctrine; it removed the anxiety inherent in the struggle to earn grace through meritorious activity. Calvin intended to direct the believer's attention away from himself and toward Christ. His doctrine was to have provided no occasion for constant spiritual pulse-taking. "Those engulf themselves in a deadly abyss," he said, "who, to make their election more certain, investigate God's eternal plan apart from his word. . . ." He acknowledged that the works of the saints might be signs of election, but he discouraged excessive self-examination.[35] What Calvin experienced as liberating, though, could appear as a terrifying ambiguity, which many Englishmen found intolerable. They yearned to be "undoubtedly sure" of their salvation, whatever the source of assurance.[36] So Puritan pastors outlined in detail the morphology of conversion; they wrote sermons and handbooks teaching the believer how to obtain "sound evidence of a good estate"; and they consistently defined the sacraments in terms of the doctrine of assurance.[37]

In 1610 Richard Rogers (1550?–1618), a lecturer at Wethersfield, described the focal point of Puritan preaching on the sacraments during the first three decades of the century.

> [I will show how] the Sacraments are meanes and helpes to set [the Christian] forward in a godly life, (as too few doe finde to be) and to leave him for other knowledge about the Sacraments (which is exceeding large) to those who have written of them at large, as M. Peter Martyr, M. Calvin, M. Beza, and to ordinarie teaching.

That Rogers alluded to Calvin, Martyr, and Beza instead of Zwingli, Oecolampadius, and Bullinger was perhaps significant, but more important was his claim that in the Lord's Supper the fearful Christian could be "assured that his soul may be comforted by Christ." [38] Rogers assumed that the essentials were established by the great Reformed divines of the sixteenth century; sacramental doctrine, as he presented it, was a mode of practical theology. And like Rogers, most Puritan preachers of the early seventeenth century neglected the technical distinctions of sacramental doctrine. Their sermons and meditations were not intended as commentaries on the whole range of traditional issues. They concentrated instead on the practical benefits of the sacraments and the requirements for admission.

35. Calvin, *Institutes* 3. 24. 4; 3. 14. 20.
36. Perkins, *Cases of Conscience, Works*, 2 : 20.
37. Richard Sibbes, *The Soules Conflict with it selfe, and Victory over itself by Faith* (London, 1635), "Introduction," n.p.
38. Richard Rogers, *Seven Treatises* (London, 1610), pp. 233, 234.

Partly as a result of their pastoral preoccupations, the ministers re-lied heavily on covenantal imagery in their explanations of the sacra-ments. The doctrine of the covenant, as expanded by second genera-tion Reformed theologians, was superbly suited for resolving the practical difficulties that troubled Puritan congregations. Predestina-tion created pastoral dilemmas: Am I among the elect? Why should I perform good deeds? Of what use is baptism if salvation depends solely on an eternal decree? To such questions about assurance, ethics, and sacraments, ministers responded with the claim that God had initiated with men a covenantal relationship with apparently mutual obliga-tions. God was thereby obliged to save men who fulfilled the covenant condition of faithful discipleship; men were obliged to lives of faith and obedience; and sacraments were necessary as visible pledges of covenantal fidelity. The relationship between covenants and sacra-ments was peculiarly intimate. Perkins said that sacramental doctrine was one source of his covenantal theology. He discovered the covenant "generally in the Word, and more specifically in the ministrie of the Gospel and administration of the Sacraments, annexed as seales unto the covenant." [39] From the beginning, Puritans spoke in the same breath of sacraments and covenants. They did so, for one reason, be-cause they were pastors to troubled people.

Baptism: The Pastoral Problem

Perkins foreshadowed his reliance on covenantal imagery when he observed in his formal definition of a sacrament that it "sealed" Christ and his graces, justifying the definition with the two Scripture verses commonly used to prove that sacraments were covenant seals, Romans 4 : 11 and Genesis 17 : 11. In Romans, Paul called "the sign of circum-cision" a "seal of the righteousness of faith" that Abraham possessed. Genesis described circumcision as "a token of the covenant" between God and Abraham. Conflating the two verses, Puritan theologians de-fined circumcision as a seal to the covenant. Since circumcision, in turn, was a prototype of baptism, the Puritans defined baptism, and by implication the Lord's Supper, as covenant seals.[40]

The covenant theme was useful, on one level, as a defense for infant baptism. Richard Sibbes (1577–1635), famed as a preacher at Gray's Inn in London, and after 1626 as master of St. Catherine's Hall, Cam-bridge, summarized the familiar argument. Since the time of Abraham,

39. William Perkins, *A Godly and Learned Exposition of the Whole Epistle of Jude containing Threescore and six sermons, Works,* 3 : 520.
40. William Perkins, *A Golden Chaine: or, The Description of Theologie, Works,* 1 : 71.

children of the faithful had been accounted members of the covenanted community. God had commanded that they receive the visible covenant sign, which once was circumcision but now was baptism.

> Whence we see a ground of baptizing infants, because they are in covenant. To whom the covenant belongs, the seal of it belongs; but to infants the covenant belongs; therefore the seal of it, baptism, belongeth to them.[41]

Covenantal language contributed far more to Puritan sacramental sermons, however, than a debating point against Baptists. Perkins contended that the covenant was "the foundation or substance of baptisme" and that baptism, in turn, was "only a seale of that covenant, and no more." [42] Sibbes concurred: "In baptism, the one thing there, is the covenant." [43] From such a premise he derived two conclusions which he held in common with other Puritan ministers. As a covenant seal, baptism provided an answer to the quest for assurance and a ground for the demand of obedience.

The sacrament was a source of assurance, first, because it introduced infants and adults into the visible Church. At least this was the claim of the Puritan ministers who remained within the Church of England. Many of their radical colleagues, who either separated from the establishment or continued the illegal attempt to alter its polity, claimed that Church membership preceded the sacrament of baptism, but the conforming spiritual brotherhood assumed that baptism was the prior mode of admittance. The sacrament did not merely seal or confirm membership but rather created it. John Downame (d. 1652), the rector of St. Margaret, Lothbury and, after 1630, of Allhallows the Great in London, began his ministry by comforting the afflicted consciences of his intimate friends and parishioners; his aptitude as a spiritual director eventually created a wider audience. Downame believed it important to remind his readers that a visible sacrament "initiated, entred, and admitted" them into the visible Church.[44] His friend Richard Sibbes clarified the potential usefulness of such a reminder:

41. Richard Sibbes, *The Faithful Covenanter*, in *The Complete Works of Richard Sibbes, D. D.*, ed. A. B. Grossart (Edinburgh, 1862), 6 : 22.

42. William Perkins, *A Commentarie or Exposition Upon the First Five Chapters of the Epistle to the Galatians, Works*, 2 : 258.

43. Richard Sibbes, *The Saints Comforts, Works*, 7 : 293.

44. John Downame, *A Guide to Godlynesse, Or A Treatise of a Christian Life* (London, 1622), p. 494; Richard Sibbes, *Commentary on Second Corinthians, Works*, 3 : 462; John Dod, *A Plaine and Familiar Exposition of the Ten Commandments* (London, 1609), p. 147; William Haller, *The Rise of Puritanism* (New York, 1938), p. 156.

For first, all that live in the Church are *Christs* to some degree. God hath prevented men with his love, in admitting them to the visible Church: and there is an obligation on them to thinke well of Christ for that, because he had care of them, before they had care of themselves, by vouchsafing them the seale of Baptisme, and making them members of the visible Church.[45]

Seventeenth-century readers would have been struck with the similarity between Sibbes's description of baptism as an expression of God's "preventing" love, and the traditional affirmation of a preventing or prevenient grace that enabled the will to perform "good works pleasant and acceptable to God." [46] Sibbes was saying that in opening the doors to the visible Church baptism became an instrument of divine grace.

Because they considered baptism as the pathway into a Church possessing the means of grace, rather than as a witness and confirmation of piety among Church members, the Puritan pastors were not concerned to establish strict requirements for prospective baptismal candidates. In contrast to radical Separatists, for instance, Perkins was remarkably generous in admitting children to baptism. He baptized the children of wicked and scandalous—even excommunicated—Christians, because he saw no reason that a parent's wickedness "should prejudice the childe in things pertaining to life eternall." [47] Throughout later baptismal controversies, insistence on rigorous admission requirements often varied inversely with the efficacy attributed to the sacrament. Puritans who would baptize only faithful adults inevitably considered baptism to be simply a sign of human faith; those who broadened the standards of admission tended also to magnify the benefits obtained through baptism. The inattention to such standards among the early conforming Puritan pastors exhibited their own positive evaluation of the sacrament.

Baptism was a source of assurance, in a further sense, as a tangible divine pledge that God would, as he had promised, save the faithful and their children. Richard Sibbes comforted distressed parents with the thought that infant baptism was evidence of an existing covenant relation:

I have assured hope that my child is gone to God. He was born in the covenant, and had the seal of the covenant, baptism; why should I doubt of the salvation of my child? If they live to years of discretion, then be of good comfort, he is God's child more than

45. Richard Sibbes, *The Christians End* (London, 1639), pp. 92–93.
46. John Leith, ed., *Creeds of the Churches* (New York, 1963), p. 270.
47. Perkins, *Galations, Works*, 2 : 264; idem, *Cases of Conscience, Works*, 1 : 79.

mine . . . he was baptized in the name of Christ, Christ will care
for him as well as for me. . . . They have received the seal of the
covenant, baptism. Christ will provide for them.[48]

Not only parents, however, but all Christian pilgrims in search of
salvation could derive assurance from baptism. God certified in the
sacrament that he, at least, would perform his part of the covenant;
ministers knowledgeable in "the right use of baptism" would therefore urge their people to meditate on their baptismal washing whenever they felt tempted to sin or remorseful because of their sinfulness.
After all, Perkins reminded them, the sacrament signified that "the
internal washing" would be "offered unto" the baptizand. Such a
pledge of union with Christ and remission of sins was "very effectual to
enforce a particular assurance" of salvation.[49] As Perkins explained in
his *Cases of Conscience,* the primary function of baptism was to be "a
token and pledge of God's favour towards us."

> In regard of this use, baptisme is of great force to releeve the heart
> in distresse. For when any childe of God feeles himselfe loden with
> the burden of his sinnes, the consideration and remembrance
> therof, that God hath pardoned them all, and given him a spe-
> ciall and certaine pledge of his pardon in baptisme, will serve to
> stay and support his soule.[50]

The need to allay anxieties that they themselves had helped arouse
thus inclined the Puritan ministers to accept a Calvinist rather than
a Zwinglian doctrine of baptism. Their sermons repeatedly conveyed
the assuring word that the sacrament confirmed and verified God's
promise.[51] The casuistical handbooks that they began to produce toward
the end of the sixteenth century, designed in part "to appease the rage,
and to quench the scorching flame and fierie darts of the divell, which
so torment all poore distressed consciences in this life," reminded read-

48. Richard Sibbes, "Lydia's Conversion," *Works,* 6 : 531; idem, *Evangelical Sacrifices, Works,* 7 : 486.
49. Perkins, *Golden Chaine, Works,* 1 : 75, 88; idem, *Galatians, Works,* 2 : 258.
50. Perkins, *Cases of Conscience, Works,* 1 : 79.
51. John Downame, *The Summe of Sacred Divinitie* (London, n.d.), p. 360;
Richard Sibbes, *The Right Receiving, Works,* 4 : 65; Rogers, *Seven Treatises,* p. 233;
Dod, *Plaine and Familiar Exposition,* p. 147; Edward Dering, *XXVII Lectures or
Readings upon part of the Epistle written to the Hebrues,* in *M. Derings workes*
(London, 1614), n.p.; Arthur Hildersham, *The Doctrine of Communicating Worth-
ily in the Lords Supper* (London, 1619), p. 23; Ezekiel Culverwell, *A Treatise of
Faith* (London, 1623), p. 357; Richard Greenham, *The Works of the Reverend and
Faithfull Servant of Jesus Christ M. Richard Greenham* (London, 1599–1600), p. 26;
William Bradshaw, *A Preparation to the Receiving of the Sacrament, of Christs Body
and Bloud* (London, 1619), p. 105.

ers who had received the baptismal seal that they had no "need to bee much dismaied." [52] The Christian possessed a pledge of love, said Perkins: that pledge was "thy baptisme, in which God promised to be thy God, and of this promise hee will not fail thee." [53]

The ministers did not ignore the ethical implications of the sacrament, which Perkins also described as a vow "to give homage to the Father, Sonne, and holy Ghost." [54] William Bradshaw was a rigorous Puritan, closely aligned with the congregationalists who complained about the absence of proper ethical and spiritual discipline in Anglican parishes. He followed the lead of Zwingli and Bullinger in tracing the origin of the word "sacrament" to "that Solemne oath, which the Romane Souldiers were wont to take." But like other ministers who accepted his etymology, Bradshaw went on to describe baptism in clearly Calvinist terms.[55] No Reformed theologian could discover signs of crypto-Zwinglianism in the frequent admonitions urging believers to recall the solemn obligation implicit in their baptism.[56] John Preston, the Puritan chaplain to Prince Charles, found himself deeply moved by the "very stile and language" of Calvin's theological treatises; he accepted without question the Calvinist position on baptism; yet he was not averse to the rhetoric of baptismal obedience: "You have given up your names to him in your baptisme: so that now well may I call you an adulterous generation, if you love him not." [57] To fall into wickedness and faithlessness was to renounce a solemn baptismal obligation—every Puritan believed that. So had Calvin himself. But they also believed that baptism represented the accommodation of an infinite and invisible Deity to the visual and conceptual capacities of men.

Finding Calvin's perspective suited to their pastoral task, the Puritan ministers gladly accepted his definition of baptism as an instru-

52. Henry Holland, "Introduction," Greenham's *Works*, n.p.; Perkins, *Cases of Conscience, Works*, 1 : 79.

53. Perkins, *Galatians, Works*, 2 : 256.

54. Ibid., p. 258.

55. Bradshaw, *Preparation*, p. 17; Downame, *Sacred Divinitie*, p. 360.

56. Rogers, *Seven Treatises*, pp. 233–34; John Preston, *The Breast-Plate of Faith and Love* (London, 1630), p. 53; John Preston, *The New Covenant, or the Saints Portion* (London, 1630), p. 349; Henry Smith, "The Wedding Garment," *The Sermons of Master Henry Smith* (London, 1622), p. 159; Downame, *Guide to Godlynesse*, p. 495; Robert Bolton, *A Three-Fold Treatise: Containing the Saints Sure and perpetuall Guide* (London, 1634), p. 39; Bradshaw, *Preparation*, p. 18; Dering, *XXVII Lectures, Works*, n.p.; Paul Baynes, *Brief Directions Unto a Godly Life* (London, 1637), p. 119; Richard Sibbes, *The Saints Cordials, Works*, 7 : 514; idem, "Lydia's Conversion," *Works*, 6 : 531; idem, *Bowels Opened, Works*, 3 : 183.

57. John Preston, *The Onely Love of the Chiefest of Ten Thousand* (London, 1640), p. 5; Haller, *Rise of Puritanism*, p. 71.

ment or means by which God performed what the sign symbolized.[58] They usually added that the sacrament nourished and strengthened faith, and thereby furthered the process of sanctification, as Calvin had said also. By instrumentally conferring the grace to nourish and increase faith, said Perkins, baptism made faith itself a more effective "instrument to apprehend or receive the grace of God." In this sense, the man who rightly used the baptismal seal would surely receive the gift that it signified. So long as baptism was joined to faith, thus being a "perfect and intire baptism," it abolished both the punishment and the guilt of sin, though sinfulness remained in the baptized.[59]

In adopting Calvin's baptismal doctrine, however, the Puritans also inherited the characteristic Reformed ambivalence about external sacraments. Salvation, after all, rested ultimately on the unconditioned election of a Deity who was "the Father and the God of all the elect, and only the elect." [60] The ministers criticized any suggestion that the sacrament conferred saving grace, or removed the stain of original sin, or justified the baptized infant, just as they denied that baptism was necessary for salvation.[61]

> The covenant of grace is absolutely necessary to salvation: for of necessitie a man must be within the covenant, and receive Christ Jesus the very substance thereof; or perish eternally; but a sacrament is not absolutely necessarie, but onely as it is a proppe and stay for faith to leane upon. For it cannot entitle us unto the inheritance of the sonnes of God, as the covenant doth, but onely by reason of faith going before, it doth seale that which before was bestowed upon us.[62]

Contempt of the sacrament, but not its want, was damnable; God saved whomever he would, "though they be not partakers of this sacrament."

58. Downname, *Guide to Godlynesse*, pp. 492–95; Bolton, *Three-Fold Treatise*, p. 38; Sibbes, "Lydia's Conversion," *Works*, 6 : 53.

59. Perkins, *Galatians, Works*, 2 : 258–60; idem, *A Reformed Catholike* (London, 1635), p. 610; John Preston, *The Saints Qualification* (London, 1634), p. 327; Richard Sibbes, *The Saints Cordials, Works*, 7 : 514; Downname, *Guide to Godlynesse*, p. 495; Rogers, *Seven Treatises*, p. 237.

60. Richard Sibbes, *A Heavenly Conference, Works*, 477.

61. Richard Sibbes, *Evangelical Sacrifices, Works*, 7 : 480; Downname, *Sacred Divinitie*, p. 364; *Rogers, Seven Treatises*, p. 237; Greenham, *Works*, pp. 27, 338; Sibbes, *Faithful Convenanter, Works*, 6 : 22. According to Norman Pettit, *The Heart Prepared* (New Haven, 1966), pp. 77–78, Preston believed that the ability of the covenant seed to "prepare for God's entrance into their hearts" rested "on the basis of baptismal regeneration." In the passages cited by Pettit, however, Preston was talking of "the baptisme of the Holy Ghost" metaphorically, referring not to the sacrament but to the outpouring of God's Spirit, which bestowed on some men "a greater measure of grace." See Preston, *New Covenant*, p. 396.

62. Perkins, *Golden Chaine, Works*, 1 : 73.

His grace could not be bound to outward elements.[63] The ministers frequently observed that God had appointed circumcision, the prototype of baptism, to be on the eighth day after birth, knowing that many infants would die before then.[64] This they interpreted as God's own repudiation of the claim that baptism necessarily preceded salvation.

Richard Rogers might say that the sacrament bound God "(in reverence be it spoken) to the performing of his covenant," but he did not for a moment believe that God was obliged to save all who were baptized. God fulfilled his covenant promise when he saved the faithful, who were synonymous with the elect.[65] Perkins also acknowledged that the baptismal seal was fruitless for the reprobate. They received the "signes alone without the things signified by the signes." That was true even of the elect until they were effectually converted; only then could the sacrament have its "good effect." [66] Sibbes explained that the baptized were only in a "general covenant" with God: "if they have no other relation to God, they may go to hell, as Judas and others did." [67]

Precisely in what sense, then, was baptism a trustworthy seal to God's promise? The question was difficult to answer partly because of the ambiguity in the notion of the covenant "seal." Sibbes distinguished four meanings: impression, as "the king's picture or image is stamped or sealed upon the wax"; distinction, as a soldier bears the insignia of his company; appropriation, as in the branding of cattle to show ownership; and ratification, as in the certifying of official documents. Sibbes believed that the Holy Spirit directly sealed Christians by imprinting on their souls a likeness to Christ, by distinguishing them from other men, by showing them that they belonged to God, and by certifying the authenticity and value of his promises.[68] He never spoke of baptism, however, in terms of impression or appropriation: the sacrament did not imprint the image of Christ or ensure that the baptizand bore the mark of election. But it did not merely distinguish professing Christians and their children from other men, or simply pledge them to obedience. Somehow baptism ratified God's covenant promise: it certified that the divine mediatorial activity symbolized by the sign had actually taken place, and it bound God to fulfill his promise of salvation. Sibbes often spoke in those terms. But he also said that "God hath appointed the sacraments to be seals

63. Perkins, *Cases of Conscience, Works,* 1 : 74, 101.
64. Perkins, *Galatians, Works,* 2 : 204; idem, *Cases of Conscience, Works,* 1 : 74.
65. Rogers, *Seven Treatises,* p. 237.
66. Perkins, *Golden Chaine, Works,* 1 : 73, 116 ff., quoting Beza.
67. Richard Sibbes, *A Heavenly Conference, Works,* 6 : 458.
68. Richard Sibbes, *Commentary on Second Corinthians, Works,* 3 : 452–55.

for us, not for himself. He himself keepeth his covenant, whether we have the seal or no, so long as we neglect it not." [69] Baptism, in other words, was appointed to assure all who were baptized of God's mercy, while truly binding God only to save the elect, whom he would save in any case.

Sibbes realized that these qualifications diminished the importance of the sacramental seal. He admitted that this "common broad seal" could not provide a final ground for assurance, which had to rest on the "privy seal" that Christ stamped upon the soul of the true Christian.

> It is another manner of seal than the outward seal in the sacrament that will satisfy and comfort the conscience in the apprehensions of wrath at the hour of death or otherways.

Baptism was still a trustworthy seal: it certified that God would, as he had promised, save the faithful. But only the Christian able to apprehend "the beginnings of faith wrought in him by the Spirit of God" could with comfort think upon his baptism.[70]

The Puritans therefore considered baptism both a divine gift and a problematic theological issue. They could not overcome the ambivalence inherent in the attempt to combine sacramental benefits and inscrutable divine decrees. The doctrine of election was not the sole problem, however. It also clarifies the Puritan ambivalence to recall the older Reformed dichotomies: flesh and spirit, finite and infinite. Perkins interpreted the significance of sacraments within the Reformed liturgy by distinguishing the "principal" worship of God, which was internal and spiritual, from the "outward" worship that included the sacraments. Precisely because of the infinity and spirituality of God, worship in spirit and truth did not require sacraments and ceremonies: "the reason is plain. God is not only a spirit or spiritual substance, but he is in every way infinite and hath sufficiency of all perfection in himself." The visible activities of finite creatures could therefore not "delight" God. Indeed, one prerequisite of true worship was an awareness of the immense "difference between ourselves and God, by reason of the greatness of his majesty" and the pure spirituality of his being. Because God was infinite spirit and omnipotent will, sacraments could have only a limited usefulness.[71]

69. Sibbes, *Faithful Covenanter, Works,* 6 : 22; idem, *Bowels Opened, Works,* 3 : 183.

70. Sibbes, *Second Corinthians, Works,* 3 : 462.

71. William Perkins, *An Instruction Touching Religious or Divine Worship, Works,* 1 : 690–95.

Conversely, the finitude and corporeality of men made sacraments necessary. Of course the primary rationale for them was Scriptural injunction: both baptism and the Lord's Supper were divine ordinances. Christ instituted baptism with the command to his disciples, in Matthew 28 : 19, to "Goe into the whole world, baptizing," and he instituted the Lord's Supper with the command that his disciples "Take, eate, drinke, doe ye this" (Matt. 26 : 26–28).[72] But outward spiritual worship was also required of men simply because "God created as well the body as the soul," and Christ redeemed the whole man, spirit and flesh. Sacramental worship was one mode of the "worship of the body." [73] More importantly, though, sacraments were required as instruments of divine accommodation to finite bodily creatures. Puritans insisted that baptism, and the Lord's Supper as well, were "visible Words" that impressed themselves upon the five senses. The Word "clothed in the sacrament" spoke more fully than the "stark word." It was better designed to influence the embodied mind, which could appropriate spiritual truth only by means of the eye and the ear, aided when necessary by the other senses.[74] Men required sacraments because they were finite and thus unable to comprehend an infinite Creator. Sacraments were accommodations to finitude, not merely to sinfulness; the Puritans insisted that Adam needed sacraments in the garden while he was "yet without sinne." The tree of life was a sacramental accommodation to Adam's finitude.[75]

Because God was infinite (and sovereign) and men were finite (and fallen), and because God was spirit and men were unities of spirit and flesh, Puritans were ambivalent about sacraments. They both affirmed and denied the need for baptism and the Lord's Supper. Perkins insisted that sacraments were not absolutely necessary marks of the Church. A Church might, for instance, lack baptism for a time and yet remain a true Church, just as the Jews continued to be a true "Church" though lacking circumcision during their thirty-year trek in the wilderness.[76]

In addition, the peculiar Puritan modification of the dichotomy between spirit and flesh drastically affected their viewpoint on the sacraments. The introspective mood of Puritan piety revealed a subtle shift in the perennial Reformed reflection on the relation of spirit

72. Perkins, *Golden Chaine, Works*, 1 : 71.
73. Perkins, *Instruction, Works*, 1 : 690–95.
74. William Ames, "Bellarmine Disarmed" (Amsterdam, 1638), trans. Douglas Horton, preliminary typescript available from Harvard Divinity School Library, p. 490; Perkins, *Reformed Catholike*, p. 610.
75. Greenham, *Works*, p. 317.
76. Perkins, *Cases of Conscience, Works*, 1 : 74.

and flesh. Like their predecessors, the Puritan pastors believed that the true Christian lived in the realm of the spirit. Increasingly, though, many of them came to view psychological interiority as the most significant expression of that spiritual realm. One could tolerate the carnal remnants of medieval worship—as the conforming Puritans were often forced to do—so long as one remembered that "principally and properly God is worshipped in our spirit." [77] When Puritan theologians differentiated spirit and flesh, of course, they sometimes had in mind the Pauline distinction between the realm of grace and the sphere of merely human achievement; they also, however, accepted an ontological distinction between matter and spirit, and thus between a fleshly body and a spiritual soul. Richard Sibbes spoke of the body as the mere "case or tabernacle" wherein the soul dwelt, and he believed that the interior spirit of man was the locus of religious experience, the "chief seat of God's good Spirit." Inward spirituality was "the chamber, the bed, and as it were the cabinet for God himself, and Christ to rest in only." [78] Just as the body was inferior to the soul, so also were external religious aids subordinate to inward spirituality.

The exaltation of inwardness manifested itself, for instance, in Puritan discussions of the interpretation of Scripture. All Reformed theologians asserted that the understanding of Scripture began with the immediate and visible activity of the transcendent Spirit on the finite spirit of the interpreter. Richard Greenham, the rector of Dry Drayton and one of the fathers of Puritan spirituality, was repeating a familiar claim when he said that "God his good spirit resteth upon the humble to cleere their understandings" before they could understand the text. The internal illumination of the Spirit preceded the understanding of the external words of Scripture. That was orthodox Calvinist doctrine, but the Puritans elaborated far more carefully than Calvin the internal spiritual qualities of the believer that were necessary for understanding the written Word. Within Puritanism generally, humility, inward purity of heart, and spiritual piety became prerequisites for understanding.[79] Inner spirituality provided the basis for proper interpretation. The focus on internal spiritual states could also be discovered in Puritan definitions of piety, or of conversion, or of churchmanship. But nowhere did the elevation of subjective internality,

77. Perkins, *Instruction, Works,* 1 : 690–95.
78. Richard Sibbes, "The Saint's Hiding Place in the Evil Day," *Works,* 1 : 408; idem, *Second Corinthians, Works,* 3 : 143.
79. Greenham, *Works,* pp. 392, 397; Richard Rogers, Richard Greenham, William Perkins, and George Webb, *A Garden of Spiritual Flowers* (London, 1610), n.p.; William Ames, *The Marrow of Theology,* 3rd. ed. (1629), trans. John Eusden (Boston, 1968), pp. 188, 255–56.

understood as a mode of the dichotomy between flesh and spirit, have more effect than in Puritan reflection on the nature of the Lord's Supper.

The Lord's Supper: Pastoral Subjectivity

The Puritan preachers spoke of the Lord's Supper primarily as a covenant seal and a source of assurance. John Preston, preaching at Lincoln's Inn, seemed often to suggest that no anxiety could survive heartfelt participation in the sacrament. He directed communicants to remind God of his covenant promises each time they received the bread and wine. When God entered into covenant with his people, Preston said, he added "his Seale to it, this Sacrament of the Lords Supper." It was "as if he should say, I have promised to forgive you your sins, let the Sacrament witnesse against me, if I performe it not." At times Preston seemed to have no compunction about restricting even the freedom of God: "when the Lord lookes upon it, hee cannot but remember his promise and his covenant of pardoning our sinnes; and when thou lookest upon it, thou art assured of it." The sacrament might well have been a cosmic court of law. The communicant could "sue" God of "his own bond written and sealed," and God could not deny his claim. Therefore "begge it," Preston told his listeners, "and you cannot misse of it." [80] Preston's language was striking, but his sacramental solution to the quest for assurance was typical of the Puritan ministers.[81] The rhetoric was more striking than the substance, since the seal obliged God only to save the truly faithful, the elect. But that did not hinder the merely presumed faithful from finding in the Lord's Supper a sense of assurance.

In describing the comforts of communion, most English Puritans relied on characteristically Calvinist themes. Zwingli was of little help: he had denied for too long that the sacrament increased faith or advanced the process of sanctification. In sacramental matters, Calvin was the pastor's theologian. Arthur Hildersham (1563–1632) was lecturer at Ashby-de-la-Zouch; his contemporaries praised him for his capacity to satisfy the doubtful, settle the wavering, and comfort the dejected. He did not overlook the pastoral potential of the Lord's Sup-

80. John Preston, *The Cuppe of Blessing*, bound with *Saints Qualification* (London, 1634), pp. 548, 551; John Preston, *Three Sermons Upon the Sacrament of the Lords Supper* (London, 1631), p. 54; Preston, *Saints Qualification*, p. 329.

81. Rogers, *Seven Treatises*, pp. 233–37; Henry Smith, "A Treatise of the Lords Supper in two Sermons," in *Sermons*, p. 70; Culverwell, *Treatise of Faith*, p. 366; Hildersham, *Communicating Worthily*, p. 23; John Preston, *A Preparation to the Lords Supper* (London, 1638), p. 121; Richard Sibbes, *Beames of Divine Light* (London, 1638), p. 155; idem, *Right Receiving*, *Works*, 4 : 69; Downame, *Guide to Godlynesse*, p. 497; Greenham, *Works*, p. 363.

per: because it confirmed God's promise of grace, he said, it could rightly be called "a principall meanes that God hath ordained for the reviving, strengthening, and increasing of our faith." John Downame claimed that the increase of faith, bringing with it assurance of Christ and his benefits, was "the chief end" of the sacrament. Preston agreed that "the one end" of the supper was the strengthening of faith, though he then proceeded to enumerate still other benefits: communion was ordained "not onely to give assurance that your sinnes are forgiven, but likewise to draw more vertue from Christ, to make up the breaches of our hearts, and to get more grace, and to bee made new creatures in a greater measure." [82]

Puritans were absorbed in the task of becoming new creatures "in a greater measure." That was their motive for attending so assiduously to the doctrine of sanctification, which they, unlike the Lutherans, understood as a gradual process restoring the image of God to the soul.[83] No strategist and comforter in the struggle for sanctification was more respected than John Dod (1549–1645), minister at Hanwell, Oxfordshire, before being suspended for his Puritan views, and later the rector at Fawsley, Northamptonshire. Dod would invite the perplexed to his dinner table, or pace with them over the floors of his parish edifice, and he did not neglect to remind them of the manifold sanctifying benefits of communion.

> Though my knowledge be small, it shall be increased: though my memory be weak, it shall be confirmed: though my affections be out of order, they shall be rectified . . . though my frailties be many, the number of them shall be diminished: and though my graces be but few and feeble, they shall be augmented, and still further strengthened.

Dod thought that the Lord's Supper and the preaching of the Word were the two "chiefe meanes" that God employed "for our cleansing and sanctifying." [84] Like baptism, the Lord's Supper also imposed an obligation of obedience,[85] but the Puritans emphasized its benefits in true Calvinist fashion.

82. Hildersham, *Communicating Worthily*, p. 21; Haller, *Rise of Puritanism*, p. 56; Downame, *Guide to Godlynesse*, pp. 492, 497; Preston, *Saints Qualification*, p. 331.

83. Luther did not emphasize gradual Christian growth as a process following justification.

84. John Dod, *Ten Sermons tending Chiefely to the fitting of men for the worthy receiving of the Lords Supper* (London, 1611), pp. 134, 95.

85. Preston, *Breast-Plate*, p. 87; Hildersham, *Communicating Worthily*, pp. 21 ff.; Preston, *Cuppe of Blessing*, p. 549; Sibbes, *Faithful Covenanter, Works*, 6:24; Downame, *Guide to Godlynesse*, p. 499; Bolton, *Three-Fold Treatise*, p. 39; Dod, *Ten Sermons*, p. 38.

Yet theirs was indeed Calvinism with a difference, for Puritan definitions of sacramental benefits represented a departure in tone and emphasis from Calvin. Because they elaborated the dichotomy between flesh and spirit especially in terms of psychological interiority, the Puritans tended to rely on subjective explanations of sacramental efficacy. Perkins described how the Lord's Supper provided confirmation of faith and assurance of salvation.

> The signes and visible elements affect the senses outward and inward: the senses convey their object to the minde: the minde directed by the holy Ghost reasoneth on this manner, out of the promise annexed to the Sacrament: He that useth the elements aright, shall receive grace thereby: but I use the elements aright in faith and repentance, saith the minde of the believer: therefore shall I receive from God increase of grace. Thus, then, faith is confirmed not by the worke done, but by *a kinde of reasoning caused in the mind,* the argument or proofe whereof is borrowed from the elements, being signes and pledges of God mercie.[86]

The sacrament was a seal with which God bound himself to stand to his word, but it worked by evoking a subjective sense of assurance in the mind of the communicant. The emphasis fell on psychological inwardness.

Perkins described a sacrament in formal terms as an external sign and an internal reality united in a "sacramentall relation." The relation was not natural; it did not, that is, effect a substantial mutation of the sign, and the internal reality was never "included in" the sign. A sacramental union was "respective."

> [The union] is respective, because there is a certaine agreement and proportion of the externall things with the internall, and of the actions of one with the actions of the other; whereby it commeth to passe, that the signes, as it were certaine visible words, incurring into the external senses, do by a certain proportionable resemblance draw a Christian mind to the consideration of the things signified, and to be applyed.[87]

The definition itself revealed a tendency to understand sacraments in terms of their impact on the understanding, to offer psychological interpretations of sacramental mysteries. Puritan ministers uniformly described the Lord's Supper as a dramatic exhortation evoking appropriate mental states. It was designed, as Hildersham said, to teach

86. Perkins, *Reformed Catholike,* p. 610 (my emphasis); idem, *Golden Chaine, Works,* 1 : 73.
87. Perkins, *Golden Chaine, Works,* 1 : 72.

men just as the preached Word did—though more plainly.[88] The ministers copiously described the symbolic content of the sacramental actions and elements, hoping that the service would thus convey doctrinal information.

Perkins, for example, distinguished between material and formal sacramental signs. In the Lord's Supper the bread and wine were the material signs. The formal signs, or the ministerial actions, constituted the didactic content of the communion. Taking up the elements, the minister sealed and proclaimed the activity of God in electing his Son as a Mediator. By blessing the elements, thus separating them from their common unto a holy use, he confirmed and taught that God sent Christ to perform his holy offices of prophet, priest, and king. When he broke the bread and poured the wine, the minister silently though graphically described the passion of Christ, and in distributing the elements, he sealed and asserted God's offer of Christ unto all and his effective conveyance to the faithful. By receiving the elements, the communicant testified to his own "apprehension" and "application" of Christ by faith.[89] The ministers attached similar significance to the actions of the baptismal ceremony, thus revealing the extent to which they considered both sacraments to be visible sermons.[90] Every action conveyed an idea, every gesture proclaimed a doctrine. Calvin had been wary of overemphasizing the merely didactic possibilities of sacramental worship, but in Puritan circles the Lord's Supper was unreservedly a vivid spectacle calling to mind the saving truths of the gospel.

Such didacticism furnished one motive for the intense Puritan opposition to the practice of placing the communion table at the east end of the chancel rather than in the body of the church. Puritan ministers disliked the eastern position, partly because of its associations with pre-Reformation "altars" and doctrines of eucharistic sacrifice, but also because the actions of the sacrament were fully visible only when the table stood openly in the midst of the chancel. The ministers were especially hopeful that their congregations would respond to the Fraction, the breaking of the bread, with the awareness that only the breaking of Christ's body on the cross could atone for their sins. In 1592 Lancelot Andrewes, who would eventually become Bishop of Winchester, complained that the attention given to the Fraction

88. Hildersham, *Communicating Worthily*, p. 23.
89. Perkins, *Golden Chaine, Works*, 1 : 73; Bolton, *Three-Fold Treatise*, pp. 39–40; Hildersham, *Communicating Worthily*, pp. 23 ff.; George Webb, in *Garden of Spiritual Flowers*, n.p.; Downame, *Guide to Godlynesse*, pp. 128 ff.; Baynes, *Brief Directions*, pp. 120–21.
90. Perkins, *Golden Chaine, Works*, 1 : 95–96.

was transforming the Lord's Supper into little more than an occasion for evoking mental images of the crucifixion, a trend that Andrewes condemned as the "worshipping of imaginations." [91] Anglicans who preferred the alternative location assumed that intellectual comprehension of the ceremony, and penitential meditation on the sufferings of Christ, were not essential to sacramental communion.

Puritans, however, were particularly concerned that communicants be able to understand and reflect upon the ministerial actions. In order to benefit from the Lord's Supper, each communicant had to be knowledgeable and spiritually prepared, mentally and emotionally receptive to the message in the sacrament. So the ministers demanded of prospective candidates a "speciall and particular examination," an internal search for faith, knowledge, love, repentance, and sincerity.[92] Preparation for communion became a focal point of sacramental piety; one suspects that it was more important to some Puritans than the sacrament itself. In *The Golden Chaine,* where Perkins laid out sacramental doctrine with systematic precision, he devoted over a third of his discussion to preparation. Like Calvin, he pointed out that communion did not require "perfection of faith and repentance," [93] but the space devoted to discussing preparation in his works inevitably magnified its importance. The quality of the communicant's spirituality often loomed as a more dominant reality than Christ's sacramental gift. Within the first decade of the seventeenth century, the ministers began to write manuals outlining the process of preparation.[94] Such manuals were not unique to Puritans, but the steady flow of meditations helped bring an introspective sacramental piety closer to the forefront of their spirituality.

One consequence was a pronounced concern about standards of admission to the Lord's Supper. The Book of Common Prayer directed ministers to exclude the notoriously evil, but few Puritans were content with that minimal standard. Perkins agreed that the scandalous should be excluded, but he also warned the respectable but faithless

91. Lancelot Andrewes, *Ninety-Six Sermons,* 5 vols. (Oxford, 1841–1843), 5 : 67, cited in David Lang Clark, "The Altar Controversy in Early Stuart England" (Th.D. diss., Harvard Divinity School, 1967), pp. 75–76. Clark notes the special interest in the Fraction.

92. Bolton, *Three-Fold Treatise,* p. 5; Sibbes, *Right Receiving, Works,* 4 : 63–64; Downame, *Guide to Godlynesse,* p. 499; Bradshaw, *Preparation,* pp. 54 ff.; Hildersham, *Communicating Worthily,* p. 13; John Preston, *Sinnes Overthrow: Or, A Godly and Learned Treatise of Mortification* (London, 1635), p. 175.

93. Perkins, *Cases of Conscience, Works,* 1 : 82; idem, *Golden Chaine, Works,* 1 : 76 ff.

94. Bradshaw, *Preparation,* one of the first manuals, probably appeared in 1608, when the preface was written. I have used the sixth edition, printed in 1619.

that their presence at the Lord's Table was a grievous sin.[95] In many Puritan congregations the faithless and unprepared were not invited to receive the sacrament. Hildersham pointed out that the admission of the scandalous had made "our assemblies and worship" contemptible to the radical Separatists, and he made the minister responsible for excluding "all such as are unworthy and unprepared." Many ministers were eager to put such advice into practice. Ezekiel Culverwell restricted the sacrament to members who could "give a reason of their hope to bee saved," and William Bradshaw claimed that "many of our Churches (at the least)" excluded all but the "faithful in outward profession, and their seed." [96] Even ministers who neglected formal examinations of prospective communicants continually warned the faithless that they ate and drank to damnation. Some Puritans at the Westminster Assembly in 1643 would launch a successful effort to procure explicit legal authority to suspend the unworthy.

Though they tried to ensure that communicants have "a true, saving and justifying faith," however, the ministers took care not to discourage weaker members.[97] Perkins believed that "every man of years, living in the Church, and being baptized" was "bound in conscience by Gods commandment, to use the Lords Supper." Only a man of faith could be a worthy communicant, but regret over hardness of heart was a sufficient indication of worthiness. Perkins demanded little more than a moral life, correct doctrinal knowledge, and seriousness of purpose. His requirements would have excluded from the Lord's Supper no serious, moral, orthodox members of a parish church.[98] Other Puritans were more rigorous, yet they attempted to avoid impossible rigidity. Preston demanded that communicants be "new creatures" and "in Christ," but he granted that "all may come that will," so long as they resolved to discontinue lives of sin. Hildersham described the worthy communicant as one who possessed a "true justifying faith" and was "undoubtedly assured" that Christ belonged to him, but he too urged "weak Christians" to receive the sacrament.[99] John Dod invited anyone willing to put away "the liking of all sinne, and the purpose of sinning."

95. William Perkins, *A Cloud of Faithfull Witnesses, Works*, 3 : 153–54.

96. Arthur Hildersham, *Lectures Upon the Fourth of John* (London, 1629), p. 129; Hildersham, *Communicating Worthily*, p. 8; William Gouge, "To the Christian Reader," in Culverwell, *Treatise of Faith;* William Bradshaw, *The Unreasonableness of the Separation* (London?, 1640), p. 144.

97. Bradshaw, *Preparation*, p. 58; Downame, *Guide to Godlynesse*, p. 127; Bolton, *Three-Fold Treatise*, p. 18; Preston, *Cuppe of Blessing*, p. 554; idem, *Three Sermons*, p. 3; Hildersham, *Communicating Worthily*, pp. 85–86.

98. Perkins, *Cases of Conscience, Works*, 1 : 81.

99. Preston, *Cuppe of Blessing*, pp. 575, 591; Hildersham, *Communicating Worthily*, pp. 85, 123.

If you have a sight of your defects, and a mourning heart for the same, and a constant endeavour to get the graces that you want, you may come to the Sacrament as soone as any other.[100]

The Puritans hoped that the Lord's Supper would provide the occasion for the extension of faith and holiness among the weak and indifferent as well as the saints. So they preached that communion was obligatory; abstention was sinful. Yet unworthy communion was equally sinful. The only alternative was repentance, holiness, and faithful attendance upon the sacrament, preceded by careful preparation.

The pastoral and practical thrust in Puritan sacramental reflection, with the accompanying disposition to concentrate on the spiritual subjectivity of the communicant, produced a certain imprecision about the issues that divided earlier Reformed theologians. About such matters as the relationship between the *res significans* and the *res significata,* the ministers were often indifferent and sometimes curiously inconsistent. They agreed that the sacrament held forth a genuine spiritual reality—the true "spiritual presence of Christ." [101] Yet they frequently combined, with no apparent sense of incongruity, sacramental themes that had once been considered incompatible.

William Perkins retained a number of Calvinist motifs. He affirmed a spiritual presence in the sacrament: "and that no fained, but a true and real presence." He denied that the Reformed English theologians differed even from Rome on that issue.

We differ not touching the presence it selfe, but onely in the maner of presence. For though wee hold a real presence of Christs body and blood in the sacrament, yet doe we not take it to bee locall, bodily, or substantial, but spirituall and mysticall, to the signes by sacramental relation and to the communicants by faith alone.[102]

The presence comprehended both the Godhead and the substance of Christ's manhood. The communicant received the Godhead "in regard of efficacie" and the human nature of Christ "in respect of substance," along with its merits and other benefits. Every believer therefore received "whole Christ, God and man." Perkins alluded briefly

100. Dod, *Ten Sermons*, pp. 118, 125. See also E. S. Morgan, *Visible Saints* (Ithaca, New York, 1963), pp. 76–77.
101. Hildersham, *Communicating Worthily*, p. 43; Dod, *Ten Sermons*, p. 26; Bolton, *Three-Fold Treatise*, p. 41; Bradshaw, *Preparation*, p. 50; Downame, *Sacred Divinitie*, p. 396; Sibbes, *The Fountain Opened, Works*, 5 : 462 ff.; Preston, *Cuppe of Blessing*, p. 534; Greenham, *Works*, p. 361.
102. Perkins, *Reformed Catholike*, p. 590.

to the Calvinist *sursum corda:* communicants were to lift their hearts
to heaven "to apprehend Christ by faith." [103] But he did not stress
the activity of the Holy Spirit, and he explained the union between
sign and reality largely as a mental event. That was his meaning
when he said that Christ's body and blood were present "with" the
bread and wine "by Sacramental relation."

> [When] the elements of bread and wine are present to the hand
> and to the mouth of the receiver; at the verie same time the body
> and bloud of Christ are presented to the minde: thus and no
> otherwise is Christ truly present with the signes.[104]

Characteristically he offered psychological explanations where Calvin
found incomprehensible mystery. In one brief phrase he even seemed
to accept Zwingli's identification of faith and sacramental eating: "to
eate his flesh is to beleeve in him and to have eternal life." [105]

John Dod provided an equally revealing example of Puritan imprecision. He spoke with Calvin of communion as the journey of the
faithful soul to Christ in heaven.

> Oh, but Christ is in heaven, and wee are in earth, and how can
> we then eat his body and drink his blood? Faith hath a long and
> an high reach, and the spirit of Christ hath as great a reach, to
> convaie the same unto us: and our communion with him is not
> carnall but spirituall.

Yet Dod also identified sacramental eating with faith: to feed upon
Christ was "to believe in him." He did not wish to minimize the reality
of the presence. He believed that Christ was nearer to the faithful
communicant "in his gracious presence" than he had been to his
earthly contemporaries, and he described the supper as "an instrument" to exhibit "Christ with all his merits" unto every believer. But
he did not carefully clarify the nature of the presence.[106]

The examples could be multiplied. Preston spoke of a "true communicating of the body and bloud" in the sacrament and yet said that
"eating of his flesh" was nothing but coming to Christ in faith. He
thought that "the very word, Remember" showed that Christ was
"rather absent than present," for remembrance was of things absent.
Preston certainly had in mind the absence of the physical body,
though his choice of words hardly seemed congruent with a strong

103. Perkins, *Cases of Conscience, Works,* 1 : 83; idem, *Reformed Catholike,* pp.
590–92.
104. Perkins, *Reformed Catholike,* p. 590.
105. Perkins, *Golden Chaine, Works,* 1 : 76.
106. Dod, *Ten Sermons,* pp. 108, 133; 12, 65, 148.

Calvinist doctrine of a true spiritual presence, and he felt no need to clarify the ambiguity.[107] The Puritan Henry Smith sounded like Calvin when he said that the faithful received Christ himself, not merely his benefits, "for Christ may not in any wise be divided from his benefits, no more than the Sunne from his light." Yet Smith, too, identified faith and sacramental eating in a thoroughly Zwinglian fashion.[108] William Bradshaw claimed that a "spiritual matter" was locked within the external signs and he called the sacrament a "blessed instrument" that effectively applied Christ and his merits, but he defined the communion as an experience of subjective remembrance.

> Hence also it appears, that we specially eate the flesh of Christ, and drink his bloud, when with a beleeving heart and mind, we effectually remember and in our remembrance, we seriously meditate of, and in our meditations are religiously affected, and in our affections thoroughly inflamed with the love of Christ, grounded upon that which Christ hath done for us, and which is represented and sealed unto us in this Sacrament.[109]

Sibbes talked of a "most special presence" of Christ in the Supper and suggested that the bread and wine were "used to raise our souls to the bread of life." Yet like Bullinger he described the presence largely in terms of its effect. As a king's influence was present throughout his kingdom, and as the sun sent beams to nourish the earth, so there was in the sacrament "a derivation of virtue from Christ, though his person be in heaven." Sibbes talked of benefits far more than of a substantial presence.[110] Furthermore his beliefs must be inferred from brief passing references in sermons mainly concerned with other matters. That in itself distinguished him from Calvin. It will not do to categorize these ministers as either Calvinists or Zwinglians: in the doctrine of the presence, the issues were too blurred.

In their opposition to Lutheran and Roman Catholic doctrine, the Puritans were unambiguous, and their sacramental arguments often illuminated broader intellectual presuppositions. Their attacks on the Lutheran physical presence, for instance, offered a precise insight into Puritan Christology. Did not the Scriptures testify that Christ ascended to the right hand of God? Was it not an essential property of all bodies to be "circumscribed or compassed of one place?" [111] Was it there-

107. Preston, *Cuppe of Blessing*, pp. 534–36; idem, *Saints Qualification*, p. 487.
108. Smith, "Treatise of the Lord's Supper," pp. 63, 56.
109. Bradshaw, *Preparation*, pp. 18, 30, 37.
110. Richard Sibbes, *A Miracle of Miracles or Christ in our nature* (London, 1638), p. 24; idem, *The Fountain Opened, Works*, 5 : 465, 529.
111. Perkins, *Golden Chaine, Works*, 1 : 76.

fore not impossible for Christ to appear physically in the Supper? In posing such rhetorical questions, Perkins was assuming a disjunction between the finite human nature of Christ and his infinite divine nature. Christ's finite humanity could not assume such a characteristic as omnipresence, which was predicable only of an infinite spiritual reality. Unlike the Lutherans, the Puritan ministers meticulously distinguished the two natures of Christ even while asserting their unity. At certain points in his exegesis Perkins felt constrained to clarify the Scriptural account itself. On the one hand, he said, 1 Corinthians 2 : 8, which recalled the crucifixion of "the Lord of Glory," must be "interpreted according to the human nature," even though the text explicitly spoke "of Christ as he is God." On the other, John 3 : 13 spoke of the descent of the "son of man" as though the manhood were intended, but "we must understand that only his deity came down from heaven." The passage must finally be "understood of his divine nature," despite its apparent reference to Christ's humanity.[112] Perkins' interpretations reflected the Christological doctrine that in Christ himself the finite corporeal humanity remained distinguishable from the infinite spiritual divine nature.

Other criticisms of Roman Catholic and Lutheran doctrine were equally revealing. Christ indeed said: "This is my body." But was it not absurd to think that at that moment he "did with his own hands take his own bodie, and give it wholly to each of his Disciples?" Did not Christ institute the sacrament before his Passion, at which time his disciples could not possibly have consumed his crucified body "after a corporall manner"? If his body were physically present in the bread, and if the bread were distributed into parts, as was customary, was it logical to claim that each communicant received "the whole bodie of Christ," as both Protestants and Roman Catholics believed? The Puritans thought that the enrichment of understanding was a major means of grace; they could not tolerate a sacramental theology that was, as they saw it, patently irrational. To acquiesce in Roman and Lutheran irrationality would be to diminish, if not destroy, a major benefit of communion. And even if that were tolerable, they considered it impious to identify the body of Christ with "bakers bread." For the Puritans Christianity was a spiritual religion; carnality was alien to it.[113]

Some Puritan theologians were sensitive to the charge that they reduced the sacraments to sources of mental stimulation. In a polemic

112. Ian Breward, ed., *The Works of William Perkins* (Appleford, England, 1970), p. 201.
113. Perkins, *Golden Chaine, Works,* 1 : 76.

against the Jesuit Robert Bellarmine, William Ames denied that Protestants conceived of them as "mere signs instituted to stimulate the mind." Sacraments were seals of God's mind and will in the communication of his grace. Ames did not think that sacraments could effect grace of their own power, but he did insist that baptism was an objective seal of God's covenant, not of human faith, and that Christ was spiritually present with the faithful in the Lord's Supper. Yet Ames did not differ from the other Puritan ministers; there was an undeniably subjective dimension in his description of sacraments, which, he said, were "efficacious, at least in adults, in proportion as they are understood." [114]

The early Puritan theologians cannot be distinguished from one another doctrinally, at least not in sacramental matters.[115] Their presuppositions about spirit and flesh, finitude and infinity, divine sovereignty and human inability, sensuous imagination and rational subjectivity created a common ambivalence about sacraments. They viewed baptism as a seal of God's promise and an instrument of grace, yet they felt constrained to discourage confidence in external seals and instruments. Their doctrine of the Lord's Supper maintained clear Calvinist themes, yet Calvinist mystery collapsed under the weight of their psychological explanation. They tried to cultivate a sacramental spirituality, but they deliberately cast their seeds on hard and rocky ground so that the harvest could not support the overindulgent.

Separatists and the Sacraments

To some English Protestants, it seemed that the conforming Puritan ministers failed either from ignorance or from timidity to put into practice their expressed convictions about the Christian life. If the sacraments were essentially communal, as Cartwright and Fenner had argued, did not Anglican practice, with its private administrations, mislead the faithful? If the validity of a sacrament depended on the abilities or the character of the administrator, as the early radicals also suggested, were not many in the Church of England devoid of a

114. Ames, "Bellarmine Disarmed," pp. 523–26; idem, *Marrow of Theology*, pp. 211–12.

115. Pettit, *The Heart Prepared*, pp. 81, 82, suggested that Ames held a higher doctrine of baptism than most of his Puritan contemporaries. But Ames did not say, as Pettit claimed, that baptism was "the very beginning of regeneration." He said something quite different: "Because in the very beginning of regeneration, whereof baptisme is a seale, man is merely passive; whence also there is no outward action required of a man to be circumcised or baptised, as in other sacraments, but only a passive receiving: therefore infants, are as capable of this sacrament, in respect to the chiefe use of it, as these of age are" (*Marrow of Theology*, pp. 182–83).

genuine baptism and deprived of the spiritual nurture of the Lord's Supper? If the Christian valued the spirit over the flesh, then was not the true Church a "spiritual body" devoid both of carnal sin and of the hated vestments and ceremonies? Could there be genuine sacraments without such "spirituall communion"? [116] Within eight years of the *Admonition to Parliament,* some of the Puritans who asked such questions began to separate from the Church of England and to deny that her sacraments possessed any validity.

The earliest known Separatist writing, a *Treatise of the Church,* was written in 1580, probably by Robert Harrison (d. 1585), who along with Robert Browne (1550–1633) led a Separatist congregation from Norwich to Middelburg, Holland in 1581. Harrison scorned the supposition that "blinde guides and dumbe dogges" could administer a valid sacrament. Anyway, he said, since corruption had destroyed the English Church, and since sacraments were seals only to that promise made to the Church, then baptism and the Lord's Supper in the English establishment were inevitably "dead synes and pretended sacraments." [117]

Browne, whose nickname among his opponents was "Troublechurch," had been a student at Cambridge while Cartwright taught there in 1570, and later a lodger with one of the patriarchs among the conforming Puritan pastors, Richard Greenham of Dry Drayton, but his hostility to episcopal authority and corrupt parishioners convinced him that gradual reform by established authorities was unlikely. Browne naturally agreed with Harrison that Anglican sacraments were "accursed" because scandalous members received and "dumbe" ministers dispensed them, but he also added a third objection: parish churches were not constituted by an explicit covenant among the members, and a Church with a false constitution could have no valid sacraments.[118] Cartwright tried to convince Browne and Harrison that sacraments, being gifts of Christ, were "good" even when administered by an unlawful minister.[119] But he failed, and before long other Englishmen were openly belittling Anglican sacraments.

At the time Browne wrote, English theologians entertained, often

116. Robert Browne, *A Treatise Upon the 23. of Matthewe* (Middleburg, 1582), in Albert Peel and Leland H. Carlson, eds., *The Writings of Robert Harrison and Robert Browne* (London, 1953), p. 214.

117. Robert Harrison, *A Treatise of the Church and the Kingdome of Christ, Writings,* pp. 39–40.

118. Browne, *Matthewe, Writings,* pp. 212–14.

119. Thomas Cartwright, "An Answere Unto a Letter of Master Harrisons by Master Cartwright," in Albert Peel and Leland H. Carlson, eds., *Cartwrightiana* (London, 1951), pp. 52–57. See also Robert Browne, "An Answer to Master Cartwright his Letter for Joyning with the English Churches," in *Writings,* p. 472.

simultaneously, two different conceptions of the covenant relation between God and man. One could speak of an unconditional covenant, thereby accenting the divine promises; but there was also talk of a conditional covenant, whereby faithful obedience was incumbent upon men. Browne's doctrine of the Church, and hence of the sacraments, rested on his preference for the conditional terminology. Only through faithful, disciplined obedience could a Church remain in covenant with God. A sacrament, therefore, was more than the confirmation of individual faith or grace; baptism and the Lord's Supper were communal seals. Browne said that churches were formed first by a covenant with God, then by a covenant of mutual love and faithfulness among the members, and finally "by using the sacrament of Baptisme to seale those conditions, and covenants." [120]

Henry Barrow (d. 1593), a former courtier who became the leader of a London Separatist congregation, and his compatriot John Greenwood (d. 1593), a clergyman from Norfolk, denied being disciples of Browne. Yet they also advanced an ecclesiology based on the idea of communal covenant conditions, and it helped convince them that the Church of England, as a false Church, possessed only "adulterate and false sacramentes." [121]

> There neither being lawfull ministery to administer, nor faithfull holye free people, orderly gathered unto the true outward profession of Christ as we have before shewed, and consequently no covenant of grace, the sacraments in these assemblies of baptisme and the Lord's Supper, gyven unto atheists, papists, whoremasters, drunkerds and theire seede, delyvered also after a superstitious manner according to theire liturgye, and not according to the institution and rules of Christ's Testament, are no true sacraments, nor seales with promise. [122]

For publishing such views Barrow and Greenwood were executed in 1593, but their successors, like Francis Johnson, who was elected pastor of the Barrowist congregation in London, continued to preach that the Church of England had broken the communal covenant conditions. It

120. Robert Browne, *A Booke which sheweth the life and manners of all true Christians*, in *Writings*, pp. 254, 261. See the excellent discussion in B. R. White, *The English Separatist Tradition* (Oxford, 1971).

121. Henry Barrow, "Reply to Dr. Some's *A Godly Treatise*: Barrow's marginal notes. . . ." in Leland Carlson, ed., *The Writings of Henry Barrow 1587–1590* (London, 1962), p. 157; Henry Barrow, *A Brief Discoverie of the False Church*, in *Writings 1587–1590*, pp. 418–19.

122. John Greenwood and Henry Barrow, *A Collection of Certaine Sclaunderous Articles Given Out by the Bishops*, in Leland Carlson, ed., *The Writings of John Greenwood* (London, 1962), p. 124.

was therefore vain to seek valid sacraments in "the Cathedrall and parishonall assemblyes of England at this day." [123]

The Separatists' repudiation of the Anglican sacraments was accompanied by a tendency to de-emphasize baptism and the Lord's Supper in their own churches. Browne maintained the traditional Protestant doctrine that baptism and the Lord's Supper were marks of the external Church, though he added the exercise of discipline as a third mark.[124] Barrow, however, denied that the sacraments were necessary marks of the Church,[125] and John Robinson, who accompanied a small band of Separatists from Scrooby in Nottinghamshire to Holland in 1608, believed also that the "Lord's visible covenant," rather than the Word and sacraments, constituted the "essential property of the visible church."

> And as the Word and sacraments may be sacrilegiously usurped by them which are no church of Christ, nor have any right at all unto them, so may the true church of Christ be for a time without them, though never without spiritual right to them. . . . It doth not then cease to be a church, no, nor a visible church neither.[126]

Later in the century, John Cook would describe as typical of all congregationalism, separating and non-separating, the belief that "the Word and Sacraments" were not "the constitution of a Church." [127] To the Separatist ministers, the Church was a covenanted community of believers and their children, inspired by the power of the Spirit, informed by the Scriptures, purified by ecclesiastical discipline. The sacraments were not of its essence.

A denigration of baptism also seemed implicit in the logic of Separatist ecclesiology. The Thirty-nine Articles, as well as Calvin's *Institutes*, defined baptism as the entrance into the visible Church. But if the visible Church were formed by a covenant, as the Separatists claimed, then in what sense was baptism the effective entrance into

123. Camplin Burrage, *The Early English Dissenters in the Light of Recent Research (1550–1641)* (Cambridge, 1912), 2 : 139. Johnson later modified his position. See also John Robinson, *A Justification of Separation from Church of England*, in *The Works of John Robinson*, ed. Robert Ashton (London, 1851), 2 : 337.

124. Browne, *Booke which sheweth*, *Writings*, pp. 257, 279; also idem, "Answere to Cartwright," *Writings*, p. 447.

125. Barrow, *Brief Discoverie*, *Writings 1587–1590*, pp. 309–12.

126. Robinson, *Justification*, *Works*, 2 : 362. See also John Cannes, *A Stay against Straying* (1639), p. 38.

127. John Cook, *What the Independents Would Have* (London, 1647) from extracts printed in *CHST* 14 (1940–44) : 11. For the distinction between separating and non-separating congregationalism, see Perry Miller, *Orthodoxy in Massachusetts* (Cambridge, 1933), pp. 53–101.

Church fellowship? When the Separatist movement was young, the issue did not arise. Browne spoke of baptism "into the bodie and governement of Christ"; but he also said that churches were formed by a covenant which was then sealed by baptism.[128] Did this mean, however, that baptism itself was the mode of entrance, or was it merely the seal of a logically prior Church membership? Was an infant considered a Church member before, or only after, being baptized? Barrow seemed to accept the traditional view.

> None can be a member of a planted church, but such as are baptised. . . . This was the practise of Christ and his apostles, they that were baptised were added and numbred to the church, and not until then receaved into the fellowship: how frendly and well affected soever they were unto the church.[129]

Baptism was the sacrament "whereby all the faithful and their seede enter into" the Church.[130] Johnson thought that children who were "baptized by the church" were "*thus* all members thereof," [131] and Henry Ainsworth (1571–1622?), who in 1596 became a teacher in Johnson's Amsterdam church, also assumed that members were "received into the church by baptism." [132]

The Separatists were compelled to examine the issue more closely, however, when the Baptists, on one hand, and the proponents of the parish churches, on the other, began to criticize Separatist ecclesiology by advancing the argument that baptism, and not a covenant vow, was the primary component of Church membership. Robinson wrote against both the Baptist Thomas Helwys, who claimed that churches were formed by the baptizing of adult believers, and Richard Bernard, vicar of Worksop, Nots, a Puritan critic of the Separatists, who claimed that baptism was the "constitution of the church" whether administered to adults or infants. Robinson could still say that one of the ends of baptism was "to initiate the parties baptized into the Church of Christ," but in order to defend his conception of the Church, he had to argue that "the covenant must be before the church, and the church before the sacrament," [133] so that infants "might be born into the church, and men of years received into it,

128. Browne, *Booke which sheweth, Writings* pp. 254, 261.
129. Barrow, *Brief Discoverie, Writings 1587–1590*, p. 427.
130. Henry Barrow, *A Brief Summe of the Causes of our Seperation*, in *Writings 1587–1590*, p. 134.
131. Francis Johnson, *A Christian Plea* (Amsterdam?, 1617), p. 282 (my emphasis).
132. Henry Ainsworth, *Counterpoyson* (Amsterdam, 1608), p. 13.
133. Robinson, *Justification, Works*, 2 : 28, 299, 334.

and both the one and the other be baptized afterwards." [134] Baptism, he said, was properly "to follow upon" admission into the church; [135] the sacrament was "after" the Church covenant "in order both of nature and time." [136] Developed in detail by Robinson, the notion that baptism was subsequent to the Church covenant, and thus to Church membership, became an accepted part of congregationalist ecclesiology. By 1623 William Ames, a non-separating congregational theologian, was able simply to assume that the "children of those believers who are in the church are to be counted with the believers as members of the church" before being baptized, and early New Englanders concurred.[137]

In such small ways did the Separatist movement seem to diminish the importance of baptism. And by 1608 at least one prominent Separatist minister was willing to carry to its logical conclusion the denigration of the sacrament implicit both in the Separatist schism and in Reformed theology. In that year John Smyth (d. 1612), who led a congregation of English Separatists from Gainsborough to Amsterdam, rebaptized himself and several members of his congregation. No man, he explained later, "can Seperate from England as from a false church except he also Seperate from the baptisme of England, which giveth England her constitution." At the same time, in his treatise on *The Character of the Beast*, Smyth repudiated infant baptism on the ground that infants were incapable of "the baptisme of the Spirit, the confession of the mouth," or of true faith and repentance. He pointed to the absence of a Scriptural precept for infant baptism, and he recalled Christ's command in Matthew 28 : 19 to make disciples by teaching, which proved to him that discipleship and its baptismal sign were intended for adults.[138] But, biblical arguments aside, Smyth was also issuing a call for consistency. Zwingli called baptism a sign of Christian profession; Calvin warned against over-

134. John Robinson, *A Defence of the Doctrine Propounded by the Synod of Dort*, in *Works*, 1 : 462.

135. John Robinson, *Of Religious Communion, Private and Public*, in *Works*, 3 : 168.

136. Robinson, *Justification, Works*, 2 : 298.

137. Ames, *Marrow of Theology*, p. 179. The Separatists also denied the sacramental character of ordination, claiming that a minister needed nothing more than "the approving and consent" of his church. Robert Harrison, *A Little Treatise Uppon the firste Verse of the 122. Psalm*, in *Writings*, p. 99. See also Henry Barrow, *A Plaine Refutation of Mr. George Giffarde's Reprochful Booke*, in Leland H. Carlson, ed., *The Writings of Henry Barrow 1590–1591* (London, 1966), pp. 340 ff. Robinson agreed, but he did advise the imposition of hands. See *Justification, Works*, 2 : 437. They were particularly opposed to ordination by bishops.

138. John Smyth, *The Character of the Beast*, in *The Works of John Smyth*, ed. W. T. Whitley (Cambridge, 1915), pp. 566–67, 574.

emphasizing its efficacy; Harrison and Browne questioned its validity in an impure Church. Smyth cut through all the ambivalence and followed the logic of his tradition to a resolute end. Smyth's decision never ceased to haunt the Puritan movement.

Nevertheless, most Puritans, including the Separatists, defied the logic that Smyth found so compelling. Barrow, for example, agreed that Anglican and Roman Catholic sacraments were false, but saw no need for rebaptism. Most Separatists agreed. The issue was politically sensitive, since Elizabeth was baptized when England was a Catholic realm. She thought, as did most Anglicans, along with Calvin, that Roman Catholic baptism was a true sacrament. The Separatists saw no truth in Roman sacraments, but some of them solved the political dilemma by saying that Elizabeth did not need a true outward seal so long as she was persuaded that her Roman baptism was valid and gave evidence of the inward baptism of the Spirit.[139] Barrow thought that this was an evasion: "As though they that had that inward grace and earnest of their adoption, need not the outward sign, and ought not seek it." He argued against rebaptism entirely on the basis of Scriptural evidence. In the time of Hezekiah, as reported in II Chronicles and Ezra, he said, the circumcision of errant Jews was never repeated.

> Whereby we are evidently taught, both that such baptisme as is delivered in the false church is no true seale of God's covenant (commonly called a true sacrament) and yet also, that such outward washing or baptisme, delivered after their superstitious manner in that idolatrous place, ought not unto such to be repeted as afterward forsake the false church, and joine unto the Church of God.[140]

Though baptism in a false church was no true sacrament, "yet concerning the outward washing it is true baptisme, and . . . the outward action need not and ought not to be againe repeated after the abuse thereof in the false church is purged away by true repentance." [141]

Barrow never completely clarified his refusal to repeat a false

139. The principal exponent of this view was the author of *M. Some Laid Open in His Coulers,* one of the anonymous Martin Marprelate treatises. Donald J. McGinn, *John Penry and the Marprelate Controversy* (New Brunswick, 1966), argues that Penry was the author. Leland Carlson, "Introduction," *The Writings of Henry Barrow 1587–1590,* p. 32, said that it was Job Throckmorton.

140. Barrow, *Brief Discoverie, Writings 1587–1590,* p. 438, 445. See 2 Chronicles 30 : 11–18; 35 : 17; Ezra 6 : 21–22.

141. Barrow, *Plaine Refutation, Writings 1590–1591,* p. 125.

Anglican baptism; he was content to rest his case on the narratives in Ezra and 2 Chronicles. Even sympathetic historians have questioned his consistency,[142] but he was utilizing with some precision a common Reformed distinction between the external and internal dimensions of a sacrament. Such a distinction had long permitted Reformed theologians to explain why the reprobate could be both baptized and damned: they received the external washing without the internal baptism of the Spirit. Barrow, in similar fashion, was arguing that a sacrament was incomplete—merely external—until it was joined to the faith and purity found only in true churches.

The distinction between external and internal baptism became commonplace in Separatist arguments. Robinson worked it out in detail.

> I conclude, therefore, that there is an outward baptism by water, and an inward baptism by the Spirit: which though they ought not to be severed, in their time, by God's appointment, yet many times are by men's default: that the outward baptism in the name of the Father, Son, and Holy Ghost, administered in an apostate church, is false baptism in the administration, and yet in itself, and own nature, a spiritual ordinance, though abused: and whose spiritual uses cannot be had without repentance: by which repentance, and the after baptism of the Spirit it is sanctified, and not to be repeated.[143]

The insistence on the permanence of the external washing was not simply a political or a polemical expedient. Reminiscent of Augustine's arguments against the Donatists in the fifth century, the Separatists' refusal to repeat baptism actually constituted an affirmation of the sacrament's objectivity. A man "once baptized," said Robinson, was "always baptized." [144] The Separatist ministers would repeat a baptism performed in jest, or in a stage play, or administered by an infidel as distinguished from an "apostate" who corruptly professed Christ,[145] but they believed that the essential matter of the sacrament, water, and the form, "baptizing into the name of the Father, Son, and Holy Ghost," existed even in the Church of Rome.[146]

142. J. Powicke, *Henry Barrow Separatist (1550?–1593) and The Exiled Church of Amsterdam 1593–1622* (London, 1900), p. 145.

143. Robinson, *Religious Communion, Works*, 3 : 185.

144. Robinson, *Justification, Works*, 2 : 417.

145. Barrow, *Brief Discoverie, Writings 1587–1590*, p. 449; Robinson, *Religious Communion, Works*, 3 : 187.

146. Robinson, *Justification, Works*, 2 : 413.

That external part of the sacrament could never be erased by human sinfulness.

In 1617 Francis Johnson, reversing an earlier position, even said that baptism was a true sacrament, though abused and misapplied, in the Roman Church. And since Rome possessed a true sacrament, it was a true Church, as was the Church of England, though both remained "in apostasy." [147] This was too much for Ainsworth, who already had broken with Johnson over the latter's desire to invest the power of excommunication solely in the elders or church officers. Ainsworth still believed, as Johnson obviously did not, that the covenant sealed by baptism was conditional, and the papists inevitably failed to fulfill the conditions of faith and repentance. But even Ainsworth followed Barrow's lead and argued against the repetition of baptism, mainly on the basis of the narratives in 2 Chronicles.[148] Separatist ambivalence, in other words, contained an affirmation as well as a denial.

The affirmation appeared clearly in their defense of infant baptism. Both Ainsworth and Robinson produced major treatises against the Baptists. They found arguments for infant baptism scattered throughout the Scriptures, but, like earlier Reformed theologians, they resisted the Baptists mainly by adducing the sacramental implications of the covenant motif.[149] Even in 1609, John Smyth recognized that the covenant theme would be his chief obstacle, and he announced a treatise devoted solely to "the covenants made with Abraham and his seeds." [150] He never published it, but his intentions were accurately directed, for the doctrine of the covenant soon dominated debates between Baptists and their opponents.

In developing the religious implications of their covenantal argument, the Separatists went beyond Zwingli. They did not emphasize an instrumental interpretation, but they also did not consider baptism to be simply "a work of man unto God, for the profession, and exercise of faith, repentance, and thankfulness," though that was included in its meaning. Baptism was "principally and in the main

147. Johnson, *Christian Plea*, pp. 34–37, 121, 214. In *An Apologie or Defence of Such True Christians as are commonly (but unjustly) called Brownists* (Amsterdam, 1604), pp. 91, 109–112, Johnson had taken essentially the same position as Barrow, even quoting at length from one of Barrow's letters.
148. Henry Ainsworth, *A Reply to a Pretended Christian Plea for the Anti-Christian Church of Rome* (1620), pp. 122, 128, 131, 139, 157–58, 171–72.
149. Henry Ainsworth, *A Seasonable Discourse, or A Censure Upon a Dialogue of the Anabaptists* (London, 1644), p. 55. See also Robinson, *Religious Communion, Works*, 3 : 183 ff, 197 ff; Johnson, *Christian Plea*, pp. 1 ff.
150. Smyth, *Character of the Beast, Works*, p. 570.

end performed, not on man's behalf toward God, but on God's behalf towards men." [151] To be sure, Barrow spoke for most Separatists when he said that salvation depended only upon divine predestination. The sacrament was not of any "present benefite to the new borne infant." [152] Robinson called it a means "by which [God] can both declare *and effect* his goodness toward infants," but he also added that baptism was not "effectual to all it is put upon." The benefits were limited to the faithful.[153] But by describing baptism as a seal of God's promise rather than man's profession, the Separatists could use it as a comforting guidepost in their quest for salvation.

> Not that I make baptisme the cause of salvation, or think that none can be saved without it. But God hath made it a most comfortable pledg and seale of his love and help to our faith, all the time that we live in this mortal life. . . .[154]

Baptism, said Ainsworth, was "more than a bare signe." It was a seal assuring the devout of forgiveness, and salvation.[155] As such, it was an integral part of Separatist piety.

As in their doctrine of baptism, so in their understanding of the Lord's Supper, the Separatists displayed some antisacramental tendencies. The Lord's Supper was neither a necessary mark of the Church, nor was it a valid sacrament as administered in the English establishment. Even their pronounced solicitude for the purity of the Lord's Supper threatened to reduce the importance of sacramental worship in Separatist churches, for some of the ministers were willing to discontinue the sacrament altogether rather than to see it administered improperly. A pure sacrament, they thought, required faithful recipients, and they not only demanded a consent to the Church covenant, godly behavior, and a profession of faith, but they also imposed on each communicant the duty of conscientious preparation.[156] Since "all the communicantes at the Lorde's table" were "joyned and commingled together into one spiritual body," to admit the sinful and unprepared was to defile both the sacrament and the

---

151. Robinson, *Religious Communion, Works,* 3 : 200.

152. Barrow, *Plaine Refutation, Writings 1590–1591,* p. 89.

153. Robinson, *Religious Communion, Works,* 3 : 201 (my emphasis); idem, *Justification, Works,* 2 : 115.

154. Barrow, *Brief Discoverie, Writings 1587–1590,* p. 451.

155. Ainsworth, *Seasonable Discourse,* p. 59.

156. Barrow, *Plaine Refutation, Writings 1590–1591,* p. 179; Greenwood and Barrow, "Sclaunderous Articles," *Writings,* p. 137; Browne, *Booke which sheweth, Writings,* pp. 278 ff.; Robinson, *Religious Communion, Works,* 3 : 166; Johnson, *Apologie,* p. 72. See also Morgan, *Visible Saints,* pp. 33–63.

faithful communicants.[157] Most Separatists also thought a worthy minister essential. The Brownist Confession of Faith of 1602 stated that no sacrament was "to be administered until the Pastors or Teachers be chosen, and ordained to their office." [158] As a consequence of all this scrupulosity, some Separatists relinquished the Lord's Supper for extended periods; their antagonists claimed that they often omitted it altogether.[159] After part of his Leyden congregation migrated to Plymouth in 1620, John Robinson did advise them to forego the Lord's Supper until a minister was available. John Paget said in 1635 that the members of Ainsworth's church, after his death, "were without Sacraments, and had neither Lords Supper nor Baptisme administred in their Church." [160] So it was true that the spiritual milieu of the early Separatist churches—with their stress on the preaching of charismatic ministers and the spiritual fellowship of covenanted congregations—was not conducive to a profoundly sacramental religious sensibility.

These antisacramental tendencies, however, the Separatist ministers also resisted. Johnson recommended frequent administration of the Lord's Supper.[161] Greenwood challenged those who faulted the Separatists for neglecting the Supper: "In that we have no sacraments amongst us, it is not by our default (whose soules gaspe and bray after them) so much as by your barbarous crueltie and tyrannical dealing with us, who will not suffer us to assemble. . . ." [162] It is also quite clear that the Separatists were not exponents of an attenuated memorialist doctrine. They had little to say about the sacramental presence —which in itself was a departure from the attitude of Calvin—but they did believe that the faithful communicant could actually "feed on our Saviour Christ." [163] A description of communion by Browne and Harrison exhibited the direction of Separatist teaching.

157. Barrow, *Plaine Refutation, Writings 1590–1591*, pp. 177–79. See also Johnson, *Apologie*, p. 72.

158. Quoted in G. F. Nuttall, "The Early Congregational Conception of the Church," *CHST* 14 (1940–44) : 202. See also Johnson, *Christian Plea*, p. 288; and Barrow, "Reply," *Writings 1587–1590*, pp. 155 ff. A few early seventeenth–century congregationalists would allow laymen to administer sacraments. Nuttall mentions two, Katherine Chidley and John Milton.

159. Greenwood and Barrow, "Certen Wicked Sects and Opinions," in *Writings*, p. 299.

160. John Paget, *Answer,* quoted in Burrage, *Early English Dissenters,* 1 : 173.

161. Johnson, *Apologie*, p. 289.

162. Greenwood and Barrow, "Sclaunderous Articles," *Writings*, p. 170.

163. Robert Harrison and Robert Browne, *Three Formes of Catechismes conteyning the most principall pointes of Religion*, in *Writings*, p. 140. See also Stephen Mayor, "The Lord's Supper in the Teachings of the Separatists," *CHST* 19 (1963) : 220.

> The preacher must take breade and blesse and geve thankes, and
> then must he breake it and pronounce it to be the body of Christ,
> which was broken for them, that by fayth they might feede thereon
> spirituallie and growe into one spiritual bodie of Christ, and so
> he eating thereof himselfe, must bidd them take and eate it among
> them, and feede on Christ in their consciences.
>
> Likewise also must he take the cuppe and blesse and geve thankes,
> and so pronounce it to be the bloud of Christ in the newe Testa-
> ment, which was shedd for remission of sinnes, that by fayth we
> might drinke it spirituallie, and so be nourished in one spirituall
> bodie of Christ, all sinne being clensed away, and then he drinking
> thereof himselfe must bydd them drinke thereof likewise and di-
> vide it among them, and feede on Christ in their consciences.[164]

On the one hand, the references to the conscience suggest a highly
subjective interpretation of the Lord's Supper; on the other, the allusions to the body and blood in the formula of distribution reflect the
1559 Prayer Book rather than the purely spiritualistic motifs of the
1552 Prayer Book. The structure and actions of the ceremony indicate
a desire to reenact the historical Supper, a desire which in itself indicates a memorialist tendency, but the language accents spiritual communion rather than historical commemoration.

The Separatists did not spend much time clarifying their doctrine of
the presence. Barrow moved toward a purely symbolic interpretation
when he said that the Lord's Supper was a "comfortable symbole of
our communion with Christ," arousing the faithful to thankfulness
and praise.[165] But Johnson sounded much like Calvin when he described the bread and wine as "signes and seales" exhibiting to true
believers "the Lord Jesus Christ and all his benefits." [166] Despite occasional ambiguities, the Separatists did not generally view the Lord's
Supper only as a memorial or a profession of commitment. They defined it as an effectual "seale, or pledge" of God's promise.[167] As such,
the sacrament strengthened the unity and fellowship of the Church.
The Separatists claimed that the Supper nourished the faithful while

164. Browne, *Booke which sheweth, Writings,* p. 284.
165. Barrow, *Brief Discoverie, Writings 1587–1590,* p. 629. Powicke, *Henry Barrow,* p. 108, insisted that the Lord's table "meant more to Barrow than a table of
remembrance," which may have been true. But Geoffrey Nuttall, *The Holy Spirit
in Puritan Faith and Experience* (Oxford, 1946), p. 93, saw the seeds of Quakerism
in some of Barrow's statements. Nuttall, I think, perceived the direction of Barrow's
thought, but the evidence is too skimpy to permit sound generalization.
166. Johnson, *Apologie,* p. 25.
167. Browne, *Booke which sheweth, Writings* p. 285; Robinson, *Justification,
Works,* 2 : 98; Harrison and Browne, *Three Formes of Catechismes, Writings,* p. 140.

also denoting their communion with Christ as members of "one mystical body." [168] It was not strange that their ecclesiological preoccupations would influence Separatist doctrine, but it was noteworthy that sacramental issues constituted such a major part of their reflections on the Church. Ambivalence was more clearly visible in their sacramental thought than in that of most other Puritans, as would be expected in a sectarian movement, but the Separatists retained a surprising appreciation for both baptism and the Lord's Supper.

The Directions of Puritan Sacramental Thought

Puritan sacramental theology was practical and pastoral. The themes varied, but whether as Separatists talking about relationship between Church and sacrament, or as preachers with sermons on assurance and obligation, the Puritans never escaped their ambivalence about sacraments, which was clearly evident in the debates of the later seventeenth century. The debates, though, did lead to a resurgence of sacramental discussions among numerous Puritan ministers, who explored thoroughly the relationships between sacramental and covenantal thinking. If sacraments were covenant seals, what was implied about admission to baptism and the Lord's Supper? What did it in fact mean to say that a sacrament "sealed" a covenant? Did sacraments convey grace as well as seal it?

It has become a commonplace, and it is largely correct, to say that the Puritan impulse led to a gradual disinterest in the sacraments. This was true among many sectarian groups, especially the Quakers and the growing Baptist movement. But there was also a countermovement, not only among men who were moving away from a Puritan past, but also among ministers who retained characteristic Puritan interests. The new involvement in sacramental matters took several forms. It was reflected in the proliferation of treatises, sermons, and public pronouncements directed against the Baptists. In some cases it developed into efforts to define a doctrine of sacramental efficacy that went beyond earlier Puritan views. Some theologians began to espouse a peculiarly Reformed doctrine of baptismal regeneration that was, they claimed, compatible with the doctrine of predestination. Others tried to popularize the doctrine that the Lord's Supper was a "converting ordinance." And even among ministers who rejected such views there was a burgeoning sacramental piety, evidenced especially in the growing popularity of eucharistic manuals and sermons. Especially visible in

168. Robinson, *Justification, Works,* 2 : 98; Barrow, *Plaine Refutation, Writings 1590-1591,* p. 152; Browne, *Booke which sheweth, Writings,* pp. 279-80.

New England, the fascination with eucharistic devotional material was also a characteristic of much English non-conformist spirituality in the late seventeenth century. Among the devotees of this sacramental piety, there was occasionally an effort to reaffirm traditional Protestant positions that had been neglected, to insist with renewed emphasis, for example, that the spiritual presence was the essential precondition of benefit from the Lord's Supper. The new interest in sacramental themes was manifest simply in the time and energy that later seventeenth-century Puritans were willing to expend in debate over such issues.

3

BAPTISMAL DEBATE IN ENGLAND

Most seventeenth-century Puritans discovered in the covenant motif a justification for the sacraments, but the discovery neither convinced their antisacramental opponents nor satisfied all their fellow Puritans. The majority believed by the middle of the century that "the doctrine of the Covenant truly stated" was the source whence "the sacraments do as it were receive a soul." [1] Yet some men complained that the notion of sacraments as covenant seals "perverted" English Christians by causing them to think too highly of baptism.[2] Others felt that the covenant had been used to defend a sacramentalism so attenuated as to be hardly worth the effort. Consequently there were numerous baptismal debates that attracted widespread interest, so that by 1655 one Puritan theologian observed that "they are almost above number that have treated of the Sacraments." [3]

The debates focused on admission to baptism, with the Baptists wanting to exclude infants, other Puritans to include them. Among the paedobaptists, some would admit infants but exclude adults unable or unwilling to profess saving faith, as well as their children, while others wanted to baptize all infants and all unbaptized adults who verbally accepted Christian doctrine. But underlying the various admission standards were divergent views of the nature of the sacrament itself. Most seventeenth-century Puritan ministers accepted Calvin's doctrine: baptism was a seal of God's promise and a means by which, in the words of the Westminster Confession, "the grace promised is not only offered, but really exhibited and conferred by the Holy

1. Richard Vines and Samuel Fisher, "To the Reader," in Thomas Blake, *Vindiciae Foederis, Or a Treatise of the Covenant* (London, 1653), n. p.
2. John Tombes, *Anti-Paedobaptisme: Or the Third Part* (London, 1657), p. 262.
3. Thomas Blake, *The Covenant Sealed, or, A Treatise of the Sacraments of both Covenants* (London, 1655), p. 2.

Ghost, to such (whether of age or infants) as the grace belongeth unto, according to the counsel of God's own will, in his appointed time." [4] God therefore used baptism to sanctify and increase the faith of his elect saints. By the third decade of the century, though, Puritans were wrestling with a new set of problems, arising in part from the intimate association of baptism with covenant doctrine.

Their reflections produced a spectrum of sacramental theories, divisible into three major groups. First were the ministers who accepted Baptist claims that baptism was no covenant seal, preferring to call it a sign of Christian profession. Second were the Puritan sacramentalists, who criticized covenantal imagery because they believed baptism itself to be an efficacious means of grace, whether as an instrument of "initial grace" for all baptized infants, as Samuel Ward would say, or an instrument of "initial regeneration" for elect infants only, which was the doctrine of Cornelius Burges. Third were the Puritans who still believed that baptism was a covenant seal, though no longer agreeing on precisely what that meant. Some of them said that the sacrament sealed both faith and a conditional covenant; others claimed that it sealed not faith but a conditional, external covenant containing "a promise of the spirit." Within this spectrum of divergent views, each theologian presented his alternative as authentic Reformed baptismal doctrine, in perfect harmony with predestination, divine sovereignty, and the spirituality of the Christian life. After 1630 Puritans seeking a viable doctrine of baptism had a wide selection.

Baptist Challenge and Sacramentalist Reaction

As early as 1622 English authorities perceived the Baptist movement as a danger. In that year King James I and Archbishop Abbot expressed anxiety at hearing "of soe manie defeccions from our Religion, both to Poperie and Anabaptisme." A reaction against Baptist sentiments became visible in 1623 with the publication of three treatises against their doctrine, but in 1631 Sir Simonds D'Ewes was still talking about "the daily growing and far-spreading" of Baptist principles.[5] By then two major groups, the Particular Baptists, who held to a strict Calvinist doctrine of election, and the General Baptists, characterized by a doctrine of conditional election, had developed thriving churches

4. Schaff, *Creeds of Christendom*, 3 : 2.

5. Burrage, *Early English Dissenters*, 1 : 266–67: Sir Simonds D'Ewes, *The Autobiography and Correspondence of Sir Simonds D'Ewes*, ed. J. O. Halliwell (London, 1845), 2 : 64. The anti-Baptist treatises were Edmond Jessop, *A Discovery of the Errors of the English Anabaptists*; [John Paget], *Anabaptismes Mysterie of Iniquity Unmasked*; Henry Ainsworth, *A Censure Upon a Dialogue of the Anabaptists*.

and attracted such able theological proponents as John Spilsbury, Henry Denne, and Hanserd Knollys. One reason for the success of both Baptist groups was their ability to raise disturbing questions about the subjects, efficacy, mode, and administration of baptism.

The underlying issue, however, was the Baptist doctrine of the gathered Church of adult believers, which required the repudiation of infant baptism. Baptists were biblical literalists who had an intense sense of spiritual immediacy and a conception of conversion that created suspicion of external forms. So also were other Puritans, but from a Baptist perspective they were blind to the implications of their doctrine and piety. The most persuasive Baptist argument was that Christ's command and example in the New Testament warranted only the baptism of the faithful. But undergirding that reading of Scripture was a conviction that Church membership did not belong to the "seed after the flesh, but after the spirit." The Baptists therefore considered baptism a covenant seal only in the carefully defined sense that it signified entrance into the "part of the covenant of grace" that was "spirituall." [6] For that reason, only believers, Abraham's true "spirituall seed," were to be baptized. Baptists preferred to think of the ordinance as a sign with which the faithful believer publicly demonstrated his obedience to the command of Christ, a symbol of inward spirituality.[7]

Some Puritan theologians decided that only thorough reexamination of baptismal doctrine would produce a convincing alternative to the Baptist position. The result was a new form of sacramentalism, which Richard Baxter described as an exaggerated reaction against "the error of the Anabaptists." Too many "incautelous [incautious] men," offended by the Baptist denigration of sacramental grace, he claimed, were too inclined "to run into the contrary extreme." [8] The sacramentalists were not, however, simply reacting against the Baptists. They were also enlarging upon an implicit pastoral ideal of the conforming Puritan tradition, namely, that Church membership was a process of

6. Henry Denne, *Antichrist Unmasked in Two Treatises* (London?, 1645), p. 41.

7. Edward Barber, *A Small Treatise of Baptisme, or Dipping* (London?, 1641), p. 8; *A Confession of Faith of Seven Congregations or Churches of Christ in London, Which are Commonly (But Unjustly) Called Anabaptists*, 2nd ed. (London, 1646), in E. B. Underhill, ed., *Confessions of Faith and Other Public Documents Illustrative of the History of the Baptist Churches of England in the 17th Century* (London, 1854), pp. 41–42; Benjamin Cox, *An Appendix to a Confession of Faith* (London, 1646), in Underhill, *Confessions*, p. 57.

8. Richard Baxter, *An Appendix containing some Briefe Animadversions on a Tractate lately published by Mr. Thomas Bedford: Written part by himself, and part by Dr. Samuel Ward* (London, 1652), in Richard Baxter, *Plain Scripture Proof of Infants Church-Membership and Baptism* (London, 1653), p. 293.

nurture facilitated by visible means of grace. In pursuing this ideal, though, they were more willing than earlier Puritans to narrow the breach between flesh and spirit, to connect spiritual grace with tangible and visible rites. Other Puritans embraced a similar view of Church membership, although they still considered the sacramentalist formulation too extreme. Nevertheless, it was being given expression by respected Puritan ministers, a fact that made the new sacramentalism seem to Baxter all the more dangerous.

The first architect of Puritan sacramentalism was Samuel Ward (1571–1643), the eminently respectable master of Sidney Sussex College and Lady Margaret Professor at Cambridge. A student of William Perkins and a delegate to the Calvinist Synod of Dort, Ward was sympathetic to Puritan reform and, despite some later lapses, an admired representative of Puritan piety. He prayed with Perkins as the great Puritan preacher lay dying in 1602, edited some of his works, listened to Lawrence Chaderton's sermons, and conversed about the spiritual life with Paul Baynes. He also complained in his diary in 1604 about plots to impose the hated surplice on Emmanuel College.[9] When William Laud became Archbishop of Canterbury in 1633, Ward received pointed criticisms for "favouring Puritans," and by 1635 he was lamenting "the times," complaining that theologians were able openly to "maintain the vilest and most feculent points of all Popery." The Long Parliament of 1640 named him to the committee that considered the Root and Branch petition to abolish episcopacy, and also invited him to represent Cambridge at the Westminister Assembly. By 1643, however, Ward had lost some of his Puritan fervor.[10] Parliamentary forces imprisoned him when they occupied Cambridge during the Civil War, by which time he was coming to be known, to the dismay of his friends, as a pluralist with no qualms about multiplying livings and

9. Samuel Ward, "Diary," in M.M. Knappen, ed., *Two Elizabethan Puritan Diaries* (Chicago, 1933), pp. 103, 115, 127. Knappen claims that Ward moved away from his youthful Puritanism. The claim was also made in the seventeenth century, though it was rebutted by Thomas Fuller, *The Worthies of England*, ed. John Freeman (London, 1952), p. 160 : "In a word, he was counted a puritan before these times, and popish in these times; and yet, being always the same, was a true protestant at all times." Certainly Ward's sacramental theology could be interpreted as a break with the Puritan consensus on this issue. For a brief discussion of Ward's Puritanism, and his influence on Oliver Cromwell, see Maurice Ashley, *The Greatness of Oliver Cromwell* (New York, 1962), pp. 46–48; and Robert S. Paul, *The Lord Protector: Religion and Politics in the Life of Oliver Cromwell* (London, 1955), pp. 31–33.

10. Ward, "Letter to Ussher," June 14, 1634, in *The Whole Work of the Most Rev. James Ussher, D. D. Lord Archbishop of Armagh and Primate of all Ireland*, ed. Charles R. Elrington (Dublin, 1864), 15 : 581. Cited hereafter as *Work*. See also D'Ewes, *Autobiography*, p. 124; Paul, *Lord Protector*, p. 33.

offices. Yet after his death Ward was still respected by Puritans who were dismayed by his pluralism as well as his doctrine of baptism.[11]

Ward himself deplored the high sacramental doctrines of some of his contemporaries. In 1635 he "openly rebuked" John Nevell, a fellow of Pembroke Hall, for saying that "the very outward act of baptism took away sin." [12] In his lectures on the Eucharist, in which he defended a strong doctrine of sacramental efficacy, Ward engaged in the customary Protestant attack on Roman Catholic doctrine, criticizing specifically the arguments of a French cardinal named Jacques-Davy Duperron.[13]

Ward also tried, however, to formulate a new Reformed sacramental theology, with particular emphasis on baptism. In a series of letters and manuscripts written around 1627, he announced that all infants were, without any doubt, justified through baptism. Baptized children who died during their infancy were assured of salvation.[14] Baptism was not an absolute necessity; were a child to die before baptism, the faith of the parents and the Church might suffice for him. Such an assurance was typical of Puritan theology, but the qualification that Ward appended to this comforting word seemed to reassert the necessity of baptism for salvation. Baptism, he said, was "by necessity the ordinary means for the ablution of original guilt in infants" and hence for their salvation.[15] Ward's point was subtle, and for that reason often misunderstood: he received at least one letter challenging "the imagined necessity of baptism to infants to salvation, as if it were indeed a medicine to save life." [16] He was simply saying, however, that while unbaptized infants could be saved, baptized infants who died in infancy

11. Baxter, *Appendix, Plain Scripture Proof,* p. 332.

12. D'Ewes, *Autobiography,* p. 124.

13. James Ussher, "Letter to Ward," March 15, 1629, *Work,* 15 : 480; Ward, "Letter to Bedell," May 28, 1630, *Work,* 15 : 511. For Duperron, see *Lexikon für Theologie und Kirche,* 3 : 607. Duperron's *Traité de l'Eucharistie* appeared in 1622.

14. Samuel Ward and Thomas Gataker, *De Baptismatis Infantilis Vi et Efficacia Disceptatio, Privatim habita, Inter Virum Celeberrimum,* in Gataker, *Opera Critica* (1698), pp. 90, 131; hereafter cited as Ward, *Baptismatis.* The title and central proposition of the debate was: *Omnes baptizati infantes sine dubio justificantur.* Gataker's transcription of the debate, which he first published in 1653, is the only document, apart from Ward's letters, in which Ward's views on baptism were preserved. Gataker published long excerpts from Ward's unpublished writings, followed by his own replies, further responses from Ward, and then Gataker had the last word on each issue. Knappen, *Two Elizabethan Puritan Diaries,* p. 45, n. 29, observed that *Baptismatis Infantilis* "professes to be an account of a discussion on infant baptism between Thomas Gataker and Ward." After comparing the work with letters from Ward to Ussher and Bedell, and their replies, I am convinced that Gataker accurately transcribed Ward's arguments.

15. Ward, *Baptismatis,* p. 131.

16. William Bedell, "Letter to Ward," *Work,* 15 : 518.

would be saved. Baptism he understood as usually prerequisite for salvation.

As an instrument for applying the merit of Christ to an infant, baptism was for Ward a "true solution for original guilt." [17] He acknowledged that "most of our divines" held that "ablution of infants from original sin [in baptism] is only conditional and expectative, of which they have no benefit till they believe and repent." [18] But this notion reduced the sacrament to a matter of "naked and inefficacious signs." Why baptize infants at all if "it produce no effect til years of discretion?" How do baptized infants dying in infancy, or non-elect infants, have any benefits from baptism if its efficacy is realized only in some distant future? [19] Ward thought it insufficient simply to say that baptism was a sign and seal of grace unless it were added that the sacrament conferred what it signified and conveyed what it sealed—and did so when the infant was baptized.[20]

Despite Ward's assurances that his doctrine was consistent with Calvin's views,[21] his definitions were ill designed to comfort Puritans who still espied in any allusion to sacramental grace the machinations of papal propagandists. He also disturbed more moderate Puritan theologians, however, by his explicit rejection of two notions that had come to be commonplace among them. He denied the priority of the covenant in sacramental theology, and he rejected the idea that a sacrament was mainly a seal. Ward did not discard the covenant, but he minimized its importance. Richard Baxter charged later that this was Ward's "great mistake of all, and the fountain of most of the rest." It was "the very core of men's ascribing to much to baptism." Earlier Puritans had believed that baptism signified and sealed a prior covenantal relationship. Ward reversed the relation: baptism, and not the covenant, was the primary means of justification for infants. This claim that "baptism is the first means of remission, and the Covenant before Baptism doth it not" was what Baxter thought "so injudicious to the Church and Covenant of God." [22] Ward denied that infants were justified by the covenant without the sacrament. It cannot, he said, "be deduced" from either the covenant of works or the covenant of grace "that all the children of the faithful . . . ordinarily are justified by the power of the covenant alone before partaking the sacrament and

17. Ward, *Baptismatis*, pp. 99, 122.
18. Ward, "Letter to Bedell, May 28, 1630, *Work*, 15 : 510.
19. Ward, "Letter to Ussher," May 25, 1630, *Work*, 15 : 505.
20. Ward, *Baptismatis*, p. 112. See also Ward, "Letter to Bedell," May 28, 1630, *Work*, 15 : 511.
21. Ward, *Baptismatis*, p. 151.
22. Baxter, *Appendix, Plain Scripture Proof*, pp. 324–25.

apart from the sacrament." Many children within the covenant would perish; infants of the faithful often fell away as adults, while infants of infidels sometimes became ardent Christians.[23] All Puritans would have agreed that some infants in the covenant were doomed; many of them, however, would have considered the salvation of covenanted children to be at least "strongly probable." [24] Ward lacked such confidence.

Ward also reinterpreted the covenant promise. Like most Puritan theologians, he thought that the covenant was conditional. When seventeenth-century theologians spoke of conditions, however, they had in mind the requirement that men respond to God with faith and repentance. According to Ward, baptism fulfilled the condition. His exegesis of Genesis 17 : 7 diverged radically from the prevailing interpretation.

> That promise, Gen. 17.7—"I will be your God, and [the God] of your seed"—is not absolute, but conditional, made under condition of the observing of circumcision, which is the ordinary means for the remission of original guilt.[25]

As the Christian analogue to circumcision, baptism became the means by which parents could fulfill the covenant condition for their children. Ward still spoke of a covenant of grace that required of adults repentance and faith, without which adult baptism was ineffective.[26] In his reflections on infant baptism, however, he advanced toward a sacramentalism independent of traditional covenantal ideas.

It is not surprising, then, that Ward criticized the tendency to define baptism primarily as a seal. He was disturbed, as he told Archbishop Ussher, that "most of our Divines do make the principal end and effect of all sacraments to be obsignation." [27] For adults who fulfilled the covenant conditions prior to baptism, the sacrament was a seal of grace. But infants could fulfill no covenants through faith and repentance, so infant baptism was of necessity more than a seal.[28] It conveyed the grace that it sealed.

23. "Ex neutro horum deduci potest, omnes filios fidelium . . . ordinarie vi solius foederis justificare ante susceptum sacramentum at absqe sacramento" (Ward, *Baptismatis*, p. 136).

24. Baxter, *Appendix, Plain Scripture Proof*, p. 330.

25. "Promissio illa Gen. 17.7 Ero Deus tuus, et seminis tui; non est absoluta, sed conditionalis, facta sub conditione observatae Circumcisionis, qae est ordinarium medium remissionis originalis reatus" (Ward, *Baptismatis*, p. 135).

26. Ibid., p. 160.

27. Ward, "Letter to Ussher," May 25, 1630, *Work*, 15 : 505.

28. Ward, *Baptismatis*, p. 99.

So that instrumental conveyance of the grace signified, to the due receiver, is as true an effect or end of a sacrament, when it is duly administered, as obsignation and is pre-existing in order of nature to obsignation: for obsignation must be of that *quod prius datur et exhibetur*. . . .[29]

As Archbishop Ussher reminded Ward, this was not "the Opinion more vulgarly received" among Reformed theologians.[30] Even William Bedell, the Bishop of Kilmore, wrote Ward exhorting him to define sacraments "not as medicines, but as seals to confirm the covenant." [31] But Ward thought that the conception of baptism as a seal was probably irrelevant in the case of infants.[32]

Ward was implicitly criticizing Calvin, who had not distinguished between sealing and instrumental conveyance. But despite his sacramental terminology, he was deeply rooted in the Reformed tradition and its predestinarian theology. For while he proposed that baptism regenerated infants, Ward also said that salvation depended on the secret and absolute will of God.

The non-elect never come to be justified by a true and lively faith, nor ever are by that bond mystically united to Christ as their seed, nor ever attain unto true repentance.[33]

But how could he acknowledge the free, mysterious character of divine election without qualifying his doctrine of baptismal efficacy? And what about infants who failed to "persevere to salvation as adults"? [34] Had he said that even apostates were justified in baptism as infants, he would have denied the Reformed doctrine of perseverance, which stated that God's elect saints, once justified, inevitably persevered to salvation. Ward could either deny that any baptized infants ever fell into apostasy—which was unthinkable for a Reformed theologian—or he could qualify his assertions about baptismal efficacy.

His qualifications took two forms. First, the original sin of non-elect infants was indeed remitted in baptism, but they would still be damned on account of the actual sins that they inevitably would commit. Second, the justification of infants in baptism was temporary: "The forgiveness of original sin which is sufficient for the justification of infants, does not suffice to justify them when they reach adulthood."

29. Ward, "Letter to Ussher," May 25, 1630, *Work*, 15 : 506.
30. Ussher, "Letter to Ward," March 15, 1629, *Work*, 15 : 482.
31. Bedell, "Letter to Ward," *Work*, 15: 508–09.
32. Ward, "Letter to Ussher," May 25, 1630, *Work*, 15 : 506.
33. Ward, *Baptismatis*, p. 137; Ward, "Letter to Ussher," May 25, 1630, *Work*, 15 : 501.
34. Ward, *Baptismatis*, p. 136.

Baptism provided a regeneration suitable only to the age and condition of children. Infants were given an "initial grace" able to save them if they died in childhood but inadequate should they pass through adulthood without spiritual rebirth, and only elect adults would truly experience rebirth.[35] Despite his caution, though, Ward became a controversial figure whose ideas emerged prominently in later English debates. Puritans in New England were still discussing him almost a century after he advanced his views. He was a new voice within the Puritan tradition.

At the same time that Ward was expounding his doctrines at Cambridge, largely through private channels, Cornelius Burges (1589–1665) published his *Baptismal Regeneration of Elect Infants* (1629). Burges was vicar of Watford, Hertfordshire, and chaplain to Charles I, whose authority he defended even after siding with Parliament during the Civil War, but he was emphatically a "divine of the Puritan stamp." [36] His criticism of the bishops for permitting the growth of popery and Arminianism brought him before the Court of High Commission in 1635; five years later he transmitted to the king the petition of the London clergy against the "etcetera oath," a measure designed to silence the Puritan criticism of the Church of England; in 1641 he utilized his membership on an ecclesiastical committee, organized by the House of Lords, as an occasion to oppose the existing Church order; and finally Burges assumed a position of leadership at the Westminster Assembly, where, after being named an assessor, or vice-president, he supported the Presbyterians.[37]

Burges was unaware of Ward's proposals, but he did echo the call for a strong doctrine of baptismal grace, hoping to secure the middle ground, he said, between the men who made baptism necessary for salvation and those who made it a "bare sign." He thought that his middle ground was the traditional domain of the Reformed tradition, and argued that his doctrine was identical with Calvin's, though he acknowledged that Calvin employed a different vocabulary. Burges even tried to demonstrate his kinship to Henry Ainsworth, the Separatist theologian, and he filled his own book with references to continental Reformed divines and confessions. But although as a Reformed theologian he acknowledged the freedom of divine election and denied that the sacramental elements had a "physical force" to

35. Ibid., pp. 160, 100, 113.
36. Daniel Neal, *The History of the Puritans*, ed. John Choules (New York, 1863), 2 : 256.
37. Alexander Gordon, "Cornelius Burges," *DNB* 3 (1949–1950) : 301–04. For Burges's activities at the Assembly, see A. F. Mitchell and John Struthers, eds., *Minutes of the Sessions of the Westminster Assembly of Divines* (Edinburgh, 1874).

confer the Spirit, Burges argued that God had "made a promise to shew himselfe . . . gratious in the ordinance of baptisme, ordinarily, when it is administered to elect infants." [38] He found in this promise sufficient justification for a reexamination of sacramental theology, which finally issued in a sacramentalist stance that afforded an alternative position to that of Ward.

Burges asked one fundamental question. When and how is the principle of regeneration communicated to elect infants? Do they ordinarily receive the Spirit in baptism? For Burges the question was entirely rhetorical.

> It is most agreeable to the Institution of Christ, that all Elect Infants that are baptized, (unlesse in some extraordinary cases) doe, ordinarily, receive, from Christ, the Spirit in Baptisme, for their first solemne initiation into Christ, and for their future actuall renovation, in Gods good time, if they live to years of discretion, and enjoy the other ordinary means of Grace appointed of God to this end.

Burges based his argument on distinctions that superficially resembled Ward's dichotomy between infant and adult justification. His differentiation of "initial" from "actual" regeneration, however, was not borrowed from Ward. Burges understood initial regeneration as a reception of the "first principle" of regeneration, a participation in the spirit of Christ as the "forme of the spiritual life." This formal or "potential" regeneration was analogous to "life in the roote of a tree." Actual regeneration was the complete actualization of this principle of life "by the spirit bringing . . . forth a new man in Christ," enabling him "actually to believe." Burges argued that initial regeneration in elect infants ordinarily began in baptism. "Elect infants doe ordinarily receive the spirit in baptisme, as the first efficient principle of future actuall regeneration." There could be union with Christ before baptism, but he ordinarily conveyed his Spirit during the administration of the sacrament. [39]

Like Ward, Burges was dissatisfied with the sacramental doctrine of the covenant theologians. Although he defined baptism as a seal, he thought the definition inadequate unless it were also conceded that the

---

38. Cornelius Burges, *Baptismal Regeneration of Elect Infants, Professed by the Church of England, According to the Scriptures, The Primitive Church, the present Reformed Churches, and many particular Divines apart* (Oxford, 1629), pp. 2, 90, 98; 120, 320. Burges appealed to Calvin, Beza, Peter Martyr, to such later continental Reformed divines as Francis Junius, Daniel Chamier, Wolfgang Musculus, and Gerhard Johann Vossius, and to the later Reformed confessions.

39. Ibid., pp. 21; 14, 20, 260.

sacrament ordinarily bestowed a "principle" or "seed" of grace. Also like Ward, he recognized the difficulty of combining doctrines of sacramental grace and divine election: he was careful to say that only "God's preordination" of elect infants unto grace and glory made the sacrament "effectual upon them, and not upon others." Burges differed from Ward, though, in two ways. He thought baptism to be effective only for an infant "under election," whereas Ward said that even non-elect infants received sufficient baptismal grace to remit original sin. From this perspective, Burges limited the efficacy of the sacrament more severely than Ward. From another point of view, he moved beyond Ward, who thought that baptism conveyed to infants a grace that was provisional and only of temporary effect. Burges described the grace of baptism as a "seed" that would ripen and produce "a further seed in due time and season," thus assuming continuity between infant baptism and adult conversion. He said explicitly that his distinction between "initial" and "actual" regeneration referred to degrees and not to distinct types of rebirth. So many people had such little benefit from their baptism, he explained, only because they were given insufficient opportunity to nourish the sacramental seed. They lacked either careful, faithful parents or a proper minister, or both.[40]

The vocabulary of the sacramentalists revealed their intention: to elevate baptism by combining two theological traditions, Reformed orthodoxy and medieval scholasticism. To speak of the Christian life in terms of potency, or form, and actualization, or matter, was to appropriate scholastic imagery. "Initial grace" was a Reformed adaptation of the medieval *gratia prima,* also given to children in baptism. Baxter recognized later the similarity between "seminal grace" and the scholastic notion of infused habits.[41] Burges and Ward carefully inserted the older language into their orthodox Calvinism, but they could not entirely eliminate the incommensurabilities. The medieval language depicted the Christian pilgrimage as a gradual development, approximate to salvation in ascending stages and levels of growth, nourished by sacramental grace from beginning to end. Earlier Reformed theologians spoke of progressive sanctification after the effectual call, and they argued about preparatory development in adults prior to the experience of saving grace, but the sacramentalist language seemed to depict the whole of a man's spiritual life, from infancy to glorification, as an unbroken continuum beginning with baptism.[42] The problem

40. Ibid., pp. 110, 115; 50, 253, 282, 277.
41. Baxter, *A Friendly Accomodation* (London, 1652), in *Plain Scripture Proof,* p. 360.
42. See Pettit, *Heart Prepared,* pp. 48–83.

was to combine that vocabulary with a traditional Puritan notion of genuine conversion as a specifiable experience, restricted to the elect, moving them into a new sphere of life, discontinuous with their past. Puritan theology often consisted of the artful manipulation of images, and Burges and Ward accordingly proposed a sacramental theology based on medieval images of organic growth combined with the more familiar Puritan image of salvation as a new creation.

Few of their Puritan contemporaries shared their vision, however, and the initial response was therefore hostile. When Ward first publicized his ideas around 1627, a close friend, John Davenant, advised that he not "sett that controversy on foot," [43] and when Burges published his treatise he complained that he received for his effort nothing but "clamors, slanders, and revilings without end or measure."

> Never since the heresies of the Sacramentarians and Anabaptists were hissed out of the Church of Christ were men so violent against [sacramental grace] and so impatient of contradiction.

No explanations, public or private, and no apologies could shelter him from the "virulent dartes which daily fly in my face where ever I become." [44] Baxter reported later that "at the first broaching" of the sacramentalist doctrine "it was so much disrellished . . . by most Divines and godly people as far as I could learn, that it did succeed and spread as little as almost any Errour that ever I knew spring up in the Church." [45] It was an inappropriate time for a Puritan to speak of baptismal efficacy. Reformed loyalists were engaged in a bitter struggle with Arminian theologians whose criticisms of Calvinism appeared to have the approval even of Charles I. In 1625 the most visible of the Arminians, Richard Montague, had exalted the efficacy of baptism in a manner repugnant to Puritans, and shortly thereafter several powerful churchmen, including Wililam Laud, then the Bishop of St. David's, informed the king that Montague's doctrines were orthodox. Calvinists feared that the new enthusiasm for sacramental theology in their own ranks might compromise their cause against the Arminians, who were finding in the doctrine of baptismal grace a weapon against the doctrine of predestination. John Davenant, the Calvinist Bishop of Salisbury, urged Ward to remain silent about baptism: "at this time when the Arminians cleav so close one to another, it is not convenient to bee at open controversies amongst our selfes." [46] A venturesome the-

43. Quoted in Morris Fuller, *The Life Letters and Writings of John Davenant, D. D. 1572–1641 Lord Bishop of Salisbury* (London, 1897), p. 329.
44. Burges, *Baptismal Regeneration*, pp. 4, 8.
45. Baxter, *Plain Scripture Proof*, p. 294.
46. Fuller, *Life of Davenant*, p. 329.

ologian who tried in 1638 to resurrect the ideas of Ward and Burges was "freely censured by many." [47]

The Issues Debated

Most Puritans were content with a baptismal doctrine built on the covenant, but the Baptists continued to attract converts, and some ministers thought that the new Reformed sacramentalism, or some other more modest affirmation of sacramental grace, was the only answer to Baptist success. Concern about baptism intensified after the lifting of censorship regulations in 1640 enabled Baptists to spread their doctrine throughout England. The political turmoil of the next two years seemed to unleash religious disorder. Daniel Featley complained in 1642 that Baptists "preach, and print, and practice their heretical impieties openly; they hold their conventicles weekly in our chief cities and suburbs thereof. . . . the presses sweat and groan under the load of their blasphemies." [48] The following year the Westminster Assembly began its attempt to restructure the Church of England, but reports of Baptist and sectarian progress constantly interrupted the deliberations. In March Burges reported that Hempstead was "possessed" with Anabaptism. There were rumors from other regions that laymen and clergy were calling sacraments "carnal ordinances." The vicar of Finchingfield, Stephen Marshall, the most influential clerical politician of the period, warned of imminent disaster: "we are afraid it will prove so great a mischief as none of us shall be able to stand before it." The Assembly importuned the House of Commons to suppress Baptists and others who persisted in pursuing to its logical conclusion the earlier Puritan stricture against reliance upon material means of grace.[49] When saints within the Parliamentary armies began not only to rip out baptismal fonts but also to repudiate the sacrament itself, some Puritans decided that the dichotomy between flesh and spirit could be carried too far.

Throughout England the theologians began to debate about sacramental practices, often in public disputations that attracted hundreds of listeners. One such debate began shortly after 1643 and eventually

47. John Tombes, *Anti-paedobaptism, or the Second Part of the Full Review of the Dispute Concerning Infant-Baptism* (London, 1654), p. 220.

48. Daniel Featley, "Epistle Dedicatory," *The Dippers dipt. Or, The Anabaptists Duck'd and Plung'd Over Head and Eares, at a Disputation in Southwark* (London, 1645), n.p.

49. S. W. Carruthers, *The Everyday Work of the Westminster Assembly* (Philadelphia, 1954), pp. 93, 94–96. See John F. Wilson, *Pulpit in Parliament: Puritanism during the English Civil Wars 1640–1648* (Princeton, 1969), p. 110.

involved numerous Puritan ministers. In that year John Tombes
(1603?–1676) attempted to persuade a special committee of the Westminster Assembly of its error on the point of infant baptism. Tombes
was "reputed the most Learned and able Anabaptist in England," [50]
but he never joined a Baptist church because he "shunned" the
thought of separation. He honored the Puritan patriarchs—Cartwright,
Hildersham, Parker, Dod, Bradshaw, "and the rest of the same stampe"
—and he thought that he was following their example when he attempted to remove the insidious custom of infant baptism from the
Church. He was genuinely surprised by the response given his views
by the Westminster committee. Only after waiting nine months for a
favorable reaction, and meeting instead with pamphlets and sermons
"tending to make the questioning of that point odious to the people,
and the Magistracie," did Tombes begin to publish voluminous treatises defending himself and his doctrine.[51]

The occasion for his first pronouncement was a sermon that Stephen
Marshall delivered in Westminster Abbey as the morning lecture to
the House of Commons. Marshall hoped that a defense of infant baptism would "reclaime some deceived soules." [52] Tombes told him that
the sermon contained "as much as can be wel said," but he charged
Marshall with responsibility for the odium attached to the Baptist
cause, and he determined to refute him, as did other antipaedobaptist
theologians.[53] Their refutation, however, helped to produce a veritable
literary crusade on behalf of infant baptism. Within a few years
Tombes could name over thirty ministers—mainly Presbyterians and
New England Congregationalists—who had directed arguments against
him.[54] Puritans had released an antisacramental impulse, but this out-

50. Richard Baxter, *Reliquiae Baxterianae, or Mr. Richard Baxter's Narrative of
the Most Memorable Passages of his Life and Times. Faithfully Published from his
own Original Manuscript, by Matthew Sylvester* (London, 1696), p. 88.

51. John Tombes, *An Apology or Plea for the Two Treatises, and Appendix to
them concerning Infant Baptisme* (London, 1646), p. 66; idem, *An Examen of the
Sermon of Mr. Stephen Marshall About Infant-Baptisme, in a Letter sent to him*
(London, 1645), in *Two Treatises and an Appendix to Them Concerning Infant
Baptisme* (London, 1645), p. 2.

52. Stephen Marshall, *A Sermon of the Baptizing of Infants* (London, 1644),
"Preface", n.p.

53. Tombes, *Examen*, in *Two Treatises*, p. 3.

54. John Tombes, *Anti-paedobaptism, Or the Second Part*, pp. 2–3. Tombes named
Marshall, John Geree, Nathanael Homes, Thomas Blake, Richard Baxter, Thomas
Cobbet, John Cotton, Robert Baillie, John Drew, Nathaniel Stephens, Daniel Feat-
ley, William Lyford, Josiah Church, William Carter, Thomas Fuller, Henry Ham-
mond, Samuel Rutherford, John Craig, John Stalham, Thomas Hall, Thomas
Shepard, John Allin, Thomas Gataker, Thomas Goodwin, Simon Ford, Giles
Firmin, Thomas Bedford, James Cranford, a Mr. Savage, and a Mr. Carter.

pouring of polemical literature represented in itself a remarkable re-affirmation of the sacrament of baptism.

Among the theologians drawn into the controversy, Richard Baxter (1615–1691), the famed preacher at Kidderminster, and Thomas Blake (1597?–1657), minister at Tamworth in Staffordshire, were prominent defenders of infant baptism and the covenantal doctrine, although they interpreted the covenant, and hence the sacrament, in slightly different ways. The discussion became more complex when Thomas Bedford, who had spoken out in 1638 for the views of Ward and Burges, insisted in 1645, and later in a series of conciliatory letters to Baxter, that the position of the Puritan sacramentalists be given full consideration. Baxter believed that it was already receiving excessive consideration; by 1652 he complained that their doctrine of sacramental efficacy, that once had been universally rejected, "hath now hit on a more fruitful season and soil," and he feared that "the error of this Doctrine is far likelier to spread and succeed in these times than ever." [55] The ensuing dispute thus reveals the diverse directions of Puritan baptismal theology in the late seventeenth century. It covered a wide range of issues, from the proper mode, subjects, and administrator of the sacrament to its efficacy, but the viability of the covenant doctrine as the regulative principle of sacramental theology was central. Was baptism the seal of a covenant? If so, did it seal an absolute or a conditional covenant? Did it seal an internal covenant? Or was it only an external seal? Did it seal only the divine promise? Or was it also a seal to faith? Such were the main issues in the debate.

Tombes: A Sign of Faith

Marshall's sermon advanced two major arguments, first that infants were within the covenant, and second that they were holy, according to 1 Corinthians 7 : 14, and therefore deserved the baptismal seal of holiness.[56] Puritan controversies were always lengthy exegetical exercises, and Tombes justified his challenge with biblical texts. Paul did teach that infants were holy, he said, but this was no federal holiness, entitling the infant to baptism, but matrimonial holiness, denoting the child as legitimate despite the paganism of one parent. Marshall claimed that Acts 2 : 38–39 contained a promise to believers and their children; Tombes replied that the promise was simply to send Christ. It did not justify infant baptism. Marshall recalled Christ's desire to have little children brought to him; Tombes insisted that Christ called

55. Baxter, *Appendix, Plain Scripture Proof,* pp. 293–94.
56. Marshall, *Sermon,* pp. 8, 41.

them for a blessing, not for baptism. Marshall pointed out that the apostles baptized entire households; Tombes answered that no text mentioned infants among those families.[57] With these and dozens of similar biblical arguments, the battle over infant baptism was fought, but Tombes thought many of these considerations were peripheral. Paedobaptism, he said, actually stood on two "pillars," Jewish circumcision and the covenant doctrine.[58]

Circumcision of Jewish infants was, in Tombes's view, "the Achilles for Paedo-baptisme." [59] Had baptism been the successor to circumcision, the Old Testament command to circumcize infants would indeed have justified the paedobaptist position. Tombes used standard arguments to cripple this Achilles. An abrogated rite, he said, could not justify a rule binding for Christians. Baptism manifestly did not succeed circumcision, for the two rites were dissimilar: females, for example, were baptized but not circumcized, and circumcision separated the Israelites from all nations while baptism united all men in Christ.

Marshall had answered such arguments in advance with equally standard paedobaptist rejoinders: the Jews had circumcized females "virtually" if not actually; the two rites signified "substantially" the same reality even though they differed "accidentally"; and circumcision as well as baptism united men in Christ, though it did so through "types" and shadows. Paul himself had in his letter to the Colossians equated circumcision and baptism, which was sufficient evidence for Marshall.[60] Throughout, Marshall's argument depended on typological exegesis: the ceremonies and activities of the Jews under the Old Covenant foreshadowed the coming of Christ and the rites of the New Testament. Baptists did not repudiate typological interpretation, though they minimized its sacramental significance. Other Puritans found in typology a major biblical justification for sacramental piety.[61]

The "other pillar" upon which paedobaptism rested was the notion of an infant's "imaginary confederation with the believing parent in the Covenant of grace." This argument, Tombes said, was "almost the first and last in this businesse," and his opponents charged that Tombes's inability to understand it underlay his other misconceptions.[62] Baxter said that the "root of his error about Baptism" was his

57. John Tombes, *An Exercitation About Infant-Baptisme* (London, 1646), in *Two Treatises*, pp. 9–23; idem, *Apology*, p. 100; Marshall, *Sermon*, pp. 15, 40–42.
58. Tombes, *Examen*, in *Two Treatises*, pp. 29–30.
59. Ibid., p. 2.
60. Tombes, *Anti-paedobaptism, Or the Second Part*, p. 272; idem, *Exercitation*, pp. 5–6; Marshall, *Sermon*, pp. 8, 10, 27 (Col. 2 : 11–12).
61. Marshall, *Sermon*, p. 36. See my discussion of the sacramental significance of typology in chapter four.
62. Tombes, *Examen*, in *Two Treatises*, idem, *Exercitation*, in *Two Treatises*, p. 1.

false description of the covenant and its seal. Thomas Blake charged that no man who had ever spoken of the covenant had "done more to darken it" than Tombes, the inevitable result being an erroneous doctrine of baptism.[63] Tombes did not reject entirely the conjunction of the covenant motif with sacramental doctrine, though he would admit covenantal language into his doctrine of baptism only with stringent qualifications.

Baptism could not seal a covenant, he said, unless it sealed also "the faith to which the promise of remission and justification is made." Tombes defended this contention with a distinction between actual and aptitudinal obsignation.

> I acknowledge baptisme in its nature to be a seale of the covenant of God, but not a seal actuall, but aptitudinall; that is, all right baptism is in its nature apt to seale . . . yet . . . onely to true believers. And God never sealed actually till a person be a beleever.[64]

Tombes knew that his distinction undercut the prevailing covenantal interpretation of baptism, but that did not disturb him. He suspected that the conception of baptism as a seal to the covenant was a "novell" invention of sixteenth-century theologians, and he used that language only because he was forced to "speake in answer to Paedobaptists according to their mind." Tombes preferred to define baptism as a sign of faith, providing an occasion for the believer to testify that he was "born again by the Spirit" and imposing the obligation of faithful obedience. It signified divine favor only to the elect believer who could testify to a "covenant already entred in heart." [65]

Moreover, baptism could not seal a conditional covenant. It was contradictory to talk of sealing a covenant yet unfulfilled: "I like not to call the Sacrament a conditionall Seal, for that which seals doth assure, and supposeth the condition." [66] And God had never promised regeneration upon fulfillment of covenant conditions.

> If God have promised regenerating grace upon condition, that condition must be performed either by himselfe or by the person to whom it is promised; if the condition be to be performed by

63. Richard Baxter, *An Answer to Mr. Tombes His Valedictory Oration to the People of Bewdeley* (London, 1652), in *Plain Scripture Proof*, p. 222; Thomas Blake, *Vindiciae Foederis*, p. 366.

64. Tombes, *Apology*, p. 152.

65. John Tombes, *Felo de Se, Or, Mr. Richard Baxters Self-destroying; Manifested in twenty Arguments against Infant-Baptism* (London, 1659), pp. 6, 25; idem, *Anti-Paedobaptisme: Third Part*, p. 54, 236, 241, 259.

66. Tombes, *Anti-Paedobaptisme: Third Part*, p. 238.

himselfe it is all one with an absolute promise; if by the person
to whom it is promised, then something may be done by a man
that may procure God's grace.[67]

Most Puritan theologians believed that baptism did not seal an absolute covenant of grace, since that would entail either the regeneration of all who were baptized or the restriction of baptism to the
elect. They distinguished a conditional and an absolute covenant, and
administered a baptism that was efficacious only on the condition of
future faith. By denying the distinction, Tombes restricted baptism to
faithful, repentant, and presumably elect adult Christians.

Finally, Tombes rejected the popular distinction between an internal and an external covenant. Puritans usually said that baptism
sealed only the latter for most men, thereby admitting them into the
external, visible church without conveying or sealing the inward spiritual grace given to the elect. They used the distinction to justify baptizing infants without knowing them to be elect, and to explain the
apostasy of baptized adults. Some used it to elevate the importance of
baptism by emphasizing the efficacy of the visible ordinances to which
the sacrament conveyed a title, thus accenting the continuity between
the external and internal covenants. But Tombes ridiculed the distinction as "gibberish," and he criticized efforts to establish continui-
ties between an outer and an inner covenant. He did think that cate-
chizing, sacraments, and prayer were "priviledges" of the external
Church, and that the infants of believers had a greater likelihood of
salvation because of the prayers of Christian parents and of the
Church.[68] But the Church was not primarily a dispensary of the means
of grace; it was a fellowship of those who possessed grace. The "promise of the Word and Sacraments" in the visible Church was not "a
promise of the Spirit." [69]

Tombes's voluntarism did not, as he saw it, diminish the importance
of the sacrament. Christ had commanded baptism, so every believer
was "by necessity of precept tied to be baptized." Those who neglected
the sacrament disobeyed a manifest duty. Tombes criticized men who
counted themselves "above Ordinances," and he resented the charge
that he dishonored baptism. If paedobaptists were consistent, he
claimed, they would be compelled not only to respect his doctrine but
also to accept it. He openly announced his determination to convince

67. Tombes, *Apology*, p. 117.
68. Tombes, *Anti-paedobaptisme, Second Part*, pp. 253, 258.
69. Tombes, *Apology*, p. 116.

one paedobaptist, the minister at neighboring Kidderminster, Richard Baxter.[70]

Baxter: A Seal to Faith and the Conditional Covenant

Perhaps Tombes sensed that Baxter was a potentially receptive convert, for at one time the latter had almost accepted the Baptist position. After baptizing only two children as a young minister, he began to have doubts about infant baptism, partly in reaction against Burges's "extream" defense of the sacrament. Additional study convinced him for a time that infants should be baptized, but, his doubts persisting, he soon discontinued the practice. Baxter had such serious misgivings that he decided not to accept a pastoral charge and to preach only as a lecturer until he resolved the issue After he became a chaplain in Colonel Whalley's regiment of the New Model army in 1645, Baxter on one occasion publicly defended Baptist views. The episode cost him "pangs of conscience" later, though he remained hesitant about infant baptism for several years.[71]

Baxter met Tombes in London during the war, and their discussion of infant baptism prompted Baxter to express surprise "that the Champion of the cause had no more to defend it." Later he recommended Tombes as a curate at Bewdley, anticipating no further sacramental discussions. But Tombes was persistent, attending Baxter's weekly lectures and posing the issue publicly. His Bewdley converts urged Baxter to respond in writing. Baxter finally agreed to a public discussion, and though Tombes was reluctant to hazard an extemporaneous disputation, they met in January, 1649, and argued "from before ten of the clock till between four and five" in an open church "in the midst of winter," and the "multitude of the crowd" was "exceeding great." [72]

Baxter based his case on the covenant. Infants had a right to the baptismal covenant seal because they had been "entered into covenant" by their parents, who possessed "so much interest in them and power of them, that their act [could be] esteemed as the infant's act, and legally imputed to them as if they themselves had done it." Tombes recognized immediately that Baxter was according greater importance to parental faith than most other English advocates of the covenantal argument, for Baxter insisted that parents who could not

70. Tombes, *Anti-paedobaptism, Second Part,* p. 79; idem, *Praecursor: Or a Forerunner to a Large Review of the Dispute Concerning Infant-Baptism* (London?, 1652), p. 20.
71. Baxter, *Plain Scripture Proof,* "Preface," n.p.
72. Ibid. See Also Baxter, *Reliquiae Baxterianae,* p. 96; Tombes, *Praecursor,* p. 2.

profess saving faith lost their covenant rights, including the right of
baptism for their children.[73] But the center of Baxter's doctrine of
baptism was still his definition of the sacrament as a covenant seal.
The sacrament completed "by solemnization and obsignation that conveyance which was before effectually . . . and certainly made by the
Covenant." [74]

Tombes did not know at first that Baxter felt himself to be battling
on three fronts. Against the Baptist view that the ordinance was a professing sign, Baxter argued that baptism was a divine seal by which
God engaged himself "to make good his promises," thus shifting attention to the objectivity of both the covenant promise and its seal.[75]
Against the Puritan sacramentalists, he stressed the priority of the
covenant, which allowed him to guard against any exaggerated notion
of sacramental grace. The covenant relationship itself was sufficient for
salvation; want of baptism would not "frustrate the salvation of those
that did truly consent in heart." [76] Against Puritans who wanted to
relax the standards of admission, Baxter affirmed, even exaggerated,
the voluntaristic and subjective character of earlier Puritan sacramental theology. This permitted him to insist that every parent—and
every adult candidate for baptism—be able to profess acceptance and
performance of the covenant conditions.

Baxter thought that Tombes's worst mistake was his definition of
the sacrament as a seal to "the Absolute Covenant." [77] He believed
that baptism was intended to seal a conditional covenant, not "the
absolute promise." [78] God engaged himself to grant salvation in the
sacrament, but the promise sealed by baptism did not give actual right
to salvation until the condition was performed.[79]

> Yet although God seal the Conditional Promise Absolutely to
> such as profess to receive it; that is, though he hereby attests that
> he owns that Promise as his Act or Deed; yet doth he not either
> Exhibit or Convey Right to Christ and his Benefits, nor yet oblige
> himself for the future, Absolutely, but Conditionally only. For
> in this Conveyance and Obligation, the Grant or Covenant is the

73. Richard Baxter, *A Christian Directory,* in *The Practical Works of the Rev.
Richard Baxter,* ed. William Orme (London, 1830), 5 : 46, 343; Tombes, *Felo de Se,*
"Preface," n.p.
74. Baxter, *Appendix,* in *Plain Scripture Proof,* p. 298.
75. Baxter, *Answer to Mr. Tombes,* in *Plain Scripture Proof,* p. 222.
76. Baxter, *Christian Directory* in *Works,* 5 : 335.
77. Richard Baxter, *Certain Disputations of Right to Sacraments and the true
nature of Visible Chritianity* (London, 1657), p. 238.
78. Baxter, *Christian Directory,* in *Works,* 5 : 331.
79. Baxter, *Certain Disputations,* p. 239.

principal Instrument, and the sign the less principal; and both to the same use: and therefore the latter cannot Absolutely Convey, or Oblige the Promiser, unless the first do it absolutely too.[80]

The "principal condition" of the promise was "saving Faith." To true believers who performed the condition, indeed to all the elect who were destined to do likewise, baptism was an effectual seal, obliging God to fulfill his promise of salvation, and therefore "a means" of "conferring" justification and glory.[81] To all others it was an empty ceremony, serving only to confer Church privileges upon men ultimately unable to benefit from them.[82]

In general, Baxter denied that baptism conveyed grace that would create faith in the faithless. The sacrament nourished and increased the grace of the believer and thus contributed to his sanctification. It did not confer any sort of "common grace" upon the "common and hypocritical receiver." Baxter did say that infant baptism conveyed a grace that could assist children to perform the covenant conditions. Infants of the faithful received in baptism pardon of their original sin, the intercession of Christ, the assistance of the Holy Ghost, and, if they died, title to the kingdom of heaven. Such a title was a benefit primarily of the covenant, of course, which baptism did no more than seal. But Baxter also proposed, very tentatively, that baptism itself conveyed a "degree of grace" to infants within the covenant. This "middle infant grace" conferred the power to obey God, but it was unable to give a "rooted, habitual determination" to the will. Baxter's proposal went beyond Calvin's baptismal doctrine, and it had affinities, which Baxter recognized, with the views of Ward. But Baxter never relinquished his insistence on the priority of the covenant. Infants could receive common grace in baptism only by virtue of their covenant relation.[83]

Baxter obviously wanted to assert the efficacy of infant baptism, but he advanced his suggestions with hesitation, fully aware, he said, that it was "a point of so great difficulty, that I may but humbly propose my opinion to trial." [84] There was a curious duality in his thought: he spoke highly of infant baptism, while granting significant concessions to the Baptists. Baxter minimized the objectivity of the sacrament by defining it as "the seal of our faith" as well as the seal of

80. Baxter, *Apology against the Modest Exceptions of Mr. T. Blake* (London, 1654), p. 121.
81. Baxter, *Appendix*, in *Plain Scripture Proof*, p. 297.
82. Baxter, *Certain Disputations*, pp. 76, 239.
83. Baxter, *Christian Directory*, in *Works*, 5 : 328; idem, *The Catechising of Families*, *Works*, 19 : 267.
84. Baxter, *Catechising of Families*, in *Works*, 19 : 267.

God's promise. Baptism was not simply an "Engaging Sign, *de futuro*," but also a professing sign that signified the present reality of a saving faith. An engagement to be faithful in the future presupposed a glimmer of true faith, without which there would be no desire to make the commitment. And any proper definition of baptism as the seal of a covenant had to include "the will's consent or heart-covenanting with God." That of course was consistent with the description of baptism as a seal to a mutual covenant, and it justified Baxter's restriction of the sacrament to the faithful and their children, though Tombes thought that Baxter's position should have led him to abandon infant baptism. Baxter replied that parental faith was legally imputed to infants. In that sense, even infant baptism was a seal to faith.[85] But some of Baxter's colleagues feared that Tombes had uncovered a weakness in the defense.

Baxter disturbed other Puritans by his ambivalent response when Tombes repudiated the distinction between an internal and external covenant. Baxter thought of baptism as an "external seal" for admitting Christ's subjects into his "visible Kingdome," the universal "visible church," [86] but since he considered the sacrament a seal of faith, he would not say that it sealed only an external covenant.

God never made any distinct covenant of outward privileges alone, to be sealed by baptism. But . . . outward mercies are the second and lesser gift of the same covenant which giveth first the great and saving blessings.

Though baptism did confer a title to visible Church ordinances, the beneficiaries should ideally have already received "saving blessings" through either an experience of faith or a prior covenant relationship with God.[87] Baxter assumed that the infants of Christian parents were included in such a covenant from birth. Their covenantal blessings were not sufficient to guarantee their salvation, but they had a

85. Baxter, *Certain Disputations*, pp. 68, 83, 147, 206; Baxter, *Christian Directory*, in *Works*, 5 : 324; Tombes, *Felo de Se*, "Preface," n.p.

86. Baxter, *Plain Scripture Proof*, p. 109. See also Baxter, *Answer to Mr. Tombes, Plain Scripture Proof*, p. 222 (incorrect pagination). By arguing that baptism entered one in the universal Church, as well as the particular church, Baxter disagreed with the early New England Puritans, who thought that the sacrament merely sealed membership in a particular visible church. Baxter thought that the children of Christians were Church members in some sense before baptism, yet everyone admitted into a visible church, he said, "must ordinarily be admitted by Baptism." See F. J. Powicke, "Some unpublished Correspondence of the Rev. Richard Baxter and the Rev. John Eliot, 'the Apostle to the American Indians,' 1656–1682," *Bulletin of the John Rylands Library* 20 (January–July, 1931) : 138–76, 422–66.

87. Baxter, *Christian Directory*, in *Works*, 5 : 326.

distinct advantage over the children of the ungodly, who received neither the blessings nor the seal of the covenant.

Baxter would have limited Church membership to godly parents and their children. He knew that many hypocrites were baptized, but he thought it only "accidental" when "any ungodly" were admitted into the Church. Though God had "fitted his ordinances" to be advantageous to the conversion of hypocrites within the Church, it was not the "first prescribed End" of the sacraments either to convert the unregenerate or to provide them—or their children—access to converting ordinances.[88] Baxter thus took his stand in an epic debate among seventeenth-century Puritans about the nature of the Church and its sacraments. Should the Church in England be a comprehensive institution embracing even the unrighteous in hopes of dispensing grace to them? Should it be a more select community of the outwardly holy and their offspring? Or should it consist purely of faithful adults? Baxter defended selectivity, though without abandoning infant membership.

He differed from many other apologists for selectivity, however, by virtue of his willingness to define Church membership in terms of sacramental nurture. The minister's task, he thought, grew out of the baptismal covenant. Baptism admitted infants into the Church, and some of these infants received in the sacrament "secret seeds of grace." By means of "holy education" the minister should develop the seeds into an "actual acquaintance with Christ." Other children eventually broke their baptismal vows; pastoral oversight should bring them to covenant renewal.[89] When Baxter published *The Reformed Pastor* in 1656, he urged ministers to expend their energies in pastoral nurture. Preaching might be the major instrument of conversion, he said, but individual pastoral instruction produced more outward success with most parishioners than "all my public preaching to them." [90] Despite his aversion to the Puritan sacramentalists, Baxter shared their understanding of Church membership as an organic, continuous development beginning with baptism. But he added that baptism initiated such a process of growth only for infants already within the covenant.

Baxter's proposals, however, met with opposition even from his allies in the struggle against the Baptists and the sacramentalists. Some Presbyterians believed that he attributed insufficient efficacy to baptism; Independents thought that he overstated its importance. The In-

88. Baxter, *Certain Disputations*, pp. 48, 51, 118, 158.
89. Richard Baxter, *Confirmation and Restauration, The Necessary Means of Reformation and Reconciliation, Works*, 14 : 450.
90. Baxter, *The Reformed Pastor, Works*, 14 : xxii.

dependents denied that baptism was the entrance to the Church. Thus they asserted their continuity with an older Congregational tradition, though not without a struggle. In 1639 John Goodwin, minister at St. Stephen's on Coleman Street in London, wrote his brother Thomas Goodwin, who was exiled in Holland. John denied that a covenant was the essence of a true Church, and that covenantal vows should be required of prospective members: "baptism doth immediately qualify for church fellowship." Thomas replied that baptism merely sealed the covenant of grace, of which a particular church was a branch. The Church covenant was therefore logically prior to baptism.[91] When about two hundred Independent delegates met at Savoy in 1658 to codify their doctrine, they ignored John Goodwin's arguments. The Savoy Declaration was an adaptation of the Westminster Confession, but it deleted the claim that baptism admitted members into the visible Church.[92] By the early eighteenth century the Independents found the Westminster Confession more satisfying than their own declaration, but in 1658 they wanted to make clear that baptism did not initiate Church membership.[93]

Blake: An External Efficacious Seal

Among the Presbyterians who believed that Baxter unduly deprecated baptism, the most articulate and outspoken was Thomas Blake, the minister at Tamworth, who entered into every sacramental controversy of the period. Blake disliked Tombes ever since they first met in the Westminster committee to discuss infant baptism, so he viewed Baxter's concessions with personal distaste. He also believed that Baxter himself often sounded and acted like a crypto-Anabaptist, and he could not appreciate Baxter's scruples about admission, which he attributed to faulty doctrine.

Specifically, he rejected Baxter's claim that a profession of justifying faith was prerequisite for every adult who desired baptism for himself or his child. Justifying faith, thought Blake, was the "great condition to which baptisme engages," so it could not be required in advance of the sacrament. A "faith short of justifying" entitled a man to baptism, and in view of the difficulty in discerning justifying faith, the only safe course was to admit all who would profess a "dogmatic faith." Blake required only that men assent to the gospel, even if their

91. John and Thomas Goodwin, "Two Letters which passed between the Reverend Mr. John Goodwin and the Author, Concerning a Church Covenant," in *The Works of Thomas Goodwin, D. D.*, ed. Thomas Smith (Edinburgh, 1865), 11 : 526–40.
92. Williston Walker, *The Creeds and Platforms of Congregationalism* (Boston, 1960), p. 398.
93. Neal, *History of the Puritans*, 2 : 178.

hearts were not drawn to a full and saving choice of Christ. And he added that the basis for the baptism of children was not the faith of their parents but the promise made to their ancestors in the faith. When asked how many generations could give right to baptism, Blake replied that men could go back "as high as Ancestors have been in Christianity." [94] Any infants with Christian ancestors were within the covenant, therefore "relatively holy," and entitled to the sign of their holiness.[95] Against Tombes, Blake joined the ranks of the Reformed theologians who emphasized the "birth priviledge" of infants born within the covenant, but against Baxter, in defense of a more inclusive administration of baptism, he noted the promise on which the privilege was based.

Baxter replied that neither he nor Tombes demanded a true justifying faith as a prerequisite for admission. He thought that "real saints in heart" would always remain unknown to the visible Church; ministers were therefore to admit men to baptism upon a verbal profession of saving faith, without searching for further evidence of sincerity. But Baxter thought the notion of a merely dogmatic faith to be contradictory. To believe in Christ meant trusting in him as Redeemer and Savior. Since baptism was, among other things, a professing sign, it presupposed a public profession of faith; and since the notion of dogmatic faith was erroneous, a profession of saving faith was mandatory. And in the case of infant baptism, remote ancestors could not give right to the sacrament, for such a privilege came only from the "immediate parents," which usually meant the natural parents, though any "true owner" of a child by nature, purchase, or adoption could devote it to God in baptism. The "further you go from the parent," Baxter warned, "the darker is the case." Baxter felt that his was a moderate position, avoiding extreme solutions; he thought that the New England Puritans were too strict in requiring "positive proof of Conversion" beyond a profession of faith and repentance.[96]

But here, as so often in the seventeenth century, disagreements over practice reflected deeper doctrinal differences. Blake agreed with Baxter's baptismal theology at only one important point—baptism did seal the covenant of grace "not absolutely but conditionally." The promise of salvation was contingent on the "performance" of the covenant conditions—faith and obedience. When the sacramental seal ratified and confirmed God's promise it assured the baptized that

94. Blake, *Covenant Sealed*, pp. 96–98, 113, 143–45, 160–64.

95. Thomas Blake, *The Birth-Priviledge: or, Covenant-Holinesse of Beleevers and their Issue in the time of the Gospel* (London, 1644), pp. 24–27.

96. Baxter, *Certain Disputations*, pp. 18–19, 37, 45, 67–68, 325; idem, *Catechising of Families*, in *Works*, 19: 271.

Christ was theirs whenever they fulfilled the conditions. The efficacy of baptism was dependent in part on faith, either before or after the sacrament.[97]

Baxter, however, made baptism a seal to the faith of the covenanted Christian. Blake claimed that the sacrament sealed the "righteousness of faith" (Rom. 4 : 11), which he described as an objective righteousness wrought *extra nobis* by a Mediator and offered to men in the covenant promise. He considered it confusing to talk of baptism as sealing the act of faith; it sealed the promise of salvation on condition of faith.[98] On that point Blake stood with Calvin. The quality of faith in the baptizand, or in the parents of a baptized infant, was less important than the divine promise.

Baxter hesitated to speak of a distinct external covenant. Blake's baptismal theology required an unequivocal distinction between the external and internal covenants.

> It is the external Covenant, not the inward, that exactly and properly is called by the name of a covenant: and to which privi-ledges of Ordinances and title to Sacraments are annext.[99]

Once again the underlying issue was the nature of the Church. Blake believed that Baxter underestimated the salvific character of Church membership and therefore deprecated unduly the import of the sacra-ment that granted entry into the Church. He claimed that external covenant membership conferred a right to baptism, which in turn certified a further right to "church-priviledges." These privileges fa-cilitated entrance into the internal covenant. Blake therefore ex-plicitly rejected the claim of Tombes that the external and internal covenants were "opposite, and [external] privilege of ordinances were not of grace, or that saving grace could be had, in God's ordinary way, without this privilege." Blake believed that the outward privi-leges contained "a promise of the spirit." Therefore baptism, by en-titling a man to the privileges of "the outward part of the Covenant," became a "step in God's ordinary dispensation of the inward." [100] Tombes charged that Blake had capitulated to Rome. Baxter was more restrained. "I suppose," he said, "it is but some common mercies that he supposeth this promise to make over the Baptized." [101] That

97. Thomas Blake, *Mr. Blake's Answer to Mr. Tombes his Letter* (London, 1646), p. 24; idem, *Covenant Sealed*, pp. 83, 181, 333.

98. Blake, *Covenant Sealed*, pp. 171, 413.

99. Ibid., p. 83.

100. Thomas Blake, *Infants Baptisme, Freed from Antichristianisme* (London, 1645), p. 28; idem, *Covenant Sealed*, p. 385; idem, *Mr. Blake's Answer*, p. 24.

101. Tombes, *Anti-Paedobaptisme: Third Part*, p. 375; Baxter, *Apology*, p. 61.

was true, but Blake attributed far more efficacy than Baxter to "common mercies," for among the mercies in the external covenant were means of grace that could carry Church members "on towards conversion." Unregenerate baptized adults might find salvation, for example, through sermons, prayers, or even the Lord's Supper, which was a converting ordinance. Blake said in effect that Baxter did not take seriously his own understanding of the Church as a field in which the minister patiently harvested the baptismal seeds.[102]

Bedford: An Instrument of First Grace

There were limits, however, to Blake's enthusiasm for the sacrament. When Thomas Bedford attempted to restate the views of the Puritan sacramentalists, Blake charged that he had "unhappily engaged. . . to carry the Sacraments higher than Scripture hath raised them." [103] Bedford was minister at Plymouth and, after 1649, rector of St. Martin Outwich in London. As a student he thought of sacraments only as visible representations of the Gospel and took "no notice of any further efficacy in them." He began to question his opinion, however, when he met with "the book of Dr. Burgess, of baptismal Regeneration," which he found persuasive, although he was as hesitant as Burges himself to "extend that efficacy of baptism further than to the elect." But Ward's letter, which Bedford later published, convinced him "that there was no necessity to restrain the efficacy of Baptism *in conferenda gratia* to the Elect; that a man may have *temporeaneam ordinationem ad salutem,* who yet is not *praedestinatus ad salutem.*" [104] In 1638 Bedford published his new views in *A Treatise of the Sacraments,* which was followed in 1645 by *A Moderate Answer to . . . Two Questions,* his main contribution to the debate of the forties.[105]

Bedford maintained a tenuous relationship to the later Puritan movement: he valued tradition and episcopal order at a time when both were highly suspect in Puritan circles. But he considered himself a Reformed theologian and expressed indebtedness to such Puri-

102. Blake, *Covenant Sealed,* pp. 211–12.
103. Ibid., p. 356.
104. Thomas Bedford, "Letter to Baxter," in Baxter, *Plain Scripture Proof,* pp. 348–49. See Alfred Goodwin, "Thomas Goodwin," *DNB* 2 (1949–50) : 112. I assume that Bedford preached regularly at Plymouth, since he dedicated his *Treatise of the Sacraments* (London, 1638) to his "loving and beloved Auditors of the Town of Plymouth."
105. *A Moderate Answer to these Two Questions 1) Whether ther be sufficient Ground in Scripture to Warrant the Conscience of a Christian to present his infants to the sacrament of Baptism 2) Whether it be not sinfull for a Christian to receiv the sacrament in a mixt Assembly* (London, 1645). See Appendix.

tan predecessors as William Perkins. He also approved some of Cartwright's strictures against Whitgift, and he was sensitive to the views
of later Puritan theologians. When Baxter criticized his baptismal
theology, Bedford began to doubt it himself, and he initiated an attempt to find "a favourable construction" of his doctrine that would
be mutually satisfying. More important, he was defending the views
of Ward and Burges, and among his supporters were such men as
James Cranford (1592–1657), the prominent Presbyterian rector of St.
Christopher, London.[106] But Bedford considered the typical Puritan
defense of the sacrament as a covenant seal insufficient to put down
the Baptist challenge. He thought it a "readier way to deal with the
Anabaptist; to say that children are to be baptized, not to confirm
them in grace, but to confer grace upon them." Sacraments were only
secondarily "seals to confirm"; they were primarily "instruments to
convey." [107]

Bedford's definition entailed a modification of covenant doctrine.
External federal holiness, he said, qualified an infant for "the grace
of baptism," which in turn conferred "admission into the Covenant
of grace." [108] The sacrament did not simply admit infants into the roll
of Christians, but was the entrance into the covenant of grace, and
there was no "other ordinance by which infants may be made partakers of Christ and the Covenant of grace except Baptism." The "first
grace," then, at least for infants, came not from the covenant but from
the sacrament. Even for adults, baptism was the sole route of entry
into the covenant, faith alone being insufficient. Most Puritans—including Blake and Baxter—thought that the truly faithful Christian
was by definition within the covenant, along with his children. For
Bedford, even earnest believers were "not completely within the Covenant, till baptized: Faith giveth them title, and interest, but the
Sacrament admission." [109]

Bedford attempted in effect to synthesize the sacramentalist views of
Ward and Burges. He accepted Ward's notion that a parent could fulfill the covenant condition for a child through baptism. Like Ward
he refused to limit the efficacy of baptism to the elect. Through the
sacrament the Spirit worked as a supernatural agent implanting grace

106. Bedford, "Letter to Baxter," in *Plain Scripture Proof*, p. 347; idem, *Vindiciae Gratiae* (London, 1656), foreword by James Cranford. See also Cranford's preface to Bedford's "Letter to Baxter," p. 354. For Cranford, see Sidney Lee, "James Cran-ford," *DNB* 5 (1908): 16–17. Bedford expressed indebtedness as well to Daniel Chamier on the continent, as well as to Ward and Burges.
107. Bedford, *Treatise*, pp. 92, 95, 153, 192.
108. Ibid., pp. 101, 192.
109. Bedford, *Moderate Answer*, p. 17; idem, *Treatise*, pp. 14, 89, 91; idem, *Vindi-ciae*, "Praefatio," n.p.

in the hearts of all baptized infants, though baptismal grace was not, as the Catholics thought, a "quality infused," and it did not convey grace *ex opere operato*. Bedford then joined Ward in defining the grace of the sacrament as temporary and provisional. In the sacrament the Spirit conferred upon infants "seminall, and initial grace," or "the seed and root of Faith." This was, as Ward had said, a grace of which infants alone were capable. It had no infallible connection with salvation unless the baptized child died as an infant; adults required a further experience of regeneration.[110]

Having limited the effect of the sacrament to the elect, Cornelius Burges had emphasized the permanent efficacy of the seminal grace given an infant in baptism. And although Bedford agreed with Ward that infant baptism could not save an adult, he took a cue from Burges and suggested that it might very well help save him. The grace bestowed in baptism was "as the seed, whence the future Acts of grace, and holiness . . . may in time spring forth." Baxter objected to this image of baptismal grace as a seed implanted in all baptized infants to bring forth "future Acts of Grace and Holiness," and he rightly accused Bedford of misinterpreting Burges. Baxter denied that baptism could effect "real Grace" in infants; to say so implied that real grace could be lost.[111] Ward would have disagreed with that implication, too, as did Bedford. But Bedford's description of baptism did, as Baxter said, create a tension between his sacramental theology and the doctrine of election.

After an exchange of letters, Baxter acknowledged that he and Bedford were nearer in judgment than he had first supposed. Tombes, however, thought that the reconciliation was superficial.

> What Mr. Bedford hath produced for the efficacy of baptism, hath been answered by Mr. Baxter in his Appendix to his *Plain Scripture*, etc. Nor doth it appear to me that Mr. B. is of his minde, notwithstanding that Letters have past between them now printed, and the syncretism yielded to in the printing of the Friendly Accommodation. . . .[112]

Baxter himself never said that he and Bedford were exactly of one mind, and even after their irenic exchange they disagreed on three issues. Bedford never agreed that remission came primarily from the

---

110. Bedford, *Treatise*, pp. 48, 70, 192; see also Bedford, *Moderate Answer*, p. 4, and *Vindiciae*, "Praefatio," n.p.

111. Bedford, *Treatise*, p. 116; Baxter, *Appendix*, and *Friendly Accomodation*, in *Plain Scripture Proof*, pp. 294, 360.

112. Tombes, *Anti-Paedobaptism, Second Part*, p. 220; Baxter, *Friendly Accomodation*, in *Plain Scripture Proof*, p. 355.

covenant rather than from baptism. Baxter never agreed that infant baptism itself was the covenant condition. And Baxter remained critical of Bedford's eclectic appropriation of the dissimilar views of Ward and Burges.[113] Perhaps the divergence between Baxter and Bedford was reflected in the fact that Baxter thought that Zwingli "meant rightly" even though he gave "too little to baptism in terms," while Bedford had nothing but contempt for Zwinglian "Sacramentarians." [114] The Reformed tradition still had room for differing attitudes toward baptism.

The Rhetoric of Debate

English Reformed theologians, however, did find it difficult to live with their differences, especially over infant baptism. Baxter was a relatively tolerant man. He never thought of Baptists as heretics, so long as they did not reject the fundamental doctrines of original sin and divine election. Infant baptism, he said, was "no such easy controversy or article of faith, as that no one should be tolerated that receiveth it not." [115] But Baxter's capacity for toleration was exceptional among Presbyterians and prelatical Puritans. And even he confessed speaking with more than usual "sharpnesse" against Tombes. Apart from Independents, who espoused toleration as a matter of principle and often fraternized openly with Baptists, most ministers felt deep dismay at the progress of antipaedobapist convictions.

The intensity of their feeling helps to clarify the cultural meaning of the quarrels over infant baptism. The theologians upset with the Baptists did not believe that they were simply discussing theological matters: the sacrament became to them a symbol of moral and political order. Many moderate Puritans interpreted the repudiation of infant baptism as a sign and cause of social disorder and associated Baptists with political radicalism. Opponents of the English Baptists always warned that they might emulate the violent uprising in 1534 of

113. Baxter, *Friendly Accomodation,* in *Plain Scripture Proof,* pp. 357, 361. Baxter thought that Bedford finally repudiated all "over-ascribing to baptisme" and acknowledged that "principally the Covenant and faith of the parent" were the channels for the remission of original sin. See Baxter, *Friendly Accomodation,* p. 364. Actually Bedford conceded only that the faith of the parent brought the child to have a "title or interest" in the covenant of grace, and he had been saying this ever since 1638, meaning only that parental faith qualified the child for "the grace of baptism." See Bedford, *Treatise,* pp. 101, 192.

114. Bedford, *Treatise,* p. 73; Baxter, *Friendly Accomodation,* in *Plain Scripture Proof,* pp. 337–65.

115. Baxter, *Apology,* n.p.; idem, *Plain Scripture Proof,* p. 10; idem, *Catechising of Families, Works,* 19 : 266–69; idem, *Christian Directory, Works,* 5 : 365.

Anabaptists in Munster on the continent. The prominence of Baptists in Cromwell's New Model Army reinforced the association between antipaedobaptism and political extremism. Years after the Restoration of the monarchy, Baxter remarked that his earlier writings contained "many enigmatical Reflections upon the Anabaptists for their horrid scandals," which included such political "crimes" as regicide and rebellion against Parliament. He had spoken in cryptic allusions, he explained, because he had then feared Baptist "Strength and Fury." [116] The growing visibility after 1642 of eschatological utopians seeking to establish the political reign of Christ on earth intensified such fears. It had long been standard Puritan doctrine that sacraments were means to proclaim the Lord's death "until he comes" (1 Cor. 11 : 26). Their usefulness would cease after Christ returned to establish his millenial kingdom. Some millenarians, therefore, anticipating the imminent kingdom, began to question such "outward customes and formes" as baptism.[117] One conclusion was natural, though mistaken: if chiliastic political extremists minimized or rejected sacraments, then Baptists who did the same were themselves potential if not actual political radicals. Baxter ridiculed the "English Anabaptists and other Fanaticks" for their dreams of "glorious Times," which produced dangerous and extravagant actions.[118] And to such respectable Puritan ministers as Baxter there was a thin line between political disorder and intolerable immorality.

Fear of immoral anarchy permeated the rhetoric of debates over the mode and administration of baptism. The procedure became problematic by 1641 when a few Baptists withdrew from a London Separatist church and then split when several became convinced that immersion was the only valid way to baptize. The earliest known Baptist treatise defending immersion appeared the same year, when Edward Barber spoke out for "that glorious principle, True Baptisme or Dipping." [119] By 1644 it was widely accepted among Baptists that the "way and manner" of dispensing the ordinance was "dipping or plunging

116. Baxter, *Reliquiae Baxterianae*, p. 109.

117. Gerrard Winstanley, "Truth Lifting Up its Head Above Scandals" (1648), in George Sabine, ed., *The Works of Gerrard Winstanley* (Ithaca, New York, 1941), p. 141; Robert Baillie, *Dissuasive from the Errors of the Time*, in A. R. Dallison, "Contemporary Criticisms of Millenarianism," *Puritans, The Millenium, and the Future of Israel: Puritan Eschatology 1600–1660*, ed. Peter Toon (London, 1970), p. 106; Louise Brown, *The Political Activities of Baptists and Fifth Monarchy Men in England During the Interregnum* (New York, 1911), pp. 6–16.

118. Baxter, *Reliquiae Baxterianae*, p. 133.

119. Champlin Burrage, *The Church Covenant Idea* (Philadelphia, 1904), p .152; Barber, *Small Treatise*, "Preface," n.p. One paedobaptist theologian, Daniel Rogers, had in 1635 recommended immersion in *A Treatise of the two Sacraments*, 2nd ed. (London, 1635), p. 70, but there is no evidence that Rogers influenced Baptist groups.

the body under water," a practice that they defended with etymological arguments and New Testament examples, frequently adding the theological point that only immersion adequately signified the participation of the saints in the burial and resurrection of Christ.[120] Tombes accepted immersion; Blake and Baxter opposed it, usually with exegetical arguments. But Baxter also believed current rumors about the moral enormity of Baptist practice, stories about "great multitudes of men and women together in the evening, and going naked into the rivers." [121] Baxter charged most Baptists with "dipping persons naked," the remainder with baptizing them "next to naked." The practice, he added, would eventually debauch the people of England.[122] The rumors were highly exaggerated, at best, but Baxter's credulity, widely shared by his contemporaries, exemplified a persistent suspicion that the Baptist movement was a potential threat to moral order.

Ethical considerations were not absent even from the controversy over the proper administrator of the sacrament. Baptists argued that any disciple able to preach the gospel and attract converts was authorized by Christ to baptize. They limited the privilege to men possessing "gifts of the spirit," which were manifest mainly in the ability to preach.[123] But they did reject the need for any ordained minister, thus exhibiting their suspicion of another rite with sacramental associations. Their practice evoked reactions, ranging from an instinctive protection of ministerial prestige to concern for ecclesiastical order and respect for the ceremony of ordination. But to the Puritans of the Westminster Assembly the challenge to the ministry also exhibited Baptist disregard for moral reform. In advocating the Assembly, ministers had promised that it would produce the rapid reformation of society, at least if it accorded them authority to discipline the scandalous.[124] Presbyterians, especially, believed that the elimination of licentiousness depended on the enhancement of the ministry. Blake insisted that a "constant standing Ministery" was essential to drive men "up to the termes of the Covenant." Therefore he considered it a "foul breach of Gospel order" when laymen replaced ministers, though neither Blake nor Baxter claimed that an improper administrator invariably nullified the efficacy of baptism. Baptist practice was rather a

120. Barber, *A Confession of Faith* in Underhill, *Confessions,* p. 42. See also Hanserd Knollys, *The Shining of a Flaming-fire in Zion* (London, 1646); and Featley, *Dippers dipt,* p. 36.
121. Featley, *Dippers dipt,* p. 36.
122. Baxter, *Plain Scripture Proof,* p. 137.
123. Barber, *A Confession of Faith;* and Cox, *Appendix,* in Underhill, *Confessions,* pp. 42, 58; Knollys, *Shining,* p. 9.
124. William A. Lamont, *Marginal Prynne 1600–1669* (London, 1963), p. 153.

threat to an authoritative ministry and hence to a moral society. Baxter scoffed at alleged Baptist naivete: they thought they advanced reformation, he said, simply when they rebaptized. He considered the task more difficult, and he believed that it depended on ministerial prestige and authority, which the Baptists were attempting to undermine.[125]

There was therefore no single issue in the Puritan baptismal debates, which were rather a series of diverse intersecting controversies. Presbyterians and Independents argued against Baptists, who along with covenantal paedobaptists opposed Puritan sacramentalists. Presbyterians fought among themselves, as did Independents. The debates did reveal the imprecision in the earlier definition of the sacrament as a covenant seal. Most agreed that baptism was the seal to an external conditional covenant, but some rejected the distinction between external and internal, and others insisted that baptism was a seal to the act of faith as well as to the covenant promise. The Reformed sacramentalists, meanwhile, claimed that the covenant imagery was insufficient as a bulwark of sacramental grace. And nobody was entirely oblivious to the question of moral, political, and ecclesiastical order, though men differed about the prerequisites for order.

Undoubtedly the Baptists, and after 1652 the Quakers, presented a greater threat to conventional sacramental theory than did the few Puritan sacramentalists. Nevertheless, the baptismal debates illustrate the vitality and diversity of sacramental thought within a changing Puritan tradition. Baptists pushed beyond familiar limits in the direction of a spirituality unencumbered by extraneous rites, and claimed to be authentic heirs of earlier Puritan worthies, but sacramentalists also transcended accepted boundaries, asserting that their exaltation of material means of grace was more consistent with the tradition. Even within the older boundaries, there was a serious attempt, represented by Blake and Baxter, to ensure that solicitude for Reformed theology and ecclesiastical purity not preclude sacramental piety. If we insist that the Quaker movement was the logical terminus of the Puritan impulse, then what do we make of the numberless Puritans who felt impelled to man the ramparts in defense of infant baptism? The sacramental ambivalence of the early Puritan movement contained an affirmation, however subdued it might occasionally have appeared, for Puritans never forgot that it was necessary for an infinite God to accommodate his revelation to the capacities of finite, em-

125. Blake, *Vindiciae Foederis*, p. 115; idem, *Convenant Sealed*, pp. 277–78; Baxter, *Reformed Pastor*, in *Works*, 14: 152, 254–69; Baxter, *An Answer to Mr. Tombes*, in *Plain Scripture Proof*, idem, pp. 210–211; *Christian Directory*, in *Works*, 5: 304, 321.

bodied men. In that divine accommodation sacramental piety found its justification.

During the seventeenth century, incipient High Anglicans in the Church of England also began to revise sacramental theology, particularly during Laud's tenure as Archbishop, but they often combined their baptismal doctrines with Arminian theology and traditional ritualism. The Puritan sacramentalists and their sympathizers, along with more cautious men like Blake and Baxter, wanted to maintain Reformed orthodoxy—to speak of sacramental efficacy, however understood, without discarding the doctrine of election or abandoning the quest for a disciplined Church. The sacramentalists proposed a stronger doctrine of baptism than most seventeenth–century Anglicans, Puritan or not, could accept, and consequently had limited influence. But their doctrines and the controversies in which they engaged denoted a growing interest in sacraments, an interest that was also visible in the Puritan debates over the Lord's Supper.

4

THE LORD'S SUPPER:

DEBATE AND DEVOTION

Late in the seventeenth century, Richard Vines, a London Presbyterian, complained that the Lord's Supper had become "an apple of contention" and division among English Christians.[1] The justice of his complaint was indisputable, though he might well have added that the controversies both reflected and stimulated an increasing interest in the sacrament within the English Puritan tradition. By the end of the century, there were at least three distinct perspectives on the Lord's Supper among mainstream English Puritans. Some continued to propagate a highly subjective spirituality that allowed a concern for inward preparation to overshadow the objective reality of the sacrament. Others argued that the Lord's Supper was an efficacious rite capable of converting the unregenerate by evoking their internal assent to the Gospel. And in sacramental manuals, confessions, and liturgies, still other Puritans reaffirmed the mystical presence as the basis of efficacy in the sacrament. Even while debates raged in the second half of the century, Puritan ministers were busily encouraging a revival of Reformed sacramental piety through a proliferation of eucharistic devotional manuals.

The debates began when questions of ecclesiastical politics became entangled with sacramental issues during the Westminster Assembly. As soon as the Assembly convened in 1643, some Puritans began to press for legal recognition of their right to discipline members by suspending them from the sacrament. Their efforts exposed two fundamentally differing assumptions about the sacrament itself. Advocates

1. Richard Vines, *A Treatise of the Institution, Right Administration, and Receiving of the Sacrament of the Lords Supper* (London, 1657), pp. 102, 247.

of suspension believed that the Lord's Supper was instituted to confirm faith and was therefore rightly accessible only to the faithful; their opponents claimed that the Supper was a converting ordinance, and consequently that it was intended even for the unregenerate, so long as they possessed competent knowledge of Christian doctrine. The controversy demonstrated once again the centrality of the covenant doctrine in Puritan sacramental theology, just as it uncovered the ambiguity in the definition of the Lord's Supper as a covenant seal.

Later seventeenth-century Puritanism is not generally associated with eucharistic preoccupations. Such heirs of Puritan spirituality as Quakers and smaller sectarian groups, who discarded sacraments, have seemed to express the inner tendencies of Puritan piety. And between the dissolution of the third parliament of Charles I in 1629 and the execution of Archbishop Laud in 1645, many Puritan ministers seemingly wrote about sacraments only to oppose Laud's program of restoring "altars" to English churches. When the proteges of Laud called for elaborate altars enclosed by protective rails, and then began inserting sacrificial terminology into their eucharistic meditations, Puritans feared the surreptitious reentry of Roman sacramental doctrine into English religious life. They wrongly accused the Laudians of holding to Roman Catholic notions of propitiatory sacrifice, corporeal presence, and a sacerdotal priesthood possessing unique power and authority. The High Churchmen, in turn, accused their opponents of Zwinglian sacramentarianism. The "altar controversy" therefore perpetuated the impression that Puritans were obsessed by an antisacramental consciousness.[2]

While they opposed the peculiar sacramental piety of Laud, however, many Puritan ministers were also engaging in positive efforts to revise—or to reaffirm—traditional Reformed doctrines. Their sacramental concerns reflected varied political and ecclesiastical interests, but they also manifested a sensitivity to the seventeenth century's changing vision of reality and how it is known. The resurgence of sacramental debate and devotion paralleled an expanding conviction that the visible, finite, corporeal creation should be incorporated more fully into the life of piety.

Sacraments in the Erastian Controversy

When Parliament invoked the Westminster Assembly in 1643, Puritan ministers viewed it as an occasion for restructuring the Church of England and reforming the society. High on the list of Puritan pro-

2. See Clark, "Altar Controversy."

posals was a statutory distinction between excommunication and "Sequestration from the Sacrament." [3] Such a measure would have permitted the exclusion from communion of errant but redeemable members, while reserving the harsher penalty for intransigent offenders. The proposal therefore protected the Lord's Supper and also facilitated the ministerial ambition to institute rigid ecclesiastical discipline as a first step toward establishing moral order throughout the land. To most Puritans, the plan seemed eminently reasonable and godly, but it had critics, especially among the Erastians.

Most ministers viewed Erastianism as a cynical and morally indifferent movement to subject the Church to the control of the state and its appointed officials. But some Erastians were themselves zealous reformers, convinced that suspension of the ungodly from the sacrament impeded the moral reformation of society, a conviction that had also been expressed by Thomas Erastus when he interrupted his labors as professor of medicine at Heidelberg to resist the presbyterian scheme of Church government in the sixteenth century. From his polemical writings the English Erastians gathered a store of arguments against sequestration, and after Parliament, in October, 1643, officially authorized presbyteries to suspend the scandalous from the sacrament, William Prynne (1600–1669) used those arguments in a sustained attack against the law. Accusing his ministerial opponents of "overmuch rigor," Prynne rebutted their contentions with *Foure Serious Questions of Grand Importance, concerning Excommunication and Suspension from the Sacrament,* in which he tried, in the words of an anonymous antagonist, to exalt the "high prerogatives and priviledges of Parliament, and the power of Civil Magistrates, Judges, and Courts of Justice" over against the power of ministers.[4] Prynne did not covet such political power as an end in itself. He believed, rather, that "speedy reformation" of the Church and society would never result from that "strict discipline, which really reforms very few, or none." [5] In Prynne's opinion, common admission to the sacrament, in a Church carefully administered by government officials who would ensure that communicants lead lives of decency and decorum, was the only means to oversee and protect the moral welfare of England.

Of the theologians who hastened to defend sequestration, the two

3. William Prynne, *Foure Serious Questions of Grand Importance, concerning Excommunication and Suspension from the Sacrament* (London, 1644), p. 4.

4. Anon., *An antidote against foure dangerous Quaeries, pretended to be propounded to the Reverend Assemblie of Divines, touching Suspension from the Sacrament* (London, 1645), p. 3.

5. William Prynne, *A Vindication of foure Serious Questions of Grand Importance Concerning Excommunication and Suspention from the Sacrament of the Lords Supper* (London, 1645), p. 57. See Lamont, *Godly Rule: Politics and Religion, 1603–60* (London, 1969) p. 122.

most influential were the Scottish commissioners to the Westminster
Assembly, Samuel Rutherford (1600–1661), whom Prynne later attacked as "one of the first broachers of this Controversie," [6] and George
Gillespie (1613–1648), the preacher at Greyfriars Church in Edinburgh.
They were not writing sacramental theology when they replied to
Prynne; they were attempting rather to defend the prerogatives of
presbyteries and to counteract the "strong influence" wielded by Erastian politicians.[7] But they became deeply involved in sacramental issues, for resolution of the controversy over ministerial authority awaited
some agreement about the criteria of admission to the Lord's Supper.
In order to deprive ministers of all authority over the sacrament,
Prynne argued that any Church member who had not been excommunicated, and who professed belief in Christian doctrine, was free to
approach the Lord's Table, and he inveighed especially against the
practice of admitting only the regenerate, or the presumably regenerate. Neither Gillespie nor Rutherford demanded infallible evidence of
regeneration. They had no interest in peering into the soul, but would
judge worthiness by visible behavior. Nevertheless, the impasse remained, for they did give ministers the right to distinguish worthy
from unworthy Church members and to demand of erstwhile sinners
a public profession of sincere repentance before being admitted to
the sacrament. A minister negligent in such affairs was an accessory
to the sin of unworthy receiving.[8]

Prynne accused his opponents of improper biblical exegesis and insufficient logical rigor. He thought that any biblical scholar should
have known that St. Paul required of communicants only sincere self-
examination. And had not Jesus admitted Judas to the Last Supper?
Furthermore, if it were dangerous for unworthy men to receive the
sacrament, would not "unprofitable and unworthy hearing of the
word" be just as dangerous? After all, Prynne said, Christ was present
in both Word and Sacrament.[9]

Rutherford and Gillespie expended considerable energy to vindicate
the logic and propriety of their exegesis. They attempted to demonstrate that morally unscrupulous Jews were barred from the Passover,
that St. Paul was as strict as the Presbyterians, and that Judas never

6. William Prynne, *The Lords Supper Briefly Vindicated and Clearly demonstrated by Scripture and other Authorities, to be a Grace-begetting, Soul-Converting,
(as well as confirming) Ordinance* (London, 1657), p. 58.

7. George Gillespie, *Aarons Rod Blossoming, Or, The Divine Ordinance of Church
Government Vindicated* (London, 1646), "To the Reader." See also Samuel Rutherford, *The Divine Right of Church Government and Excommunication* (London,
1646).

8. Gillespie, *Aarons Rod*, pp. 343, 487.

9. Prynne, *Foure serious Questions*, pp. 2, 4.

partook of the first sacrament, having left the Supper before the sacrament was instituted. Gillespie ridiculed Prynne's contention that the sacrament was instituted during the Supper while Judas was present. In any case, he wanted only to suspend "known wicked persons" from the Lord's Supper, and Judas's wickedness was not publicly known before his departure. When Prynne argued that Jesus, for one, knew Judas to be sinful, Gillespie replied that Jesus knew this as God, and that Presbyterians did not claim divinity for their ministers.[10]

Prynne argued against each of these claims, but the key to his defense was his description of the Lord's Supper itself. Gillespie recognized that the underlying issue in the controversy was "the nature of the Ordinance." [11] With that claim Prynne agreed, and in his reply to an *Antidote against foure dangerous quaeries,* an anonymous pamphlet written against him in 1645, he introduced into the debate a definition of the sacrament as a "converting ordinance." [12] By 1660, William Morice, a lay theologian and secretary of state for Charles II, reported that Prynne's definition had become the main object of contention.

> Whether the sacrament be a converting Ordinance, is the pole where upon the sphear of this whole dispute doth hang and turn, we cannot move any way but we meet with a new meridian tending unto and centered in this pole . . . and if we can therefore elevate this pole to such a degree, as to prove the sacrament to be a converting ordinance, then those which are yet unconverted may lawfully have accesse, thereby to attain conversion. . . .[13]

Prynne's innovation was a stroke of genius that not only altered the contours of the admission controversy but also informed English and American sacramental discussion for well over a century.

Prynne's doctrine of sacramental efficacy had almost been anticipated in the sixteenth century by Erastus himself, in the course of elaborating similar arguments about Judas, the Passover, and Pauline sacramental practice. Erastus propounded no lofty conception of the Lord's Supper, to be sure. His doctrine of the presence barely moved beyond Zwingli's early memorialist views. But he did think that the sacraments were "Provocations and Allurements to Religion and Piety; and that men grow better by frequenting, than by being robb'd of them, provided they are rightly and faithfully instructed." Turks and pagans he would exclude, but he wanted to admit all orthodox

10. Gillespie, *Aarons Rod,* p. 473.
11. Ibid., p. 538.
12. Prynne, *Vindication of foure Serious Questions,* pp. 35–41.
13. William Morice, *Coena quasi Koine: or the Common Right to the Lords Supper Asserted, Wherein That Question is Fully Stated* (London, 1660), p. 310.

Church members, even if they lacked "the *farther pitch* of Internal
Fellowship of the Soul and Spirit" or failed to live exemplary lives.
It was not that the Lord's Supper itself could produce internal fellowship with the Spirit; Erastus did not encourage men to seek salvation
in the sacrament. But he implied that communion could improve a
man's religious condition.[14] The implication was not fully developed,
so when Theodore Beza set out to castigate Erastus for his errors, he
quickly passed over the contention that the Lord's Supper was an
allurement to piety.[15] But the doctrine was suggestive, particularly for
theologians who, like the English Puritans, were fascinated with
the morphology of conversion.

As a young man, Prynne shared that fascination. He thrived on the
Puritan sermons of John Preston at Lincoln's Inn, wrote treatises on
Calvinist theology, and joined the Puritan crusade against the Anglican
hierarchy—a step that cost him both of his ears during Laud's tenure
as Archbishop of Canterbury.[16] It is not surprising, therefore, that his
version of Erastus's doctrine was couched in the vocabulary of conversion. Rather than describe the Lord's Supper merely as an allurement
to piety, Prynne called it a "converting ordinance," thus coining an
effective slogan to demolish the bar to the sacrament.

At the center of Prynne's doctrine was a distinction between two
kinds of conversion. Pagans, he said, were ordinarily converted by the
Word, or in extraordinary cases by miracles, and the "conversion" of
the infants of Christian parents was "ordinarily effected by the Sacrament of Baptism," by which they were made members of the visible
Church. In either case, however, conversion was simply formal entry
into a visible community, involving for an adult no more than a
"meere externall formal profession of the Doctrine." In such instances,
which Prynne thought normal, there was need for a second conversion,
an "inward spirituall embracing and application of Christ." For these
formal Christians, and for them only, the Lord's Supper was a "regenerating and converting Ordinance." Prynne also recalled the traditional Reformed doctrine that the sacrament was an appendix to the
Word; he concluded that it was potentially as effective for conversion
as preaching, adding that any ordinance able to increase grace could
beget grace.[17] He granted that unconverted heathen, along with infants

14. Thomas Erastus, *A Treatise of Excommunication* (London, 1682), pp. 2–5, 16,
21–29, 73.
15. Theodore Beza, *Tractatus pius et moderatus de vera Excommunicatione et
christiano Presbyterio* (Geneva, 1590).
16. See Ethyn Kirby, *William Prynne, a study in Puritanism* (Cambridge, Mass.,
1931); and William Lamont, *Marginal Prynne 1600–1669* (London, 1963).
17. Prynne, *Vindication of foure Serious Questions*, pp. 40–41.

and the insane, were to be excluded, but since virtually the entire
adult population of England met the requirements of formal membership, Prynne's qualifications did not detract from the effectiveness
of his argument.

Gillespie and Rutherford replied, first, by saying that the Lord's
Supper was a "confirming and sealing ordinance," appointed to "seal
unto a man that interest in Christ and in the covenant of grace which
he already hath." Second, they insisted that while sacraments were
"exhibitive signes," so that "the thing signified" was "given and exhibite to the soul," the exhibition was to believers only and did not
entail the "giving of grace where it is not." Third, they criticized
Prynne's understanding of conversion. There was, they thought, only
one type of conversion—"A conversion from nature to grace"—and
one "converting Ordinance," the Word.[18] Gillespie acknowledged that
some men might experience conversion during the Eucharist, but he
explained this fact as a consequence of the "preaching, exhortation,
and prayer" accompanying the administration of the elements.[19]
Prynne would later answer this argument by including exhoration and
prayer within the circle of sacramental actions: "the Word of Bene-
diction, Consecration, Institution used at the Lords Supper, is an essential part of it, without which it neither is nor can be a Sacrament." [20]

Neither Rutherford nor Gillespie intended to rob the sacrament of
efficacy. The Lord's Supper was still "the nourishment of those in
whom Christ liveth," increasing "the conversion which was before" by
adding "a new degree of faith." [21] Like Calvin, they linked sacramental efficacy with the doctrine of sanctification, which described the
Christian's growth in faith and holiness. Moreover, the sacrament
sealed God's promises to the elect.[22] Since the seal applied to the
worthy communicant "in particular, the very promise that in generall
is made to him," he could leave the table with assurance of God's
mercy.[23] Prynne wanted to say more, and in his attempts to push beyond traditional sacramental ideas he dealt with two questions that
occupied the Puritans throughout the subsequent half-century. The
first issue was the precise relation between the covenant and its seal.
Although hesitant to describe the sacrament as a seal, on the grounds
that the term was not biblical, Prynne agreed to accept the popular

18. Gillespie, *Aarons Rod,* pp. 489, 496–98; Rutherford, *Divine Right,* pp. 521–23.
19. Gillespie, *Aarons Rod,* pp. 502, 524.
20. Prynne, *Lords Supper briefly Vindicated,* p. 20.
21. Rutherford, *Divine Right,* pp. 340, 523.
22. Gillespie, *Aarons Rod,* p. 500.
23. Rutherford, *Divine Right,* p. 253.

terminology if he could distinguish a "double-sealing." As a visible external seal, the sacrament offered God's promise only on condition of future repentance, but the elect communicant who embraced Christ's promises received an internal, invisible sealing "by the Spirit." [24] Prynne did not refine the distinction, but by exposing the flexibility in the definition of the Lord's Supper as a seal, and by demanding precise distinctions, he uncovered an issue that persisted throughout the century. What did it mean to call the Lord's Supper a seal to the covenant?

Prynne also raised the fundamental question of the relation between presence and efficacy in the Lord's Supper. At times he himself spoke as if Christ were uniquely present in the Lord's Supper. "We have a more immediate intercourse with God and Christ in this Sacrament, then in any other Ordinance whatsoever." [25] The sacrament applied the promises and merits of Christ "far livelier than the word preached doth." But that did not entail a high conception of the presence, for Prynne spoke of merits and benefits instead of spiritual substance, and he thought that the Lord's Supper communicated the benefits of Christ more effectively only because it reached all the physical senses as well as the "heart, and soule." [26] He explicitly denied that Christ was uniquely present when he criticized the theologians who had

> . . . bred a strange schisme between the Sacrament and ordinances of God themselves, as if the Lord's supper were far holier, and Christ more really, immediately, and in another manner present therein, than he is in Baptism, Prayer, or the Word preached; when as in truth, Gods Sacraments, Ordinances are all of equal holinesse. . . .[27]

At the time Prynne wrote these words, few if any Puritan theologians in fact desired to make a sharp theoretical distinction between Word and Sacrament. It was the admission controversy itself that produced the insistence on the unique character of Christ's presence in the Lord's Supper. Some disputants ignored sacramental doctrine throughout the debate: one anonymous author, writing around 1646, defended Prynne's position on admission without once calling the

24. Prynne, *Vindication of foure Serious Questions*, p. 40.
25. Ibid., p. 42.
26. William Prynne, *A Seasonable Vindication of Free-Admission and Frequent Administration of the Holy Communion To all Visible Church-Members, Regenerate or Unregenerate* (London, 1656), p. 44. See also Prynne, *Vindication of foure Serious Questions*, pp. 37, 43.
27. Prynne, *Seasonable Vindication*, p. 44.

Lord's Supper a converting ordinance.[28] After 1651, however, specifically doctrinal questions received greater attention, and a variety of theologians within the Puritan tradition developed a broad spectrum of views on the Lord's Supper.

Debate

The debate resumed after John Humfrey (1621–1719), the vicar of Frome Selwood in Somersetshire, published two sermons in 1651 in which he restated the demand for free admission to the sacrament. Humfrey had been ordained by a classis of presbyters in 1649. A Royalist who never accepted the Solemn League and Covenant, he was shortly thereafter reordained by a bishop. But since he was, as Samuel Petto wrote to Increase Mather in New England, decidedly "not a Conformist," Humfrey then renounced his episcopal ordination. After being ejected by the Uniformity act in 1662, he went to London and gathered a congregational church.[29] Well before that time, however, Humfrey had developed one of the three major doctrinal positions that originated during the controversy over admission: he argued that the sacrament was an efficacious seal to a conditional covenant. The most articulate opponent of free admission, Roger Drake, would reply that the Lord's Supper was primarily a seal of faith, while the most innovative of Humfrey's allies, the layman John Timson, developed the notion that the sacrament sealed an absolute divine promise.

28. Anon, *The antidote animadverted* (London, n. d.), pp. 1–8. The nature of the sacrament was also ignored in Henry Burton, *A Vindication of the Churches Commonly Called Independent* (London, 1644); and Thomas Bakewell, *The Ordinance of Excommunication rightly Stated* (London, 1646). The issue was taken up briefly in John Saltmarsh, *The Opening of Master Prynnes new Book, called A Vindication* (London, 1645), pp. 12–22; and in W. L., *The Sacramental Stumbling Block Removed* (London, 1648), p. 29. Both writers denied that the Lord's Supper was a converting ordinance. George Williams, "Called by thy Name, Leave us Not: The Case of Mrs. Joan Drake," *Harvard Library Bulletin* 16 (April, 1968) : 123, quoted a seventeenth-century Englishman who reported that John Dod had called the Lord's Supper a converting ordinance. Certainly, however, Dod's use of the term was unrelated to the tradition that I am discussing, if indeed he did actually use it. Dod never called the Lord's Supper a converting ordinance in any of his written work.

29. John Humfrey, *An Humble Vindication of a Free Admission Unto the Lords Supper, Published for the ease, support, and satisfaction of tender Consciences (otherwise remediles) in our mixt Congregations as it was delivered at two sermons* (London, 1651). See Alexander Gordon, "John Humfrey," *DNB* 10 (1908) : 235–37; and see also "Letter from Samuel Petto to Increase Mather," January 2, 1678/9, Prince Collection, Mather Papers, III, 1, Boston Public Library. It is not correct to call Humfrey one of the "clergy of the Establishment," as Horton Davies does in *The Worship of the English Puritans*, p. 239.

Though other theologians added various minor modifications, these three established the terms of later argumentation.

Humfrey's interest in sacramental practice was not a by-product of any involvement in ecclesiastical politics. He was neither an Erastian nor was he indifferent to purity within the Church; he reverenced the "pantings and breathings" of his Puritan contemporaries "after a fellowship of the Saints on Earth, as neer as may be to the Church in Heaven." [30] Humfrey's support for "an Anti-Erastian free admission" was mainly due to his biblical scholarship and his sense of pastoral responsibility, and he more than any other man injected into one stream of Puritan piety the idea that the Lord's Supper could be an instrument of conversion.[31]

According to the narrative of the Last Supper in Matthew 26 : 27, Jesus commanded all of his disciples to partake of the wine: "Drink ye all of it." The words impressed Humfrey, as did the testimony in the Gospel of Mark that "they all drank of it," so he decided to open the Lord's Supper to all of Christ's seventeenth-century disciples. Humfrey's invitation was not indiscriminate; he required preparation and excluded scandalous sinners excommunicated by the Church, as well as infants and the insane. He also demanded that every communicant be baptized and have at least an "historical faith." But these minimal requirements were sufficient; the absence of grace was "no hindrance." If ministers waited until they discerned effectual faith in their parishioners before inviting them to the Lord's Supper, Humfrey warned, then they would never administer the elements, "seeing that cannot be discerned by any." [32] He was convinced that the sacrament itself would convert the unregenerate believer.

The Lord's Supper, he said, "works in every one, as his state and need requires, in the converted for their strength and establishment, and in the unregenerate for their conversion." [33] It could convert the unregenerate within the Church because they already possessed sufficient "common grace" to benefit from it. Humfrey was never certain precisely how their common grace differed from the "special grace" of the regenerate, but his argument presupposed that the two kinds of grace differed only in degree—a presupposition that he occasionally expressed openly.

30. John Humfrey, *A Rejoynder to Mr. Drake, or a A Reply Unto his Book Entitled A Boundary to the Holy Mount* (London, 1654), p. 147 and "To the Reader."

31. John Humfrey, *A Second Vindication of a Disciplinary, Anti-Erastian, Orthodox Free-Admission to the Lords-Supper* (London, 1656), p. 109. See chapter seven for Humfrey's influence in New England.

32. Humfrey, *Rejoynder*, pp. 169; 34, 66, 180.

33. Humfrey, *Humble Vindication*, p. 59.

As as for my part, I am persuaded the serious exercise of common grace, the confirming and encreasing thereof, and that [by the sacrament] . . . is the way of God's own working speciall grace also, yet most freely, as is suitable to the nature of it.

Since the sacrament nourished and increased common grace, frequent communion was a "means of regeneration." Like Prynne, Humfrey distinguished a "conversion of assent," by which the convert came to believe Christian doctrine, from a "conversion of consent," by which he embraced Jesus as his savior. The confirming of assent by the sacrament produced consent. By holding forth Christ to the intelligent believer, the Lord's Supper reminded him, as a visible gospel, of the covenant made by Christ's death, and thereby often produced "effectual conversion" in intelligent Christians.[34]

After more than half a century of serious speculation on covenantal themes by English Puritans, Humfrey was convinced that "the very body of our Religion" consisted in "the knowledge of the Covenant, and Application of it." Naturally he thought the covenant to be the "foundation of the sacraments," so he defended his position by clarifying the relation between the covenant and its seal. Like Prynne, however, he was reluctant to speak of sacraments as covenant seals. Many "poor souls," he noted, had found themselves in "some trouble about the notions of sealing and the like, when they sunk too deep in them." [35]

Humfrey would use the customary language only if he were permitted two distinctions. First, he said, the sacrament sealed the conditional, not the absolute covenant. Since the Lord's Supper did not seal an interest in Christ "absolutely," men who failed to repent and believe, to meet the covenant conditions, would never receive its full benefits.[36] But the sacrament did convey grace enabling the elect to fulfill the requirements of the covenant, thus obviating any need to limit administration to those who presumably had already met the conditions of faith and repentance. Second, Humfrey added, the sacrament was not a "seal of faith," unless that simply meant that it increased and confirmed faith, or provided Christians an occasion to engage themselves to believe.[37] But to stop at that was to minimize the objectivity of sacramental sealing: "God doth not attest our Faith but the truth of his own promises." [38] From that perspective Humfrey

34. Humfrey, *Rejoynder,* pp. 208; 200, 211.
35. Ibid., pp. 64, 168; 33–34.
36. Humfrey, *Humble Vindication,* p. 48.
37. Humfrey, *Rejoynder,* p. 201; idem, *Humble Vindication,* p. 45.
38. Humfrey, *Humble Vindication,* p. 42.

could criticize ministers who would bar unregenerate Christians with
the argument that sacraments did not seal "blanks."[39] The Lord's
Supper, he said, sealed the promise of God, not the piety of men.

To many Puritans it seemed that Humfrey had excessively minimized the importance of faith in sacramental thought and practice.
The major spokesman for the ministers offended by Humfrey's doctrine was Roger Drake (1608–1669), who became known as the "fierc-
est-champion" of a fenced communion table. Drake was a physician
who had defended Harvey's views while studying at Leyden, receiving
a medical degree there in 1639. He entered the ministry after 1646 as
a staunch Presbyterian, and within five years he was arrested after
being implicated in Love's Plot, an attempt to reach an accommodation with the Scots and enthrone Charles II, who had sworn to establish Presbyterian polity. After being pardoned, Drake became the minister in 1653 of St. Peter's Cheap, where he was active at the time that
he published his protestations against the views of John Humfrey.[40]

Drake insisted that every communicant was obliged to profess faith
and repentance, which hopefully would reveal traces of saving grace.[41]
A purely historical faith, which Drake defined as a merely "intellectual
discretion," was insufficient; a "cordial discretion" of saving faith and
love was necessary to discern the Lord's body.[42] Drake never claimed
that a presbytery could infallibly identify saving grace, but since any
communicant without inward grace drew upon himself guilt and dam-
nations, pastors were to exclude the obviously unregenerate.[43]

Prynne wrote his sacramental treatises because he wanted to reform
the morality of English society; Humfrey wrote his in order to press
upon his fellow Puritans an expanded view of pastoral responsibility;
Drake was concerned to preserve the purity of the Church and the
sanctity of the sacrament. To accomplish his end, he relied on familiar
biblical arguments about the Passover, Judas, and Pauline scrupulosity,
but he agreed that the underlying issue was the nature of the Lord's
Supper. "Prove actuall receiving a converting ordinance," Drake wrote,
"and we shall be . . . zealous for free admission." The traditional Reformed description of the Lord's Supper as a confirming, rather than a
converting ordinance, he continued, was "one of our grand arguments

39. Humfrey, *Rejoynder*, p. 170.

40. Gordon Goodwin, "Roger Drake, M.D.," *DNB* 5 (1908) : 1353–54; Prynne,
Lords Supper Briefly Vindicated, p. 58.

41. Roger Drake, *The Bar, against Free Admission to the Lords Supper, Fixed,
or an Answer to Mr. Humfrey his Rejoynder, or, Reply* (London, 1656), p. 85.

42. Roger Drake, *A Boundary to the Holy Mount, Or, a Barre against Free admission to the Lords Supper* (London, 1653), p. 191. See also Drake, *Bar*, p. 43.

43. Drake, *Bar*, p. 330.

against free admission." It was so grand, in fact, that "if it be not cannon-proof our cause must needs be in a great deal of hazard." [44] Drake would grant that God might convert a sinner at the Lord's Table; any ordinance was potentially a "morall instrument" of conversion that God could use "arbitrarily." But he was certain that the "actuall receiving" had nothing to do with such a conversion, which he preferred to attribute to the preaching and prayers associated with the sacrament. Chance conversions did not prove the Lord's Supper a converting ordinance: "Although a man may be converted *at*, it is not *by* the Sacrament, it is occasionally, but not intentionally a converting Ordinance." [45] Drake challenged Humfrey to produce one instance of a person's being converted by or at the sacrament.[46]

Drake thought that a multitude of doctrinal errors were implicit in Humfrey's lax policies about admission, and he especially criticized Humfrey's covenantal doctrine. Drake thought that the sacrament sealed both a conditional and an absolute covenant. The conditional covenant—he who believes shall be saved—was offered to all the world; the absolute covenant encompassed only elect saints who had received an effectual call.[47] In administering the sacramental seal, the preacher was a minister of both covenants: every sacrament sealed the "general offer" of the covenant to all men, but only to God's elect did the Lord's Supper "instrumentally apply" the benefits of the covenant, sealing "absolutely" an interest in the death and satisfaction of Christ. Drake wished to limit communion, so far as possible, to sanctified believers presumably within the absolute covenant. Therefore he added that the conditional covenant was sealed even to absentees, so that there was no need to admit everyone.[48]

Since he limited participation to those assumed to be faithful, Drake felt obliged to add one further clarification: the Lord's Supper was a seal "to faith as well as to the Covenant." If sacraments were only "seals properly of the Covenant," as Humfrey wanted to say, then Drake saw no way to exclude even infants and "distracted persons," as well as profane and scandalous sinners, for all were subjects of the conditional covenant. But since the sacrament was also the seal of faith, Drake felt that he had reason to exclude the faithless. Humfrey's objections notwithstanding, it would be contradictory, he said, to apply seals to "blanks." [49]

44. Drake, *Boundary*, pp. 92, 154.
45. Drake, *Bar*, p. 24; idem, *Boundary*, p. 161.
46. Drake, *Boundary*, p. 91.
47. Drake, *Bar*, pp. 113, 373.
48. Drake, *Boundary*, p. 51; idem, *Bar*, pp. 113, 373.
49. Drake, *Boundary*, pp. 128–29.

Drake believed that sacraments were intended to convey to the faithful two privileges: "more degrees of Sanctification as well as further evidence of Justification and Adoption." By providing "progressive grace" to the faithful believer, thus increasing his faith, and by visibly sealing God's promise, the sacrament verified the syllogism of assurance: he that believes shall be saved; I believe; therefore, I shall be saved. The Lord's Supper was intended for the man who could, in humility, apply to himself the conclusion of the syllogism.[50]

The exchange between Drake and Humfrey compelled English ministers once again to reconsider the meaning of the Lord's Supper, and the subsequent argumentation revealed how great the inroads of sacramentalism into the Reformed tradition really were. In 1654 Anthony Palmer (1618?–1697), an Independent, published *The Scripture Rail to the Lords Table* to rebut Humfrey. In the same year, however, John Timson, a layman from Great Bowden in Leicestershire, championed free admission, convinced, as he announced later, that he had never read "any author that came up to my opinion or judgment in these things in any measure" until he read Humfrey's *Vindication of Free Admission*.[51] As Humfrey's 1656 description revealed, Timson was a product of Puritan nurture and preaching.

> He was, it seems, bred up under the famous Robert Bolton, and so one of the Old Puritans, who using often with some of his neighbours to seek God together in the holy duty of religious conference, (Mal. 3. 16) and being deeply affected (as I suppose) with the evil of the neglect in many places of the Sacrament (himself being one that received the first impression of that grace which is in him, at this Ordinance) they were in the end convinced wholly of this opinion, and satisfied their Minister about the same.[52]

Timson characterized himself as being "point blanck" against Prynne and the Erastians, and he disclaimed direct dependence on Humfrey as well. Part of his book, he said, was completed and sent "towards the Presse" before he "even knew of Mr. Humfrey's rejoinder." [53] The tenor of his argument was entirely compatible with the claim that he

50. Drake, *Bar*, p. 129; idem, *Boundary*, p. 42.
51. John Timson, *To Receive the Lords Supper, the Actual Right and Duty of all Church-Members of Years not Excommunicate* (London, 1655), "To the Reader." See also John Timson, *The Bar to Free Admission to the Lords Supper Removed: Or, a Vindication of Mr. Humfreys Free Admission to the Sacrament of the Lords Supper* (London, 1654).
52. Humfrey, *Second Vindication*, "Epistle to the Reader." For Bolton, see E. Bagshawe, ed., *Mr. Boltons Last and Learned Worke of the Foure last Things, Death, Judgement, Hell, and Heaven* (London, 1639).
53. Timson, *To Receive the Lords Supper*, "To the Reader."

himself was converted at the sacrament; he seemed far more concerned about the religious significance of the Lord's Supper than its political or ethical implications.

It was not Timson's piety that was unique, however, but rather his doctrine, as he carried the covenant theme further in the direction of a consistently sacramental interpretation of Christianity than any of his predecessors in the debate. Timson was convinced that there was a general misunderstanding about "the nature and largeness of the Gospel Covenant made to the Church." So far as he was concerned, the "whole Church" was "in covenant with God," and he was not talking simply about a conditional covenant, which lacked any "promise . . . to give a sinner grace to beleeve." [54] To limit the discussion to the conditional part of the covenant was to rob the unregenerate, even within the Church, of consolation. Timson would extend the "whole" covenant of grace unto the entire Church: "Those in the Church . . . are the immediate objects of the absolute promises, in order to the Lord's putting these promises into execution." [55]

The absolute promise, Timson warned, was made "to the use of means." He did not want Church members to become overly confident of their position as immediate objects of the promise and therefore to neglect the Word and sacraments.

> The promises of the first grace are not only free, but absolute, not so depending upon condition of faith in a strict sense, as many other promises doe: yet not so absolute, but that the ordinary means of salvation ought to be observed diligently in order to attainment of the first grace.[56]

The promise extended to the unregenerate within the Church was in fact their "main encouragement to the use of means," which, according to Timson, had produced effectual conversions in every age and time.[57]

Timson was intent on pursuing a consistent Reformed sacramentalism. Baptism, he said, publicly marked men as Church members and thus as "objects of the absolute promises." Grace and glory were "bestowed upon baptized man." [58] Without the baptismal washing, men were ultimately strangers from the covenant, isolated from God and from all hope. Baptism, in turn, conferred a title to the Lord's Supper, by which the grace promised could be received.[59] Timson was

54. Ibid., "To the Reader."
55. Ibid., p. 95.
56. Ibid., p. 94.
57. Timson, *Bar Removed*, p. 31; and idem, *To Receive the Lords Supper*, p. 97.
58. Timson, *Bar Removed*, pp. 31, 50.
59. Timson, *To Receive the Lords Supper*, pp. 75, 99.

sufficiently Calvinist to express some reluctance about limiting the freedom of God; he acknowledged that the blessing of grace was promised and given "freely according to the good pleasure of God's own will." But he observed that God had made "many promises to the use of means," which therefore were "ordinarily successful and blessed to the attainment of grace." [60] In that sense, the Lord's Supper sealed an absolute covenant. Timson was proposing to the Presbyterians that they build their doctrine of the Church and the Christian life upon a sacramental principle.

Timson soon had support, for before the end of 1654, Thomas Fuller (1608–1661), the celebrated historian of English Christianity, joined forces with the ministers who were trying to topple the bar that the Westminster Assembly had erected around the table. Thomas Blake, the Presbyterian rector of Tamworth, was disturbed that John Humfrey was "so much by some applauded," for they differed on minor points, but Blake agreed that the Lord's Supper was a converting ordinance, and in 1655 he spoke out in *The Covenant Sealed* against a rigid policy of exclusion.[61] That same year, however, John Collings (1623–1690), the Presbyterian vicar of St. Stephens in London, observing that free admission was "the great bone of contention in the Church of God this day," attacked Humfrey in a polemic entitled *Responsoria Bipartita*, though Collings apparently felt that theology was irrelevant to the controversy, for he gave only cursory attention to the claim that the Lord's Supper was a converting ordinance.[62] But within a short time, William Prynne, confident that Humfrey's sermons would finally "remove the bar," wrote a series of sharply worded tracts against the "false, vain, absurd, irreligious Objections, Cavils, Whimsies, Delusion of those Novellists" who refused to administer the sacrament to all their members, and Prynne made ample use of sacramental doctrine to buttress his arguments.[63] Humfrey wrote a review and analysis of the controversy in 1656, but if he intended for his summary to mark the termination of debate, he was disappointed. Most English theologians who wrote on the sacrament after 1656 felt obliged to take some position on the issue of free admission.[64]

60. Timson, *Bar Removed*, p. 59.
61. Blake, *Covenant Sealed*, p. 248.
62. John Collings, *Responsoria Bipartita, Sive Vindiciae Suspensionis Ecclesiasticae Ut Et Presbyterii Evangelici* (London, 1655), "The Preface," pp. 14–15, 36–37.
63. Prynne, *Lords Supper Briefly Vindicated*, "To the Reader."
64. Humfrey, *Second Vindication;* Richard Baxter, *Certain Disputations of Right to Sacraments and the true nature of Visible Christianity* (London, 1657); Morice, *Coena quasi Koine;* and see the various meditations on preparation that I discuss later in this chapter. See also Wilfred W. Biggs, "The Controversy concerning Free Admission to the Lord's Supper, 1652–1660," *CHST* 16 (July, 1951) : 178–89.

Drake's aversion to free admission was characteristic of most seventeenth-century Puritans; the divines in the Westminster Assembly voted overwhelmingly to bar the Lord's Supper to the unworthy, and though Parliament always guarded its status as the supreme court of appeals in local disputes over admission, the policy of sequestration became the law of the realm.[65] Historians of English political and social life have recognized that the debates over admission offer clues to the nature of political alignments during the Civil War and insights into the seventeenth-century preoccupation with moral order in the society.[66] But the controversy was also a sign of intellectual changes within Puritanism. By means of combining eucharistic theory with the doctrine of conversion, Humfrey and his supporters were moving away from an earlier Puritan consensus, toward a peculiarly Reformed sacramentalism. Sixteenth-century Puritans had never attributed regenerative efficacy to the Lord's Supper. Drake recognized however, that the new doctrine of sacramental efficacy not only threatened ministerial authority and ecclesiastical purity, but also overshadowed concern about a distinctive eucharistic presence and the special sanctity required of communicants. Among other things, Drake and Humfrey were arguing about two modes of sacramental worship: the first would reserve "holy things to holy men," the second would extend efficacious rites to unholy men.[67] In either case, the Lord's Supper assumed an elevated status.

From the beginning of the debate over admission, however, the Puritans who sought to fence the table had accused their opponents of failing to recognize the unique quality of the sacramental presence. John Collings criticized Timson for his suggestion that the Lord's Supper was nothing but "a notional remembrance of the history and passion of Christ." [68] Drake took offense when Humfrey denied that the Supper "excells other ordinances." In the sacrament, Drake insisted, a godly man "eats Christ more than at the word." He also disliked Humfrey's claim that the bread was the body only when "taken and eaten . . . not otherwise." [69] Drake believed that the bread was "Christs body by consecration" even before it was eaten; "otherwise

65. A. F. Mitchell and John Struthers, eds., *Minutes of the Sessions of the Westminster Assembly of Divines while Engaged in Preparing their Directory for Church Government, Confessions of Faith, and Catechisms* (Edinburgh, 1874), p. 257; Lawrence Kaplan, "English Civil War Politics and the Religious Settlement," *Church History* 41 (Sept., 1972) : 307–25.
66. William A. Lamont, *Godly Rule: Politics and Religion, 1603–60* (London, 1969); idem, *Marginal Prynne*; Kaplan, "English Civil War Politics."
67. Humfrey, *Humble Vindication*, p. 38.
68. Collings, *Responsoria Bipartita*, p. 37.
69. Humfrey, *Rejoynder*, p. 190.

the Minister would utter an untruth in speaking those words, Take eat, this is Christs body, et." [70] But Humfrey was content to explain sacramental efficacy as a mental event: "the work of the Sacrament on the receiver being only by way of sign, as the understanding is exercised thereon." And he refused to set the Lord's Supper "above other ordinances." [71] Timson voiced the same belief and implied that most Puritans erred by "putting too much holinesse in the consecrated elements." [72] Despite their stress on sacramental efficacy, Humfrey and Timson persistently minimized the objective presence. A vivid accent on the presence of Christ would have undermined their attempt to keep the Lord's Supper on exactly the same level as the Word and thus to open the sacrament to the unregenerate. Their sacramental piety rested entirely on the conviction, prominent in the earlier Puritan tradition, that the sacramental Word, like all words, was addressed to the understanding.

Devotion and the Spiritual Presence

In the course of the century, even Puritan preachers who considered Humfrey's doctrine to be nothing "but an upstart among us" began to exhibit greater interest in the possibilities of sacramental piety.[73] Earlier Puritans had written sacramental treatises, and at least two, William Bradshaw and Arthur Hildersham, published popular manuals on preparation for communion. But in the late seventeenth and early eighteenth centuries there was an impressive dissemination of Puritan sacramental meditations throughout England and New England, many of them intent on reaffirming traditional Calvinist doctrine.

Meditations were written by such prominent English nonconformists as Jeremiah Dyke (d. 1620), minister at Epping in Essex; Richard Vines (d. 1656), minister at St. Lawrence Jewry in London; Thomas Doolittle (d. 1707), a well-known Presbyterian who resigned at the Restoration; Stephen Charnock (d. 1680), chaplain to Henry Cromwell and later pastor of a Presbyterian congregation in London; John Flavel (d. 1691), a Presbyterian who was the incumbent of Willersley, Gloucestershire before being ejected in 1662; John Quick (d. 1706), leader of a Presbyterian congregation in London; Theophilus Dorrington (d. 1715), another London nonconformist; Richard Baxter

70. Drake, *Bar*, p. 364.
71. Humfrey, *Rejoynder*, p. 51; idem, *Second Vindication*, p. 28.
72. Timson, *Bar Removed*, pp. 28, 36, 40.
73. Vines, *Treatise*, p. 247.

(d. 1691), minister at Kidderminster; Matthew Henry (d. 1714), non-conformist divine at Chester; and Jabez Earle (d. 1768), pastor of a Presbyterian congregation in Drury Street, Westminster.[74] These efforts were emulated by other nonconformist ministers in both England and New England, and the manuals proved to be highly popular. There were twenty-six editions of Doolittle's *Treatise concerning the Lord's Supper* between 1665 and 1727. Dorrington's *Familiar Guide to the Right and Profitable Receiving of the Lord's Supper* went through over twenty printings. More typically, Henry's *Communicant's Companion* underwent a respectable eight printings within its first twenty years. Sacramental piety found an increasingly secure place in the spirituality of many churches and ministers of the Puritan tradition.

The authors of the sacramental manuals universally repudiated free admission and denied the converting efficacy of the Lord's Supper, but they also differed noticeably among themselves. For some the spirituality of the communicant was a far more vivid reality than the presence of Christ in the rite. Jeremiah Dyke wrote nearly six hundred pages and managed to avoid any clear, extended description of the *res sacramenti*. One can gather from occasional references and allusions that the "Body and Blood" of Christ were somehow present in the Lord's Supper, and that communion nourished and increased faith. But the main topic of Dyke's meditation, *The Worthy Communicant*, was not sacramental theology. He wrote rather about the interior life of the communicant, about duties, motives, and psychological states. He expounded upon "preparation for the sacrament, and the necessity of it," describing with great care the need for self-examination and meditation prior to communion and dutiful obedience following it.[75] Such preoccupation with the preparation and internal worthiness of the communicant tended naturally to magnify the subjective dimension

74. Jeremiah Dyke, *A Worthy Communicant: Or A Treatise, Shewing the Due Order of receiving the Sacrament of the Lords Supper* (London, 1642); Vines, *Treatise*; Thomas Doolittle, *A Treatise Concerning the Lord's Supper*, 1st ed., London, 1665 (Boston, 1727); Stephen Charnock, *The Works of the Learned Divine Stephen Charnock* (London, 1699) 2; John Flavel *Sacramental Meditations Upon divers Select Verses of Scripture*, 1st ed., London, 1689 (Boston, 1708); John Quick, *The Young Mans claim unto the Sacrament of the Lords-Supper*, 1st ed., London, 1691 (Boston, 1700); Theophilus Dorrington, *A Familiar Guide to the Right and Profitable Receiving of the Lord's Supper*, 1st ed., London, 1695 (Boston, 1718); Richard Baxter, *Monthly Preparations for the Holy Communion*, 1st ed., London, 1696 (Boston, 1728); Matthew Henry, *The Communicant's Companion: Or, Instructions and Helps for the right Receiving of the Lord's Supper*, 1st ed., London, 1704 (Boston, 1716); Jabez Earle, *Sacramental Exercise: Or, The Christian's Employment, Before, At, and After the Lords Supper*, 1st ed., London, 1707 (Boston, 1715).

75. Dyke, *Worthy Communicant*, pp. 33 ff.

of eucharistic worship and to slight Calvin's concern for an objective sacramental presence. Some Puritan manuals defined the sacrament as little more than "Glasses for our Understanding, and Monuments for our Memories," and then moved on to the more pressing question of the communicant's holiness.[76]

A scrupulous accent on preparation, in turn, sometimes caused conscientious communicants to fear the punishment for unworthy communion more than they rejoiced in the prospect of the sacramental gift. Richard Baxter lamented the tendency to mourn over the corruptions of communicants instead of studying "the love of God in Christ" in the sacrament.

> The Sacrament of the Lord's Supper is become more terrible, and uncomfortable to abundance of such distempered Christians, than any other Ordinance of God; and that which should most comfort them doth trouble them most.

To remedy this situation, the manuals often added a comforting exhortation to the doubtful, a theme that was especially favored by the New England Congregationalists. But Baxter also proposed another solution, namely, that ministers try to alleviate misconceptions about the sacrament.[77] He was suggesting that introspection was not the sole mode of eucharistic meditation, which should be based on the message and mystery of the sacrament itself. In emphasizing the objective realities of the Lord's Supper, Baxter was not alone. Not all the writers limited themselves, as did Dyke, to dissecting the soul of the communicant. Some Puritans claimed that their colleagues who exalted sacramental efficacy, as well as those who concentrated simply on psychological interiority, had forgotten the older Reformed affirmations about the sacramental presence.

By 1656 Richard Vines, among others, was pressing for a Puritan alternative, based on Calvinist precedent. A graduate of Cambridge who began his pastoral labors in 1638 at the rectory of Weddington, Warwickshire, Vines (1600–1656) became a member of the Westminster Assembly in 1643, where he acquired special prominence for his numerous sermons to the Long Parliament. Master of the Temple for several years, he then moved to St. Laurence Jewry in London.[78] While there Vines announced that a one-sided emphasis on the efficacy of the

76. Doolittle, *A Treatise*, p. 4 (but see p. 160 for a somewhat stronger statement).
77. Baxter, *Monthly Preparations*, pp. 15; 14.
78. Alexander Gordon, "Richard Vines," *DNB* 20 (London, 1910) : 369–71; Wilson, *Pulpit in Parliament*, pp. 112–13.

sacrament had been one of the four chief errors in the continuing debate over the Lord's Supper.

Two of these errors—the Lutheran teaching that Christ's "very
body" was present "with, or in or under" the elements, and the Roman
Catholic dogma that the substance of bread and wine was changed into
"the very substance of Christ's Body and Blood"—Vines dismissed with
arguments that had been used by Reformed theologians for a century.
Such doctrines were irrational, latently idolatrous, and contrary to
the nature of the finite resurrected body. A third view, that Christ was
"really present" but "we know not the manner how," he merely
ridiculed.[79] The last unacceptable interpretation was a one-sided
stress on efficacy: "that Christ is present in this Sacrament by his
efficacy and power, to realize and exhibit vertue to, and by the
Ordinance." In opposition to these four "parties," as Vines called
them, he affirmed a fifth position: "That the Bread and Wine are
sacramentally Christs Body and Bloud." The "efficacy" of the body
was "not all" that the sacrament exhibited; the faithful believer received "first and principally" the body and blood of Christ, "not the
benefits of Christ apart and abstract, but Christ himself." Vines would
gladly have called this a "reall presence" had the term not occasioned
misunderstanding, for he was quite certain that "the Body of Christ"
was "really, though spiritually eaten by a Beleever." [80]

Vines believed that English Reformed theologians had been "unjustly" depicted as sacramentarians, who were guilty of defining the
Lord's Supper as a naked sign, an empty shadow that merely represented the death of Christ in much the way that "the Picture of
Hercules resembles and represents Hercules." In fact, he said, Puritan
ministers agreed that sacraments were seals and instruments, offering
and exhibiting the "very bodie and bloud of Christ," which meant that
the believer experienced "not representation only, but communion or
participation also." Christ was in heaven, to be sure, but that did not
preclude a real spiritual presence: "It is somewhat a grosse conceit to
ask, How Christ in heaven, and a believer on earth can be united?"
The mystical union, Vines explained, was effected by the "Spirit and
faith." But rather than offering psychological interpretations of the
Supper, Vines shared and affirmed Calvin's sense of sacramental mys-

79. In 1641 William Bray, chaplain to Archbishop Laud, asserted that Christ had
"not said the *manner* how" he was present in the sacrament, and Bray urged theologians not to "search into that which is not written." Vines may have been thinking of him. See William Bray, *A Sermon of the Blessed Sacrament of The Lords
Supper Proving that there is therein no proper sacrifice now offered* (London, 1641),
p. 19.
80. Vines, *Treatise*, pp. 110–11, 125.

tery and he quoted the *Institutes* to express it: "When I have said all, I have said but little, the tongue is overcome, yea the minde is overwhelmed." [81]

Vines moved away from the early Zwinglian identification of sacramental eating with faith. He said that God offered and presented the body of Christ "to my faith," which then went forth to "take Christ in." The objectivity of the sacramental gift was not dissolved into the exercise of faith. And the believer did not merely receive the divine nature: "the human nature of Christ is the root of this Union." Vines even moved slightly beyond Calvin by exalting the Lord's Supper over every other rite: "the sweetest and neerest intercourse with our Lord, is here set forth as in no other Ordinance." [82]

It would be a mistake to take Vines literally when he describes the Puritans who accented the unique sacramental presence as a "party." The reaffirmation of Calvinist eucharistic doctrine did not assume the form of a self-conscious partisan movement, but was common to Presbyterians and Independents who otherwise disagreed about sacramental matters. The Independent John Howe told Baxter that even the admission standards proposed by the Presbyterian rigorists were insufficient. Independent churches wanted more than a profession of visible faith by communicants; they demanded credible evidence of saving faith.[83] But both Presbyterian and Independent theologians could unite in a Calvinist interpretation of the presence.

The leading Independent divine of the mid-seventeenth cenutry was John Owen (1616–1683), chaplain to Cromwell and vice-chancellor of Oxford. After the restoration of the monarchy in 1660, Owen retired to a private estate at Stadhampton, but he continued to write and to preach in secret to a small congregation. Within three years the Congregationalists of colonial Boston attempted to lure him to America, but Charles II would not permit Owen to depart. Finally he returned to an active ministry in England, accepting in 1673 the pastorate of an Independent congregation in Leadenhall Street. Here he preached a series of eucharistic sermons that clearly contradict any suggestion that Independency was invariably synonymous with anti-sacramental spiritualism.[84]

81. Ibid., pp. 50, 124, 326–27.
82. Ibid., pp. 42, 283, 292, 327.
83. John Howe to Richard Baxter, Baxter MSS. 59.3 f. 196, in Dr. Williams's Library, London, quoted in Lamont, *Godly Rule*, p. 145.
84. John Owen, *The Works of John Owen, D. D.*, ed. William Goold, (Edinburgh, 1851) 9 : 521–622; J. Rigg, "John Owen," *DNB* 14 (1909) : 1318–22; C. E. Whiting, *Studies in English Puritanism From the Restoration to the Revolution, 1660–1688* (New York, 1931), pp. 75–81.

Owen taught that there was a "real exhibition" of Christ unto every worthy communicant. Christ was present, he said, not only by symbolic representation, but also "by obsignation," sealing the covenant with his blood each time the sacrament was administered, and "by exhibition," tendering his body and blood unto the faithful. By virtue of the divine institution, there was a "sacramental union" between the elements and the body and blood, ensuring that Christ was truly communicated to the faithful. In the light of Owen's intense interest in pneumatology, he was surprisingly silent about the activity of the Holy Spirit in the sacrament, and he did not assert that the "substance" of the human nature was present in the Lord's Supper. He did, however, affirm the sacramental significance of the human nature:

> The special and peculiar object of faith, the immediate object of it in this ordinance, in its largest extent is . . . the human nature of Christ, as the subject wherein mediation and redemption was wrought. . . . This we are to have a peculiar regard unto when we come to the administration or participation of this ordinance.

And Owen stressed even more than Calvin himself the uniqueness of the sacramental presence. There was, he said, a special and peculiar communion with Christ in the Lord's Supper: "It is a common received notion among Christians, and it is true, that there is a peculiar communion with Christ in this ordinance, which we have in no other ordinance." In addition, Owen shared Calvin's sense of sacramental mystery: communion with Christ, he said, "was always esteemed the principal mystery in the agenda of the church." [85] Owen's references to the sacrament were not numerous, but by celebrating the uniqueness of the Lord's Supper, and by giving attention as he did to the doctrine of the presence, he did manifest a genuine kinship with men like Vines who were seeking to reaffirm the essentials of Reformed doctrine and piety.

Certainly not every Puritan shared this appreciation of the Lord's Supper, but the seventeenth-century English confessions demonstrate that the theology of Vines and Owen would have been acceptable to most Presbyterians and Independents. The Westminster Confession avoided explicitly instrumental language and omitted specific mention of the Holy Spirit's activity in its paragraphs on the Lord's Supper, but otherwise it approximated Calvin's doctrine.

> Worthy receivers, outwardly partaking of the visible elements in this sacrament, do then also inwardly by faith, really and indeed,

85. Owen, *Works*, 9 : 524, 620; 8 : 560 ("agenda" meant "liturgy").

yet not carnally and corporally, but spiritually, receive and feed
upon Christ crucified, and all the benefits of his death: the body
and blood of Christ being then not corporally or carnally in, with,
or under the bread and wine; yet as really, but spiritually, present
to the faith of believers in that ordinance, as the elements themselves are, to their outward senses.[86]

When the Independents met at Savoy, they affirmed precisely the same
confessional position.[87]

The change in Puritan sacramental attitudes was visible, however,
not in the Westminster Confession, which simply codified a traditional
doctrinal consensus, but in the liturgical developments of the later
seventeenth century. While some heirs of Puritanism were moving
toward Quaker spiritualism, others were gradually discarding their
sense of discomfort about the corporeal instruments of eucharistic worship. In the sixteenth century, Puritan ministers had occasionally
objected to any suggestion that the words of institution in the liturgy
were words of consecration spoken for the elements as well as the
communicants. In response to criticism from Reformed theologians,
the authors of the 1552 *Book of Common Prayer* had excised the in-
vocation to the Trinity to sanctify the bread and wine and in its place
had inserted a prayer seeking God's blessing on the worshippers, and
even the Prayer Book of 1559 had avoided a petition for the consecration of material elements. But the Puritan service book prepared at
Westminster, the *Directory*, specifically instructed the minister to sanctify and bless both by prayer and the words of institution "the elements of Bread and Wine" so that they would be "set apart" to a
holy use.[88] And when the Restoration bishops met with the Presbyterians at Savoy in 1661 to discuss possible changes in the *Book of
Common Prayer*, the Presbyterians criticized the liturgy because it
lacked a petition for consecration of the elements.[89] Richard Baxter
drew up an alternate service, known subsequently as the Savoy Liturgy,
in which he attempted to modify the severely introspective character
of Puritan sacramental worship, to provide for a consecration of the
elements by Word and prayer, and to emphasize that the Holy Spirit

86. In Leith, *Creeds of the Churches*, p. 226. See also the Westminster Catechisms
in Thomas F. Torrance, ed., *The School of Faith: The Catechisms of the Reformed
Church* (London, 1959), pp. 222, 226–27, 276.
87. See Walker, *Creeds and Platforms*, pp. 399–400.
88. Bard Thompson, ed., *Liturgies of the Western Church* (Cleveland, 1961), p.
369; E. C. Ratcliff, "The Savoy Conference and the Revision of the Book of Common Prayer," in *From Uniformity to Unity 1662–1692*, ed. Geoffrey Nuttall and F.
Owen Chadwick (London, 1692), p. 116, n. 2.
89. Ratcliff, "Savoy Conference," p. 116.

enabled the faithful believer truly "to feed on Christ by faith." [90] Still opposed to kneeling and offended by ceremony, the Puritans were unable to reach agreement with the bishops, but their liturgies expressed a Calvinist sacramental doctrine that was fully consonant with the theology of men like Vines.

Two diverse modes of sacramentalism characterized the Puritan movement in the late seventeenth century. One small group of ministers saw the Lord's Supper as a converting ordinance, capable of evoking from nominal Christians a heartfelt assent to the gospel. In some ways they had a low view of the sacrament, describing its converting efficacy in terms of its power to evoke a mental response and showing little interest in the sacramental presence. But they were aware of the positive possibilities of sacramental piety; it would be inaccurate to describe them as ecclesiastical politicians exploiting theology for ulterior motives. In their own way they tried to turn the Puritan tradition toward a basically new doctrine of the Lord's Supper. The Puritan sacramental meditations also encouraged a subjective sacramental spirituality, but they often restated genuinely Calvinist doctrines, while asserting the uniqueness of the sacrament in a way that Calvin had never done. The authors of the meditations maintained orthodox Reformed views about such matters as the relationship between the infinite divine nature of Christ and his finite human nature, which precluded any corporeal presence, but in the realm of piety, their meditations reflected the conviction that the visible could manifest and reveal the invisible, that the elements of bread and wine offered a means of contact with an infinite spiritual Deity.

The Visible: Types and the Creatures

The resurgence of Puritan interest in a sacramental piety did not reflect simply disputes over admission but also changing convictions about the usefulness of sensory experience as an avenue to spiritual truth and an ingredient in religious devotion. Throughout the sixteenth and seventeenth centuries, of course, Puritan theologians had spoken of the availability of God's revelation in the visible creation. Natural theology was a familiar mode of religious thinking within the Puritan tradition, though all Puritans, of every period, denied that reason or the senses unaided by revelation could grasp such mysteries

90. Thompson, *Liturgies,* pp. 385–86, 394–95, 399, 402. Ratcliff, "Savoy Conference," p. 123, observed that "the doctrine of Baxter's service is markedly higher than the doctrine expressed or implied in the communion office of the Prayer Book of 1552 to 1559."

as the Trinity and the miracle of regeneration. Nor was the empirical epistemology of Baxter and others an innovation. Earlier English Reformed divines could have accepted the Baxterian dictum that all knowledge originated in the senses: "even faith and reason suppose our senses, and their true perception; and if that first perception be false, faith and reason could be no truer." [91] The burgeoning scientific interests of the seventeenth century, however, confirmed the value of meditation on the wonders of God in the creation. Certainly late seventeenth century Puritans observed "the book of nature" with increasing care and attention, thus facilitating the fuller incorporation of the sensory into the life of piety.[92]

The "improvement of the creatures" became an increasingly popular mode of Puritan meditation. Baxter announced in 1649 that there had been no change in his fundamental conviction that "the object of Faith" was infinitely distant from "the object of sense," but there was no reason, he added, that the senses could not be "serviceable" in Christian meditation.

> Why, surely it will be a point to our spiritual prudence, and a singular help to our futhering of the work of faith, to call in our sense to its assistance: if we can make us friends of these usual enemies, and make them instruments of raising us to God, which are the usual means of drawing us from God, I think we shall perform a very excellent work. Surely, it is both possible and lawful, yea, and necessary too, to do something in this kind: for God would not have given us either our senses themselves, or their usual objects, if they might not have been serviceable to his own praise, and helps to raise up to the apprehension of higher things.[93]

Puritan ministers did not suddenly discard the introspective piety of their predecessors, but long before the end of the century they began to devote equal attention to the visible creation as a stimulus for devotion. Enthusiasm for "the lovely characters of Divine goodness" in the "outward world" could on occasion indicate a disillusionment with a Puritan past, as with some of the Cambridge Platonists.[94] But orthodox Presbyterians and Independents also urged their congregations to cultivate "reverent and admiring thoughts upon the prospect of the

91. Baxter, *Catechising of Families, Works,* 19 : 13.
92. See Gerald Cragg, *From Puritanism to the Age of Reason* (Cambridge, 1966), p. 53; J. Paul Hunter, *The Reluctant Pilgrim: Defoe's Emblematic Method and Quest for Form in Robinson Crusoe* (Baltimore, 1966).
93. Richard Baxter, *The Saints Everlasting Rest, Works,* 23 : 375.
94. Cragg, *Puritanism to the Age of Reason,* p. 53, quoting John Smith.

creatures!" [95] By 1664 Puritan laymen could turn to such devotional handbooks as John Flavel's *Navigation Spiritualized* to learn the techniques of "spiritualizing the creatures." Its success prompted Flavel in 1699 to publish a second manual of the same type, *Husbandry Spiritualized,* containing further instructions on "the heavenly use of earthly things." [96] By that time the Independent minister at the Leadenhall Street meetinghouse in London, Joseph Caryl, concluded that the construction of "a ladder out of the earthly materials, for the raising ourselves in spirit up to heaven, is the art of arts." [97]

Viewed in retrospect, the proliferation of sacramental manuals appears to have been, among other things, one expression of this piety of sensation. Baxter and Flavel both recognized the similarities between reflection on the visible creation and sacramental meditation. Study God and his glory in the natural creation, Baxter urged, and you might begin to taste more of Christ in everyday bread and beer than "most men have in the use of the sacrament," an aphorism that elicited Flavel's praise.[98] The sacrament itself celebrated redemption rather than creation, but Puritans recognized that eucharistic meditation was analogous to reflection on the mysteries of the cosmos. John Owen noted that the eucharistic bread and wine were the "cream of the creation: which is an endless storehouse, if pursued, of representing the mysteries of Christ." In sacramental devotion, as described by Thomas Doolittle, "mean and visible signs" called to mind "sublime and invisible things." [99] Puritans had always said that the sacrament was a visible gospel that appealed to the senses; it is understandable that expanding confidence in the ability of the senses to derive spiritual benefit from the visible world would provide support for sacramental piety.

In justifying his program of meditation, Baxter pointed out that "the expressions of God in Scripture" themselves "set forth the excellencies of spiritual things in words that are borrowed from the objects of sense." [100] All Puritans would have agreed, for since the beginning of the century they had been writing handbooks on typology designed

95. Stephen Charnock, *A Discourse on the Wisdom of God, The Complete Works of Stephen Charnock* (Edinburgh, 1864), 2 : 27.

96. John Flavel, *Husbandry Spiritualized: The Heavenly Use of Earthly Things,* in *The Works of John Flavel* (London, 1968), 5 : 3.

97. Joseph Caryl, "To the Christian Reader," in Flavel, *Husbandry Spiritualized, Works,* 5 : 9.

98. Baxter, *Saints Everlasting Rest, Works,* 23 : 300; Flavel, *Husbandry Spiritualized, Works,* 5 : 4.

99. Owen, *Works,* 9 : 540; Doolittle, *Treatise,* p. 4; see Gordon Wakefield, *Puritan Devotion: Its Place in the Development of Christian Piety* (London, 1957), p. 47.

100. Baxter, *Saints Everlasting Rest, Works,* 23 : 375–77.

to illustrate the revelatory capacity of the visible images in the Scripture. Such works as William Gould's *Moses Unvailed* (1620) or Thomas Taylor's *Christ Revealed* (1635) helped to focus attention on typological exegesis in the English Puritan tradition. Both men would have accepted the definition given by Samuel Mather, a nonconformist minister in Ireland, whose *Figures and Types of the Old Testament* appeared posthumously in 1683. A type, Mather wrote, was "some outward or sensible thing ordained of God under the old Testament to represent and hold forth something of Christ in the New." [101]

The Puritans recognized the correspondence between typology and sacramental theology and defined types explicitly as "Sacraments and seals of faith on the part of the beleeving Jew." Like a sacrament, a type exposed and revealed spiritual realities; it embodied a hidden "Spiritual Sense." As signs and seals representing evangelical mysteries and assuring Israel of spiritual blessings, types were in fact efficacious precisely "after that manner of efficacy that is in sacraments."

> The Types were not only Signs, but Seals; not only Signs to represent Gospel Mysteries unto them; but also Seals to assure them of the certain and infallible exhibition thereof in God's appointed time. As we say of our Sacraments; *Sacramentum est verbum visible*, the Sacrament is a visible Promise, and holds forth the Covenant of Grace to the eye and other Senses, as the Word to the Ear: So it was with the Types of old. The types were visible Promises, and not only Signs, but Pledges and Assurances of the good they represented. They did represent those great Mysteries not only by way of resemblance to the understandings, but by way of assurance to the Faith of God's people.

There was for the Puritan no essential difference between a type and a sacrament, except that one foreshadowed and the other followed the historical advent of Christ.[102] It was characteristic that fully one third of Taylor's typological handbook, *Christ Revealed,* was devoted to a discussion of sacraments. Nor is it surprising that typological arguments were central to the sacramental debates that stirred the English Puritan churches. Proponents of rigorous standards of admission to the Lord's Supper rested their case in large part on arguments about "typical" Jewish rites, especially the Passover. Defenders of infant baptism relied on the analogy between the Christian sacrament and the Jewish rite of circumcision, which they defined as a "Type of the

101. Samuel Mather, *Figures and Types of the Old Testament*, Dublin, 1683, ed. Mason Lowance, Jr., (New York, 1969), p. 52.

102. Ibid., pp. 344, 55, 59.

future Exhibition of the Covenant and Blessings of it." [103] There was no absolute consensus about the relationship between Jewish types and Christian sacraments. Some Puritans claimed that the Passover and circumcision typified the Lord's Supper and baptism; others argued that since one sacrament could not prefigure another, Israel's typical rites foreshadowed either the experience of the Christian or the sacrifice of Christ, which were then represented or effectually exhibited in the Christian sacraments.[104] In either case, though, sacramental worship rested on typological exegesis.

Because of the intimate relationship between typology and sacramental thought, the changing conceptions of "types" in the course of the seventeenth century illuminate both the piety of sensation and the resurgence of eucharistic interest. Conservative exegetes insisted that types and antitypes could be found only in Scripture. Somewhat more adventurous Puritans claimed that the Christian's experience might be an antitype of Old Testament figures, though the type itself was still found in Scripture. Occasionally a Puritan might describe Christian sacraments as types of eschatological blessings. But by the end of the seventeenth century, some ministers began gradually to view the physical world itself as a repository of types that revealed the mysteries of the spiritual realm. Flavel, for instance, found the natural order to be an abundant fountain of types. The observation of nature, he said, "serves excellently to shadow forth" theological truth.[105] A vast range of natural events, objects, and experiences within the physical creation became concrete figures and shadows embodying spiritual truth, as typological methodology transcended the Scriptural canon. A biblical hermeneutic became a mode of interpreting the book of nature, and the expanded typology became an instrument of the piety of sensation.

There is no proof that the developments in Puritan writings on sacraments, types, and the physical creation were causally related. But it is revealing that the expanding interest in natural theology, the new meditative practices, hermeneutical developments, and sacramental piety all converged toward a common ideal: the rehabilitation of the visible. Of course Puritans had never been totally estranged from the sensory aspects of worship, so long as the senses remained subordinate to the understanding. The visible was acceptable when it was con-

103. Ibid., p. 181. See also Thomas Taylor, *Christ Revealed: Or the Old Testament Types Explained* (London, 1635). A second edition of Taylor's manual was entitled *Moses and Aaron* (London, 1653).

104. Cf. Vines, *Treatise*, p. 14, with Mather, *Figures and Types*, p. 183.

105. Flavel, *Husbandry Spiritualized, Works,* 5 : 61; See Mason Lowance, Jr., "Images or Shadows of Divine Things: The Typology of Jonathan Edwards," *Early American Literature* 5 (Spring, 1970) : 141–81.

gruent with didactic intentions and biblical prescriptions. Only when sensory aids distracted the worshipper's attention, or resembled Roman ceremonial, or lacked biblical warrant did Puritans object to them. Thus Puritan ministers had insisted that the celebration of the sacraments be visible to congregations, believing that the elements and gestures were providentially adapted to move the mind through the senses.

The growing appreciation of the visible in Puritan devotion after 1650 did not mark a drastic transformation of the tradition, but rather a gradual accretion of patterns present in earlier Puritanism. On occasion a minister might break away from familiar limits, as happened when Baxter decided to accord a guarded usefulness to pictures and images in worship: they could be used, he said, as "objects of our consideration, exciting our minds to worship God." [106] But even this innovation, astounding as it might sound, remained well within the boundaries of accepted Puritan theory, which stipulated that the senses were handmaidens to the understanding. To speak of a piety of sensation is simply to record an increasing interest in sacramental manuals and handbooks on "spiritualizing the creatures," which paralleled a changing vision of reality in English intellectual life, but which also displayed continuity with earlier Puritan history.

Roman Catholics, and many Anglicans, would have found the worship of the dissenters barren and drab, even in congregations affected by the new sacramental and meditative concerns. And of course many churches were untouched by sacramental piety, especially among the Independents, whose strictness about the worthiness of communicants often led to the virtual elimination of eucharistic worship.[107] The renaissance of sacramental piety in English Puritanism was a program advanced by a corps of articulate leaders rather than a broad popular movement fundamentally transforming the character of English dissent. But the eucharistic developments do provide an insight into the complex potentialities of seventeenth-century Puritan intellectual history and its intimate relation to the life of piety.

106. Richard Baxter, *Christian Directory, Works*, 5:481. See the discussion in Irwonwy Morgan, *The Nonconformity of Richard Baxter* (London, 1946), pp. 202–5.
107. Geoffrey Nuttall, *The Holy Spirit in Puritan Faith and Experience* (Oxford, 1946), p. 94.

5

NEW ENGLAND:

AMBIVALENCE AND AFFIRMATION

The Puritan ministers who came to New England after 1628 shared fully the ambivalence of their English colleagues toward the sacramental traditions of western Christendom. One reason for their immigration to America was an intense desire to shake off the yoke of such "popish" ceremonies as kneeling at the Lord's Supper and using the sign of the cross in baptism. The celebrated minister of St. Botolph's Church in Old Boston, John Cotton, assured the emigrants to Massachusetts in 1630 that the voyage was eminently justified because it would allow them to enjoy the "liberty of the Ordinances." [1] He also sanctioned the journey for other reasons, but the conviction that the first settlers had "come hither for ordinances," [2] for the freedom to worship and especially to receive the sacraments without ceremonial encumbrances, soon became part of the sustaining mythology of the New England churches.

New England ministers wanted not only to discard extraneous ceremonies, however, but also to safeguard their congregations from sacramental doctrines that subverted the pure faith. Even before leaving England, they were disposed to minimize the effect of baptism and the Lord's Supper in the manner of such conforming Puritans as Preston and Sibbes. John Cotton (1584–1652), who remained at St. Botolph's until 1633, spoke there in conventional Reformed terms of

1. John Cotton, *Gods Promise to His Plantation* (London, 1634), p. 9.
2. Peter Bulkeley, *The Gospel-Covenant: Or, the Covenant of Grace Opened* 1st ed. (London, 1646), p. 268; Cotton Mather, *Magnalia Christi Americana: Or, The Ecclesiastical History of New-England, From Its First Planting in the Year 1620 unto the Year of our Lord, 1698* (London, 1702), 1 : 17.

sacraments as covenant seals: baptism was a pledge of salvation that admitted infants "into the protection and provision" of God, and the Lord's Supper, which spiritually exhibited "both Christs body and blood," yielded "plentiful nourishment" to the worthy receiver.[3] But Cotton also cautioned his parishioners to "sit loose from the Ordinances," never presuming to trust in externals.[4] He journeyed to New England aboard the *Griffin* with Thomas Hooker (1586–1647), who was lecturer at Chelmsford in Essex before Laud drove him into Holland. The two shipmates would not always agree on theological technicalities, but when they disembarked in 1633, Hooker shared with Cotton both an unexceptional Reformed sacramental doctrine and a suspicion of undue reliance upon outward means of grace.[5] And certainly the atmosphere of early New England was not designed to transform such men into sacramentalists. Some historians have claimed that there were pronounced disagreements about sacramental efficacy among the ministers of the first generation of settlers.[6] But in fact, the influential theologians of the colony shared a common ambivalence, and a common theological understanding, about sacramental matters.

The New England ideal of pure churches, composed of members who had been reborn of the Spirit and bound together by explicit covenants, stood in tension with historic conceptions of sacramental efficacy and traditional patterns of sacramental practice. The ministers, and many of the laity, were particularly preoccupied with "the manner of the Spirit's work, in the conversion of a sinner."[7] The essence of their piety was the longing for a personal experience of the Spirit. John Cotton described the delights of spiritual rebirth while warning his congregation that communion with Christ required participation in his Spirit. In comparison with Cotton, Thomas Shepard (1605–1649), the minister at Cambridge, was restrained and cautious in speaking of the indwelling Spirit. For years he harboured the suspicion that Cotton's pneumatology bordered on heterodoxy.[8] But Shep-

3. John Cotton, *The Way of Life, or Gods Way and Course in Bringing the Soule Into, keeping it in, and carrying it on, in the wayes of life and peace* (London, 1641), pp. 364, 366, 378.

4. John Cotton, *Christ the Fountaine of Life* (London, 1651), p. 22.

5. Thomas Hooker, *The Poor Doubting Christian Drawn to Christ* (Boston, 1643), pp. 77–79; idem, *The Paterne of Perfection: Exhibited in Gods Image on Adam: And Gods Covenant made with him* (London, 1640), pp. 345–75.

6. Pettit, *Heart Prepared*, pp. 93, 108, 114, 117; C. J. Sommerville, "Conversion *Versus* the Early Puritan Covenant of Grace," *The Journal of Presbyterian History* 44 (June, 1965) : 178–97.

7. Thomas Shepard, *The Sound Believer: A Treatise of Evangelical Conversion*, in *The Works of Thomas Shepard*, ed. John Adams Albro (Boston, 1853), 1 : 117.

8. Thomas Shepard, *The Autobiography of Thomas Shepard*, ed. Nehemiah Adams (Boston, 1832), p. 386.

ard's own piety was suffused with a yearning for the Spirit that illustrates the temper of New England devotion:

> I was stirred up to pray for the Spirit; not only for particular graces of it, but for the Spirit itself. The ground of my prayer was . . . Because I felt an Absence of the Spirit exceeding much. I found I was sensual and carnal, and carried and acted by my own spirit in every thing. However, I felt a little of God's Spirit smoking forth in some weak desires after it; I felt not the power of it, according as Paul did, bound by it, led with it. Acts I. "Power from on high." [9]

Puritans attributed the work of creation to the Father, of redemption to the Son, and of application to the Spirit, and the processes of application through which the Spirit transformed and sanctified the will and understanding elicited their constant scrutiny.[10] Puritan assumptions and preoccupations therefore produced intense religious feeling but did not comport with a vigorous sacramental piety.

Yet the New England churches clearly decided by 1637 that neither the infinite gap between the Creator and the creature nor the longing for an experience of the Spirit should entail an absolutely unbridgeable chasm between the visible, finite, created order and the realm of grace, the domain of the Spirit. In that year, after a period of temporary spiritual lassitude, the followers of Anne Hutchinson, a Boston midwife with pronounced theological convictions, charged that most ministers in the colony had succumbed to covenantal legalism. In amplifying their charges, the Hutchinsonians discarded the entire range of presuppositions that supported Puritan sacramental thought. They claimed, among other things, that only the immediate witness of the Spirit could evidence the presence of justifying faith, and that salvation resulted solely from the Spirit's direct activity, entirely apart from the instrumentalities of the material creation, whether ordinances of the visible Church or creaturely faculties of men.[11]

For a time John Cotton, now the teacher at First Church in Boston, offered vocal support to the Hutchinsonians. But before long other ministers began to perceive a multitude of heresies in the new movement, and though the ensuing debates did not explicitly involve bap-

9. Thomas Shepard, *Meditations and Spiritual Experiences of Mr. Thomas Shepard* (Boston, 1749), p. 79.
10. Thomas Shepard, *The First Principles of the Oracles of God, Works*, 1 : 340.
11. See especially David Hall, ed., *The Antinomian Controversy, 1636–1638* (Middletown, Connecticut, 1968); and William K. B. Stoever, "The Covenant of Works in Puritan Theology: The Antinomian Crisis in New England" (Ph.D. diss., Yale University, 1970).

tism or the Lord's Supper, the sacramental implications were manifest. The dissenters were undermining covenantal doctrines and deprecating the means of grace, while suggesting that the believer somehow transcended creaturely finitude. Anne Hutchinson herself claimed to receive immediate revelations from God, without the aid of the audible or visible Word. Had the Hutchinsonians triumphed, there would have been little reason for New England churches to retain the sacraments, which were, after all, covenantal accommodations to the embodied finitude and persisting sinfulness of the believer. Did not the "Seal of the Spirit," as the dissenters described it, make sacramental seals superfluous? Cotton assured his fellow ministers of his continuing belief that "the Spirit useth not only the word and other Ordinances but also the two seals of the Covenant of Grace, baptism and the Lords Supper," [12] but more zealous dissenters surprised even Cotton by their cavalier dismissal of the ordained means of grace. One Antinomian layman proclaimed that baptism was anachronistic: "In the New Testament there are no signes, no not our baptisme, for the baptisme of water is of no use to us, when once wee are baptized with the Holy Ghost." [13] By 1637, when the Bay Colony banished Anne Hutchinson, others among her followers were openly expounding Baptist views. The experience with the Hutchinsonians, however, intensified the conviction of the orthodox that enthusiasm for the Holy Spirit did not require the antisacramental spiritualizing of religion.

After 1637 the ministers of New England reacted harshly to extreme criticism of the sacraments. The followers of one Samuel Gorton enraged them by calling "baptism an abomination, and the Lord's Supper the juice of a poor silly grape turned into the blood of Christ by the skill of our magicians." [14] The churches continued to make every effort to protect the Lord's Supper from the incursions of the profane and to defend infant baptism from the reproaches of the Baptists. They barred the Lord's Table to all but regenerate members; their ministers published five treatises against Baptist theologians; they rushed unpublished anti-Baptist manuscripts to the wavering souls among the faithful; and when all else failed, they justified, with intricate logical maneuvering, outright repression of Baptist opinions. The authorities whipped a Baptist named Painter from Hingham, for example, "not for his opinion, but for reproaching the Lord's ordinance" by expressing his opinion.[15]

12. Hall, *Antinomian Controversy*, p. 81.
13. Charles F. Adams, ed., *Antinomianism in the Colony of Massachusetts Bay* (Boston, 1894), pp. 183–84.
14. John Winthrop, *The History of New England from 1630 to 1649*, ed. James Savage (Boston, 1853), 2 : 175.
15. Winthrop, *History*, 2 : 213–14. See George Phillips, *Reply to a Confutation of*

New England churches, then, simultaneously denigrated and defended baptism and the Lord's Supper. The efforts of their ministers, as theologians and as architects of Church polity, to maintain the tension between comprehensive and sectarian patterns of worship, and between spiritual enthusiasm and structured order, left them with a handful of unresolved issues and critical problems.

Baptism and the Church

The administration of baptism was an exalted and solemn occasion in New England churches. Only ordained ministers baptized, and only on the Lord's Day, invariably during the afternoon service. After a series of exhortations to the membership in general, and to the parents, the minister—either the pastor or teacher of the local church —baptized a child by sprinkling or, more frequently, by pouring water upon his head.[16] According to John Davenport, the minister in New Haven, adults were occasionally immersed in New England rivers, and at least one pastor, Charles Chauncy, demanded the immersion of infants, though his suggestion evoked such an outcry that he finally agreed to keep such opinions to himself.[17]

Despite their vigor in defending and their solemnity in dispensing baptism, however, the ministers unintentionally deprecated the sacrament, for their covenantal ecclesiology led them to deny that baptism conferred Church membership on either infants or adults. Several English Puritans suspected that their friends in New England failed to view the sacrament as the door of entrance into the Church, and when they inquired about it around 1638, Richard Mather (1596–1669), the minister at Dorchester, confirmed their suspicions. Suspended by Laud in 1633, Mather had arrived in New England two years later, intent on preserving the purity of the Church. There he learned, if he was not already persuaded, that pure and properly

---

some grounds for Infants Baptisme (London, 1645); John Cotton, The Grounds and Ends of the Baptisme of the Children of the Faithfull (London, 1647); Thomas Cobbet, A Just Vindication of the Covenant and Church-Estate of Children of Church-Members (London, 1648); Thomas Hooker, The Covenant of Grace Opened (London, 1649); Thomas Shepard, The Church Membership of Children and their Right to Baptisme (Cambridge, 1663).

16. Thomas Lechford, Plain Dealing: Or Newes from New England (London, 1642), p. 18; and John Cotton, The Doctrine of the Church, to which is committed the Keyes of Heaven (London, 1642), p. 7

17. Winthrop, History, 1 : 398; Charles Chauncy, "Letter to John Davenport," Prince Collection, Cotton Papers, II, 20, Boston Public Library. The ministers would accept the immersion of adults, but they preferred sprinkling or pouring. See Thomas Hooker, A Survey of the Summe of Church-Discipline (London, 1648), pt. 3 sec. 2, pp. 28–32; and Cotton, Grounds, p. 3.

formed churches discarded the tradition of admitting new members by means of baptism. Only papists and Baptists, he said, thought that the Church was "made by Baptisme."

> But we do not believe that Baptisme doth make men Members of the Church, nor that it is to be Administered to them that are without the Church, as the way and meanes to bring them in, but to them that are within the Church, as a seale to confirme the covenant of God unto them. . . . Now a seale is not to make a thing that was not, but to confirme something that was before; and so Baptisme is not that which gives being to the Church, nor to the Covenant, but is for the confirmation thereof. To bring in Baptisme before the Covenant, and before the Church, with whom God makes the Covenant, and then to bring in the Church afterwards, is to make Baptisme a seale unto a Blanke, or to a falshood.[18]

Mather was expressing a common New England belief. When Francis Higginson and Samuel Skelton came to Salem in 1628 as the first ministers to the colony, they announced, after consultation with Elder William Brewster at Plymouth, that they baptized children not to make them Church members but to signify that they were already within the fellowship. Their membership was conveyed by the explicit covenant made by their parents in forming a particular visible church, and baptism was merely a "seal" of the "church membership of the children with their parents." [19]

The ministers who came to New England after 1628 agreed with the decision of the Salem church. Thomas Hooker, who took his congregation to Hartford in 1636, argued that "the baptizing of Infants doth not make them members of the Church, for they are members before they be baptized, and baptisme doth but seale up the covenant unto them." [20] Richard Baxter tried to persuade John Eliot, the New England missionary to the Indians, that baptism itself was "the only Regular compleat entrance into the church visible," but Eliot was convinced, like Hooker, that membership preceded baptism. John Norton of Ipswich defended the same view in his *Answer* to the questions of several Reformed ministers in Holland: the baptized, he said, "must be legitimate members before baptism." [21] In England John

18. Richard Mather, *Church-Government and Church-Covenant Discussed* (London, 1643), p. 12.
19. Nathaniel Morton, *New England's Memorial* (Cambridge, 1669), p. 77.
20. Hooker, *Covenant of Grace Opened*, p. 64.
21. F. J. Powicke, "Some Unpublished Correspondence of the Rev. Richard Baxter and the Rev. John Eliot, 'The Apostle to the American Indians,' 1656–1682," *Bul-*

Cotton for a time had assumed that baptism initiated Church membership, but he changed his mind before arriving in the colony. While still aboard the *Griffin,* Cotton refused to baptize his own newborn son, convinced that the ceremony must await admission into a "settled congregation." He later rebuked English critics for their assumption that "Baptized persons" were "Church-members . . . by their Baptisme." [22]

Such a doctrine, however, threatened to make the sacrament of baptism irrelevant to the majority of worshippers in each congregation, since most were unable to meet the rigorous requirements for actual Church membership, which alone entitled their children to be baptized. The probable results of this situation became especially clear after 1633 when, probably under the leadership of Cotton, New Englanders began to require of prospective members a credible narration of a specifiable experience of saving grace.[23] By insisting that a divinely initiated conversion experience be the requirement for subscribing to the Church covenant, which in turn was the prerequisite for admission to baptism, the ministers created the conditions for the restriction of the sacramental washing to a small spiritual elite and their children. Some laymen feared that "in short time" their children "for the most part" would have to "remain unbaptized." [24] Thomas Lechford, an English layman and critic of the New England Way who had lived in the colony a short time as a lawyer, predicted in 1642 that "the major part" of New Englanders would be unbaptized "in twenty years." [25] Indeed, if baptism had become the personal possession of a spiritual aristocracy, the sacramental practice of the New England churches would have lost all resemblance to the baptismal traditions of historic Protestantism.

Not every minister in New England accepted the view that baptism merely sealed Church membership. The Weymouth congregation wanted Thomas Lenthall as their minister in 1639 because he be-

letin of the John Rylands Library 20 (January, 1939) : 164–65; John Norton, *The Answer to the Whole Set of Questions of the Celebrated Mr. William Apollonius* (1648), trans. Douglas Horton (Cambridge, 1958), p. 57.

22. Winthrop, *History,* 1 : 131, and John Cotton, *The Way of the Churches of Christ in New England* (London, 1645), p. 9. For Cotton's earlier view, see idem, *God's Mercie Mixed with His Justice, Or His Peoples Deliverance in Times of Danger* (London, 1641; reprint ed. Gainsville, 1958), p. 38. For New England, see also Thomas Shepard, *A Treatise of Liturgies, Power of the Keyes, and of matter of Visible Church* (London, 1653), pp. 100, 141–44; and Thomas Cobbet, *The Civil Magistrates Power in matters of Religion Modestly Debated* (London, 1653), p. 37.

23. Morgan, *Visible Saints,* pp. 64–113.

24. Lechford, *Plain Dealing,* p. 39.

25. Ibid., "To the Reader."

lieved that "only baptism was the door of entrance to the church." [26]
In 1653 Richard Mather exchanged a series of letters on the issue
with an unidentified neighbor. Disturbed by news that a church of
Indians had been formed before they were baptized, Mather's cor-
respondent contended that a man became a member of the Church
"at his baptism: and not before." Mather repeated the argument that
men were members "afore their baptisme"; the sacrament was a token
and seal of the covenant and "the church with whom God makes his
. . . covenant must needs be presupposed and be before baptisme." [27]
In 1659 a Chelmsford layman named Adams drew a reprimand from
his church for maintaining with unseemly persistence that "all Baptized persons" were Church members.[28]

Richard Mather represented the consensus among the early colonial
Puritans, who generally accepted the subordination of baptism to the
Church covenant. The theory created problems, however, especially
with infant baptism, for it required that someone determine which
children were legitimate members of the Church and therefore fitting
subjects for baptism. Was a child within the Church covenant only
if his immediate parents were regenerate members of covenanted
churches? What if a faithful grandparent claimed the right of baptism for his grandchild whose parents were manifestly outside the
Church? What was to be done with servants, or with adopted children?
And what was to happen to the children of those who themselves received baptism in New England churches but never experienced the
conversion that entitled them to full membership?

The problems arose as early as 1634, when John Cotton allowed a
grandfather to claim the right of baptism for his grandchild, but only
on the condition that he raise and educate the child.[29] Cotton argued
in 1645 that an infant's right to baptism ordinarily was derived from
the covenant of "the next immediate parents (or of one of them at
least)."

> Infants cannot claime right unto Baptisme, but in the right of
> one of their parents, or both: where neither of the Parents can
> claime right to the Lords Supper, there their infants cannot
> claime right to Baptisme.[30]

26. Winthrop, *History*, 1 : 347.
27. *MHSC*, 4th ser. 8 (1868) : 69–72.
28. John Fiske, "Church Records of Rev. John Fiske," transcribed by David
Pulsifer, Beinecke Library, Yale University, p. 223.
29. Increase Mather, *The First Principles of New-England, Concerning the Subject of Baptisme and Communion of Churches* (Cambridge, 1675), p. 2.
30. Cotton, *Way of the Churches of Christ*, pp. 81, 87.

At the same time, though, Cotton acknowledged that a faithful man could "entitle another mans childe to Baptisme" by adopting the infant, and he later extended the right of baptism to the slaves of church members. According to a letter copied by Increase Mather, Cotton was even willing by 1648 to admit to baptism the infants of "Church members with us baptized in their infancey" who were yet unconverted and thus ineligible for the full rights of membership.[31]

Cotton's extension of baptismal rights to slaves, adopted infants, and the children of unregenerate Church members remained well within the accepted logical boundaries of New England ecclesiology, for in each case the warrant for baptism rested on an association with a local covenant church. His generosity was entirely consistent with the claim that the sacrament sealed prior membership in a particular church. But Puritans also believed that the sacrament sealed the divine covenant of grace, which was logically distinct from the Church covenant, and in 1648 Cotton appealed to the covenant of grace itself as a basis for baptism: the sacrament could be administered to infants on the grounds of "the Faith of their former Ancestors in Elder Ages." [32] By no stretch of the imagination, however, could the names of faithful ancestors be entered on the membership rolls of New England churches. In effect, Cotton was acknowledging that baptism might in some cases be considered logically prior to the Church covenant, though he ostensibly did not recognize the implications of his position.

Most of the other ministers made similar adjustments to the ineluctable progress of propagation. By 1642 Thomas Allen of Charlestown was extending baptism to the children of parents outside the Church covenant. George Phillips of Watertown strongly implied, shortly after 1642, that he also accepted the extension of baptism, though he said later that he disliked the principle espoused by Cotton that children were entitled to baptism by "the faith of their forefathers." [33] Hooker, however, resisted his "secret desire and inclination" to baptize the children of non-confederate parents and continued to base infant baptism on "the faithful covenant" of "the next parents," specifically denying any appeal to distant ancestors in the faith.[34] Though most ministers followed the new practice, there was considerable confusion. The Massachusetts General Court called a

31. Ibid., p. 88; Cotton, *Grounds*, p. 187. See also Increase Mather, *First Principles*, p. 5.
32. Increase Mather, *First Principles*, p. 6.
33. Phillips, *Reply to a Confutation*, p. 122; Walker, *Creeds and Platforms*, pp. 239 ff.
34. Hooker, *Survey of the Summe*, 3. 2. 12–16.

synod in 1645 to resolve the indecision, observing that "the apprehensions of many persons in the country" with regard to "baptisme, and the persons to be received thereto" were "knowne not a little to differ." [35] But the synod, which met at Cambridge intermittently from 1646 to 1648, failed to insert any directives in the Cambridge Platform, probably for fear of needlessly antagonizing opponents of the extension of baptism.

The most troubling critics of New England baptismal practice, however, were the Baptists, who argued that the sacrament itself constituted the visible Church. The paedobaptist ministers often grouped their Baptist antagonists with Roman Catholics, who also claimed that baptism was the foundation of the Church, but they knew that the similarity was purely formal, since the Baptists administered the sacrament only to the regenerate and thus actually grounded the Church on spiritual experience. Every pious New Englander cherished the experience of conversion, which certified the indwelling of the Spirit, but most also believed that spiritual immediacy could transform men into pneumatic enthusiasts. They knew also that ecclesiastical continuity required sacramental structures: infant baptism both symbolized and guaranteed the continuity of the Church covenant. With the exception of an occasional renegade—like Roger Williams or Henry Dunster, the first real president of Harvard—the leading ministers were united in their opposition to Baptist admission policies, partly for doctrinal reasons but also because persistent tales of sixteenth-century Anabaptist excesses had created suspicions about all Baptists. In Massachusetts Bay the authorities passed a law against Anabaptist "incendiaries of commonwealths and infectors of persons in main matters of religion." Convicted Baptists were often punished with imprisonment, public whippings, and banishment.[36]

As a rule, ministerial argumentation against the Baptists consisted of long exegetical excurses on familiar proof-texts. Most New Englanders believed that the New Testament contained, either explicitly or inferentially, outright commands for infant baptism—such as Christ's directive that little children be brought to him.[37] The paedobaptist ministers also noted Paul's observation (1 Cor. 7 : 14) that the child of

---

35. Nathaniel Shurtleff, ed., *Records of the Governor and Company of the Massachusetts Bay in New England*, 5 vols. (Boston, 1853–54), 3 : 71.

36. Shurleff, *Records*, 2 : 85. See especially William G. McLoughlin, *New England Dissent 1630–1833: The Baptists and the Separation of Church and State*, 2 vols. (Cambridge, Mass., 1971), 1 : 3–48.

37. Cotton, *Grounds*, pp. 4–7, 150 ff.; Hooker, *Covenant of Grace Opened*, p. 63; Cobbet, *Just Vindication*, pp. 108 ff.

one believing parent was "holy." Originally set forth to discourage
Christians from indiscriminately divorcing pagans, the text proved to
New England divines that the children of a faithful parent were "Ec-
clesiastically and Federally holy" and therefore proper subjects of the
sacramental covenant seal.[38] Or again, in Acts 2 : 39 Peter assured the
Jews that they and their children had received God's promise of salvation. According to the Puritan ministers, Christians and their children
were contemporary beneficiaries of all God's promises to the Jews, and
since baptism was the seal of such promises, true Christians had in
Peter's sermon an implicit command to baptize their children.[39]

In the end, the New England ministers always returned to the
"types." Their defense of sacramental piety against the Baptists rested
on typological exegesis. Among the manifold scriptural arguments for
infant baptism, the most popular continued to be the claim, taken
from Genesis 17 : 1–14, that God's covenant with Abraham, inclusive
of his seed and sealed with circumcision, was identical in substance
with the Christian covenant, which consequently also extended to children and required an analogous seal. Typology demonstrated that
Jewish and Christian seals were truly analogous, for when the paedobaptist ministers subjected to typological analysis Old Testament references to circumcision, or the passing through the sea, or the cloud in
the wilderness, it became evident to them that these were sacramental
signs and events, which like baptism pointed to Christ, though by way
of anticipation. Since the seals of the old and new covenants were substantially identical, Christians might legitimately appeal to the Old
Testament to justify their sacramental practices.[40]

The Baptist debates were devoid of original argumentation; the
New England paedobaptists simply resurrected timeworn proofs and
commonplace exegesis. Yet the controversy shaped and informed the
development of mainline sacramental doctrine within the colony. Baptists probing for a sensitive spot continually asked what "good" it did
to baptize children.[41] Consequently, the New England preachers felt
constrained to clarify their own position by developing and defending
a respectable doctrine of baptismal efficacy that could silence their crit-

38. Cobbet, *Just Vindication*, pp. 2–30; Cotton, *Grounds*, pp. 113 ff.; Hooker,
Covenant of Grace Opened, pp. 41 ff.
39. Cobbet, *Just Vindication*, pp. 21–36; Cotton, *Grounds*, p. 26.
40. Cotton, *Grounds*, pp. 38 ff.; Hooker, *Covenant of Grace Opened*, pp. 2 ff.;
Phillips, *Reply to a Confutation*, pp. 14 ff.; Cobbet, *Just Vindication*, pp. 37 ff.;
Bulkeley, *Gospel Covenant*, 2nd ed., (London, 1653), pp. 161 ff.; Shepard, *Church
Membership of Children*, pp. 6 ff.
41. Shepard, *Church Membership of Children*, p. 21.

ics and yet satisfy their own religious needs. Their efforts demonstrate, as nothing else does, the indecision of the first generation of colonial ministers concerning the sacraments.

The leading ministers were convinced that no sacrament conveyed regenerating grace. None of them ever claimed that baptism conveyed the "habit of faith," which was rather the fruit of the covenant of grace.[42] None of them suggested that baptism transmitted a provision of grace that made infants "capable" of salvation. When the ministers spoke of capability in children, they were referring to the qualifications required for baptism, not to the consequences of being baptized. They were fond of arguing, on the basis of the doctrine of election, that infants were capable of receiving faith from the Spirit and were therefore proper recipients of the seal of faith. Cotton confessed that such infant faith could be recognized not by its effect, but only by the testimony of the Scripture.[43] Despite its invisibility, however, Hooker thought that his proof of an infant's capacity for such faith was "the maine thing of the businesse" in his controversy with John Spilsbury, an English Baptist who had said that infants were incapable of grace and therefore unfit for baptism. Because some infants were inevitably among the elect, Hooker insisted, a "portion and provision" of grace must have been "appointed by God, and bestowed of God on some children." If such infants were capable of grace, they also had a capacity for faith, which, indeed, was proved by the fact that God must "work faith in the hearts of all elected infants that dye in their infancy," faith being required for salvation. Since infants were capable of both grace and faith, Hooker thought, then Spilsbury's argument against infant baptism was clearly specious. Hooker even claimed that infants were "more capable" of grace and therefore more appropriate subjects for baptism than adults, most of whom were habituated in sin and more prone to resist the Spirit.[44] It was not bap-

42. According to Pettit, *Heart Prepared*, p. 117, Peter Bulkeley said that "the habit of faith" was conveyed "in baptism." Bulkeley actually said, however, that the habit was given "in the Covenant of grace," and he himself did not explicitly connect the habit of faith with baptism. See Bulkeley, *Gospel Covenant* 1st ed., pp. 33, 47, 298–99.
43. Cotton, *Grounds*, pp. 13–16.
44. Hooker, *Covenant of Grace Opened*, p. 24. Pettit, *Heart Prepared*, pp. 92, 105, considerably overstated Hooker's doctrine of baptismal efficacy largely because he misinterpreted the passages in which Hooker argued that infants were "capable." Pettit thought Hooker to be saying that infants received *in baptism* a "portion and provision of grace" that made them in some sense more "capable" of conversion. Actually Hooker was arguing, against Spilsbury, that infants were capable of grace and therefore fitting subjects for baptism. Consequently Pettit was mistaken when he distinguished between the baptismal doctrine of Hooker and Shepard on the grounds that the latter "unlike Hooker . . . never suggested that the baptized are

tism that created their capacities, however, but the interior activity of the Spirit.

Since the New England ministers considered sacraments to be covenant seals, their doctrine of baptismal efficacy depended entirely upon what Peter Bulkeley at Concord called "the efficacy of the covenant." [45] Hooker stated the conventional argument when he said that "the utmost power" a sacrament possessed was the capacity "to signifie, seale, and exhibite" the spiritual good of the covenant of grace.[46] Thomas Cobbett, the minister of Ipswich, agreed that the covenant was "the maine instrumentall force, in the fruit of the initiatory seale, and the application of it." [47] Baptism was more than a badge of Christianity, it was the confirmation of a covenant promise. But the sacrament itself did not create the covenant nor did it actually enter infants into the covenant, since their federal holiness existed prior to baptism, which merely guaranteed visibly that God's promise was trustworthy.[48]

Unless the covenant itself somehow facilitated regeneration, therefore, it was hard to see how the baptismal seal could comfort and re-

---

'capable.' " Pettit also understood Hooker to be saying that baptism implanted a "gracious principle" into the baptizand, thereby facilitating his conversion. But Hooker assumed that the "gracious principle" was conveyed after and apart from baptism: "The Sacrament of Baptisme is a seale of our first entrance; and the Supper is our nourishing in the family of Christ: And this being the scope of Baptisme sealing our first work into Christ; in which we are merely passive: but when we are setled on Christ, the truth is this, wee have a gracious principle put into us, and so we work by our selves, and by the help of the Spirit: but at the first the Spirit makes us willing that we may will it. This is the confession of all our othodox divines." See Hooker, *Covenant of Grace Opened*, p. 16.

45. Bulkeley, *Gospel Covenant*, 2nd ed., p. 23.
46. Hooker, *Covenant of Grace Opened*, p. 10.
47. Cobbet, *Just Vindication*, p. 143.
48. Pettit, *Heart Prepared*, p. 117, believed that "in Bulkeley the efficacy of baptism is brought to its highest point," and he quoted Bulkeley as saying that "we have made a covenant with Him in our baptism." The quotation seems to imply that baptism itself created the covenant relationship, which would mean that Bulkeley held a higher view of baptism than those ministers who believed that the sacrament simply sealed a prior covenant membership. Bulkeley's complete statement, however, was somewhat ambiguous: "Wee have made a covenant with him in our Baptisme, in our conversion and turning unto God, and coming to the Lords Supper." See *Gospel Covenant*, 1st ed., p. 47. At other points Bulkeley explicitly stated that there was "no sufficient reason, to deprive children of the seale of the Covenant now," precisely because such infants of Christian parents were already "within" the covenant, an argument indicating Bulkeley's agreement with the view that baptism simply sealed a pre-existing covenant relationship. Both circumcision and baptism, he said, were administered to children "in token of their being in covenant." See *Gospel Covenant*, 2nd ed., pp. 161–62. It seems to me that Bulkeley's doctrine of baptism did not differ from that of the other leading Puritan ministers in the colony.

assure the anxious parents of New England. In fact, the ministers of New England were never quite clear about "the efficacy of the covenant" that was sealed by baptism. Cotton suspected that Arminian notions of free will were lurking behind all the talk about covenants and their conditions, and he wanted to quash any suggestion that God could be manipulated by a contract. "Wee doe not promise life to any by the Covenant," he said, "unlesse they be elect." [49] Though the conception of conditionality was integral to the covenant imagery, Cotton would gladly have abandoned any discussion of conditions. He granted theologians their right to "speak of conditions," but he warned them to remember that "the Lord doth undertake both for his own part and for our parts also." God would freely maintain and preserve his elect, whose effectual calling was not "built upon any Conditionall Promise" or covenantal transaction, but rested on the "absolute free Promise unto the Soule" of the elect Saint.[50] The covenant relationship was thus effectual for salvation only for the elect, the preordained beneficiaries of absolute promises.

No other New England minister was quite so wary as Cotton about covenants and conditions, but the other ministers also believed that in the end everything depended on the absolute promise. Shepard wrote that the covenant of grace was "absolute": God fulfilled his own conditions. He had "undertaken to fulfill the Covenant absolutely" for his elect.[51] Hooker spoke freely of covenant conditions, yet he too thought that Christ performed the requisite duties for the elect: "the Lord Christ as the Second Adam, he performs the Condition also; not only requires new heart, but puts new spirits into us; not only commands us to beleeve, but enables us." [52] Even Peter Bulkeley (1583–1659), whose fascination with the covenant seemed at times to lead him to the brink of Arminianism, acknowledged that salvation depended finally on "absolute promises." [53]

All the talk about absolute promises created sacramental problems. If only the elect within the covenant had the absolute promise of life, then both the covenant and its baptismal seal seemed to be worthless

49. Cotton, *Grounds*, pp. 33, 68.
50. John Cotton, *The Covenant of Grace: Discovering the Great Work of a Sinners Reconciliation to God* (London, 1655), pp. 18, 29.
51. Thomas Shepard, *Certain Cases Resolved Specially, tending to the right ordering of the heart, that we may comfortably walk with God in our general and particular Callings* (London, 1650), p. 13.
52. Thomas Hooker, *The Application of Redemption* (London, 1657), p. 302.
53. Bulkeley, *Gospel Covenant*, 2nd ed., p. 324. Increase Mather, in the introduction to Samuel Willard's, *Covenant-Keeping the Way to Blessedness* (Boston, 1682), said that for Bulkeley the promises were in part conditional but "absolute as to the subjects of them," so that Bulkeley was no Arminian. Mather also noted that Cotton was not "free to use the word conditions, lest they should make those things to be causa regnandi, which are but Via ad Regnum."

for everyone else. The ministers might have said that baptism sealed the absolute promise to every infant receiving the sacrament, but that would have been interpreted as a periphrastic affirmation of the baptismal regeneration of all baptized children. New England Puritans recoiled from any suggestion that they made baptism "the wombe of regeneration.." [54] Or they might have claimed that baptism sealed a conditional covenant, thus making the efficacy of the sacrament contingent on future faith and repentance. As a matter of fact they did make this claim, though it was a peripheral distinction for most of them.[55] But was the sacrament then barren and void of effect, a superfluous ceremony performed simply because Scripture seemed to command it?

Surely the ministers seemed at times to discount altogether the effect of the baptismal seal, especially when they persisted in saying that baptism usually sealed only an external covenant. The covenant of grace, said Hooker, could be "considered in a double notion." "I finde a double covenant," he explained, "an inward and an outward." In the inward covenant stood the faithful elect, who by baptism were sealed for salvation. For most men, however, the sacrament sealed only an external covenant membership, and since Hooker held that "covenant grace is one thing, and saving grace is another," he was able to protect himself from any insinuation that he overstated the efficacy of baptism. His claim that the sacrament frequently sealed a mere external holiness also enabled him to counter Baptist charges that he and other paedobaptists attributed holiness to infants who could fall from grace, thereby denying the Reformed doctrines of perseverance and original sin. After all, Hooker never said that infants within the covenant necessarily possessed true saving grace, or that their covenant holiness freed them from original sin. But with such restrictive qualifications, baptism seemed to offer little comfort to the anxious.[56]

Most New England ministers shared Hooker's opinions. Shepard announced that baptism was annexed to an outward covenant and that baptized infants were therefore by no means "always in inward covenant." [57] Cotton also distinguished "a double state of grace"; saving grace, which sanctified the inner man and from which there was no

54. Cotton, *Grounds*, p. 148.
55. Cobbet incorporated the language of conditionality into his doctrine of baptism, though without emphasis in *Just Vindication*, p. 51. Cotton at least mentioned it, though obliquely, in *Grounds*, pp. 148, 168, 176. Shepard gave it his own distinctive twist in *Church Membership of Children*, pp. 5 ff., but outside of Shepard's theology, it was not stressed.
56. Hooker, *Covenant of Grace Opened*, pp. 2, 20, 41–44. See also Cotton, *Grounds*, pp. 43, 125, 173; Cobbet, *Just Vindication*, p. 21; Phillips, *Reply to a Confutation*, pp. 39, 43.
57. Shepard, *Church Membership of Children*, pp. 2, 6.

fall, and federal grace, by which the children of believing parents were holy. Because of their federal grace, such children had right to the "outward dispensation of the Covenant and to the seale of it," but neither the covenant nor its seal would benefit the non-elect "seed of the flesh."

> But the seed of the flesh, though the Lord gave his Covenant even unto them also, and the seal thereof; yet he hath not established it unto them forever; whence afterward it cometh to passe that they reject the Covenant and the faith of it.[58]

The distinction between the inner and outer covenants made it clear that the elect would be saved even without baptism—New England ministers denied that baptism was necessary for salvation—and that the non-elect would perish despite their baptism.[59]

Hooker therefore reminded his readers that John had baptized scribes, pharisees, publicans, and soldiers without their necessarily being saved. He acknowledged that God engaged himself in the sacrament to "worke grace" in the hearts of baptized infants, but, he added, God dispenses such grace only "as he sees fit," so that neither covenant membership nor its seal could ensure salvation. Though believing parents entered the covenant "personally for themselves and their children," God dispensed his "internall and spirituall" adoption according to his arbitrary will: "as to accept the father somtime and the sonne somtime, and sometime the one and sometime the other, as he pleases." [60] Hooker therefore wrote on several occasions of the emptiness of all outward privileges, including the baptismal seal.[61] And his skepticism was shared by his colleagues; Cotton once suggested that infant baptism was of value mainly as an "incentive" to parental faith.[62]

It sometimes appeared as if New England ministers were able to say only that baptism was a pledge and engagement to obedience. They preached with unqualified zeal about baptismal obligations. Hooker commanded baptized children to "lay hold of the covenant"; Shepard taught that infant baptism was an "engagement" obliging infants to forsake sin when they matured; Bulkeley urged that his lis-

58. Cotton, *Grounds*, pp. 43, 53, 54.
59. Hooker, *Covenant of Grace Opened*, p. 66; Cobbet, *Just Vindication* p. 50; Phillips, *Reply to a Confutation*, pp. 41–43; Norton, *Answer*, p. 54.
60. Hooker, *Covenant of Grace Opened*, pp. 34, 43, 56.
61. Thomas Hooker, *The Soules Humiliation* (London, 1638), p. 38; idem, *The Saints Dignitie and Dutie Together with the Danger of Ignorance and Hardnesse* (London, 1651), p. 157.
62. Winthrop, *History*, 1 : 132.

teners "labor" to keep their baptismal covenant; Cotton insisted that baptized children be trained in "obedience" to God as part of their sacramental nurture.[63] It has been claimed that their repeated exhortations about baptismal duties implicitly made the sacrament a "cause of faith," as it had been in "historic sacramental theology." [64] But this is to read into Puritan doctrine an implication that the ministers would not have accepted. Certainly Zwingli had emphasized baptismal obligations without intending to affirm an implicit notion of baptismal efficacy. No Puritan believed that a pledge of obedience could actually create the capacity for truly obedient discipleship.

Yet the Puritans were ambidextrous theologians: what the right hand took away, the left hand could retrieve. For almost every negation in their baptismal doctrine there was a qualifying affirmation. Baptism did not convey saving grace, yet it was a means of grace. The sacrament could not save an infant, but it could facilitate the process of salvation. It sealed an external covenant, but the efficacy of that covenant, and hence of its seal, was not to be taken lightly.

In the Cambridge Platform of 1648, New Englanders asserted that covenanted, baptized children were "in a more hopefull way of attayning regenerating grace." [65] Speaking as individuals, they sometimes surpassed even this optimistic prediction. Cotton cautioned that baptism was annexed only to the outward covenant, but then he turned around and proclaimed that this external dispensation harbored the means of salvation. Having discerned the perils of spiritual immediacy during the Hutchinsonian affair, he was by 1647 fully convinced that God normally accommodated his activity to creaturely finitude and sinfulness through visible means of grace suited to the nature and capacity of men. Baptism was one of these means of grace; it was distinctive because it provided access to others. Membership in the external covenant sealed by baptism entitled an infant to the visible ordinances of the Church, and Cotton denied that the ordinances mediated only "common graces."

> Where then must they seek the influence of Christ in saving graces, if not in the visible Ministry and keyes of the Church? Is not this to evacuate the saving benefit of living in visible Church-fellowship under visible Ministry, visible sacraments, and cen-

63. Hooker, *Covenant of Grace Opened*, p. 84; Shepard, *Church Membership of Children*, p. 24; Bulkeley, *Gospel Covenant*, 2nd ed., p. 52; John Cotton, *The Way of Life*, pp. 382–84.
64. Perry Miller, "The Puritan Theory of the Sacraments in Seventeenth Century New England," *The Catholic Historical Review* 22 (January, 1937) : 409–25.
65. Walker, *Creeds and Platforms*, p. 224.

sures? Where did all the Saints of God receive their saving graces of conversion, faith, repentance, sanctification, but in attendance upon Christ the head [of the Church] in the visible use of visible church ordinances.[66]

Cotton's doctrine of the means of grace elevated baptism, for it enabled him to argue that the sacrament entitled the children of the faithful to the "means" by which the elect among them would eventually experience "the grace of the new birth." It was precisely for this end, Cotton said, that "the seale of the Covenant" was administered to infants.[67]

Cotton's claims were modest: the sacrament did not itself convey the saving grace; it was not the doorway into the Church; it did not create the covenant relationship. But it did seal and confirm the right of admission to the locus of salvation. Baptism granted a title "to the meanes of grace, with promises of efficacy to the elect seed, and offers thereof to the rest, so farre as to leave them without excuse." [68]

For Cotton, then, baptism was a title to efficacious ordinances within the Church. Hooker suggested a second mode of baptismal power: the sacrament was an effective seal if the covenant that it sealed conveyed salvation. Despite his distinction between covenanted and saving grace, Hooker believed that God had engaged himself through the covenant "to communicate spirituall good to children." Since baptism was a seal of this divine engagement, it possessed a certain instrumental efficacy. Whenever baptism was lawfully administered, the Spirit would "go along with it" to assure the faithful of God's fidelity to his covenant promises. The sacrament would not save the reprobate—for God had not promised to deliver them—but it was, in Hooker's words, an objective "instrumental cause" in a fully Calvinist sense.[69] In view of the faithfulness of God, the sacramental confirmation of a divine promise was synonymous with its fulfillment. In the heavenly economy, to seal was to convey; the sealed promise was equivalent to the deed.

Hooker was careful, in good Calvinist fashion, to specify the limitations of the baptismal promise: it encompassed only the elect. There was, however, a further possibility implicit in the sacramental rhetoric; perhaps covenantal affiliation, sealed by baptism, might be a sign of election. It was possible to infer from the rhetoric an even more audacious conclusion: that the covenantal relation was a basis

66. John Cotton, *Of the Holiness of Church Members* (London, 1650), pp. 19, 41.
67. Cotton, *Grounds*, pp. 125, 145–46.
68. Ibid, p. 125.
69. Hooker, *Covenant of Grace Opened*, pp. 13–15.

for salvation. Could it be that God elected a child for salvation purely because he was within the covenant? In that case, the demography of natural generation would have vastly affected the population of the spiritual kingdom of God. When pressed, no Puritan theologian would seriously have entertained such a thought without immediately appending a host of qualifications. Yet the New England ministers often left the impression that the circumstances of birth could determine the course of a man's spiritual history. Despite his obeisance to the freedom of God in election, John Cotton took comfort in recalling that God had promised "upon the faith of the Parent, salvation to his household."

> But this wee further claime in the behalf of the children of believers . . . that the children of believers doe come on themselves to believe, by reason of the Covenant of grace which God hath made with believers and their seed, for by that Covenant hee hath promised to write the law of faith (as of all other saving graces) in their hearts, that they also may come in Gods time and way to enjoy all the other saving priviledges of the Covenant, as did their Fathers before them.

The children of the faithful were like the early Jews, who found conversion "more easie and naturall" than did the Gentiles. In fact, Cotton sometimes seemed to imply that all the offspring of faithful parents were to be included among the elect saints chosen by a suddenly predictable deity. This confidence in the efficacy of the covenant, in turn, apparently justified equal confidence in the baptismal seal. In baptism, Cotton wrote, God assured faithful parents that the Spirit would "sooner or later . . . performe that work in our Children, which he hath wrought in our selves." The sacrament was therefore a trustworthy seal of "regeneration, and righteousness promised." [70]

No theologian in New England had a higher conception of baptism than Thomas Shepard, who told his son that the sacrament was a happy privilege "whereby god is become thy god, and is beforehand with thee that when ever thou shalt returne to god, he will undoubtedly receive thee." [71] Shepard brought to explicit formulation the thought that was implicit in Cotton's rhetoric: the external covenant, sealed by baptism, was in some sense "absolute." If it were only conditional, he explained, then God was no more in covenant with

70. Cotton, *Grounds*, pp. 69; 137; 77–78; 140, 172.
71. *PCSM* 27 (1932): 355. In comparison with the other first generation New England divines, Shepard did not have a "low conception of baptism," as Pettit claimed in *The Heart Prepared*, p. 108.

Church members than with pagans and infidels, which was absurd. To be in the external covenant was to be a likely candidate for salvation, because God had extended special promises to "the seed of his people (indefinitely considered)." Here and there a child might fall away, but as a group the children of the faithful would be drawn to accept "special grace and mercy." And God would never cut them off until they "positively rejected" the means to procure the special benefits of their parental covenant.

> [God will] prune, and cutt, and dresse, and water them, and improve the means of their eternal good upon them, which good they shall have, unless they refuse in resisting the meanes; nay that he will take away this refuseing heart from among them indefinitely, so that though every one cannot assure himself, that he will do it particularly for this or that person, yet every one, through this promise, may hope, and pray for the communication of this grace, and so feel it in time.[72]

As the external covenant was thus somehow absolute, so also was the baptismal seal. Shepard thought it wrong to suppose that "Circumcision and Baptism, seal only conditionally." Challenged to show the immediate benefit of infant baptism, he argued that God gave to "many" baptized children "such hearts as they shall not be able to refuse the good" of the means of grace. Shepard therefore suggested, using Calvinist language, that the sacrament was an "instrument and means" by which God conveyed his grace.[73]

For similar reasons, Peter Bulkeley of Concord told his fellow colonists that they were "exalted in privileges of the Gospel above many other people." Their covenant with God was uppermost among those privileges: God conveyed salvation "by no other way, but by way of Covenant," which descended from fathers to children and so continued forever. The efficacy of the covenant would never be "disanulled," and baptism was proof of covenant membership: the "seales of the covenant (the Sacraments) are given to us, and therefore the covenant is made with us also." Bulkeley acknowledged that there could be "an interruption for a time" in the transmission of covenant membership, but he strongly implied that no parent needed to be unduly anxious about the salvation of a baptized child, not because baptism created the covenant relationship or directly infused grace, but

72. Shepard, *Church Membership of Children,* pp. 4–5, 6.
73. Thomas Shepard *Theses Sabbaticae, or the Doctrine of the Sabbath, Works,* 3 : 75; Shepard, *Church Membership of Children,* pp. 5, 22.

because it confirmed the veracity of God's promises to his covenanted people.[74]

The New England ministers faced the problem, endemic to the Reformed tradition, of reconciling predestination and baptismal efficacy, and they offered a Calvinist solution. Baptism was not simply a pledge of obedience or a badge of Christian profession; it was a seal or confirmation of God's covenant promise, and God was true to his promises. That was what Calvin meant when he called the sacraments instruments of divine grace: precisely because God was faithful, they conveyed what they signified when rightfully used. Like Calvin, then, the New England ministers tried to hold in balance a comforting doctrine of baptism and a proper respect for God's sovereign electing decrees, with their antisacramental implications. It was no easier for them than for Calvin, however, to maintain the balance. In 1663 John Davenport, the minister at New Haven, would quote John Cotton's views on predestination to rebuke excessive confidence in covenants and covenant seals on the part of ministers who ventured to suggest that faith and repentance were "indefinitely given" to infants "in covenant and baptized." [75] Those ministers defended their own position, though, with other quotations from Cotton. Thus did the duality within the founders' theology issue in divisiveness within the New England churches.

To Protect the Lord's Supper

When asked to explain his habit of leaving the meetinghouse whenever the Lord's Supper was administered, Goodman Badger of Wenham claimed to believe that the communion table had been set up to "write on." [76] Goodman Badger, however, was not typical. The ministers of New England made a serious effort to ensure a fitting reverence for the sacrament among the people; they expected their congregations to have an articulate understanding of the Lord's Supper, which was administered with great solemnity to communicants who had been carefully instructed in its meaning. The lawyer Thomas Lechford, a temporary resident in Massachusetts Bay, described the service for the curious in England:

74. Bulkeley, *Gospel Covenant*, 1st ed., p. 33; idem, *Gospel Covenant*, 2nd ed., pp. 23, 153, 159.

75. John Davenport, *Another Essay for Investigation of the Truth* (Cambridge, 1663), p. 29.

76. Fiske, "Church Records," p. 75.

Once a moneth is a Sacrament of the Lords Supper, whereof notice is given usually a fortnight before, and then all others depart-
ing save the Church, which is a great deale lesse in number than
those that goe away, they receive the sacrament, the Ministers and
ruling Elders sitting at the Table, the rest in their seats, or upon
forms: All cannot see the Minister consecrating, unless they stand
up, and make a narrow shift. The one of the teaching Elders
prayes before, and blesseth, and consecrates the Bread and Wine,
according to the Words of Institution; the other prays after the
receiving of all the members: and next Communion, they change
turnes; he that began at that, ends at this: and the ministers deliver the Bread in a Charger to some of the chiefe, and peradven-
ture gives to a few the Bread into their hands, and they deliver
the charger from one to another, till all have eaten; in like manner, the cup, till all have dranke, goes from one to another. Then
a Psalme is sung, and with a short blessing the congregation is
dismissed.[77]

The ministers urged communicants to spend at least a day in preparation, and there were periodic efforts to institute a weekly eucharistic
observance.[78] In 1655 the governor of the Bay Colony requested that
Richard Mather advise him whether the sacrament should be celebrated "every Lord's day," as in the New Testament Church (Acts
20 : 7). Mather decided that a "frequent use of that Ordinance" was
commendable, but he hesitated to say that "this degree of frequency
be of necessity, so that if it be not so it will be sinne." [79] Nevertheless, whether a church administered the sacrament weekly, as occasionally happened, or observed communion only one day each month,
the Lord's Supper was an exalted symbol of New England piety.

By some turn of irony, however, the ministerial solicitude for the
sanctity of eucharistic worship inhibited the growth of a widespread
sacramental devotion in New England. The efforts to protect the
Lord's Supper isolated it from the unregenerate majority within the
congregation, and by implying that the Supper was a meal for a spiritual aristocracy, the ministers reinforced the attitude, common among
Reformed congregations, that sacramental communion could be a dangerous venture for the spiritually mediocre. The personal diaries of
such men as Thomas Shepard and Michael Wigglesworth, the pastor

77. Lechford, *Plain Dealing*, pp. 16–17. See also Cotton, *Doctrine of the Church*,
p. 7; idem, *Questions and Answers Upon Church Government*, in *A Treatise of
Faith* (London?, n.d.); idem, *Way of the Churches of Christ*, p. 68.
78. Winthrop, *History*, 1 : 399.
79. *MHSC*, 5th ser. 8 (1868) : 72–75.

at Malden, clearly demonstrate the existence of a heart-felt sacramental piety, but for more than half a century there was, as later ministers complained, a dearth of sacramental manuals and devotional guides in the colony.[80]

The churches agreed that only visible saints—presumably regenerate members of particular Reformed churches who possessed ability to discern the Lord's body, knowledge of Christian doctrine, and "grace to examine and judge themselves before the Lord"—were to be admitted to the Lord's Supper. They required that members baptized as infants offer a further "profession of repentance and faith" before approaching the sacrament.[81] But the status of the Lord's Supper in New England created persistent difficulties, and even such mundane matters as payment for bread and wine agitated some of the churches. At Chelmsford members of the congregation balked at using the church treasury to pay for the sacramental elements that they could not receive, so the church voted that communicants alone were to reimburse the deacons for communion expenses.[82] Far more pressing, however, was the issue of admission, which created the impression that New Englanders had separated from the Church of England, since members of English parish churches were, as a rule, barred from the Lord's Supper when they came to the colony.

In 1630, before he arrived in the Bay Colony, John Cotton had criticized Samuel Skelton and the Salem church for denying the sacrament to several "godly and faithful servants of Christ" from parish churches in England, including the future governor of the colony, John Winthrop, while admitting a member of an English Congregational church led by John Lathrop. According to Cotton, the action of the Salem church wrongfully implied that no man was eligible for the Lord's Supper unless he was a member of "some particular Reformed Church," and that no Anglican could fit this description save "Mr. Lathrop's and such as his." [83] By 1633, however, Cotton began to change his mind, and three years later, in a sermon preached at Salem, he retracted his condemnation. The covenant, he acknowledged, was "not made to the Righteousness of Faith at large, But to them that are

80. Thomas Shepard, "Diary," New York Public Library; Michael Wigglesworth, *The Diary of Michael Wigglesworth 1653–1657*, ed. Edmund Morgan (New York, 1965).

81. Cotton, *Way of the Churches of Christ*, p. 5; idem, *Holiness of Church Members*, pp. 19, 41.

82. Fiske, "Church Records," pp. 215, 340.

83. In Thaddeus M. Harris, *Memorials of the First Church in Dorchester From its Settlement in New England To the End of the Second Century* (Boston, 1830), pp. 53–56. Reprinted in David D. Hall, "John Cotton's Letter to Samuel Skelton," *William and Mary Quarterly*, 3rd ser.22 (July, 1965) : 478–85.

Righteous by the Faith of the Seed of Abraham, that is, to such Believers as are Confederate with Abraham," and thus to members of
"particular covenanted churches." [84] In effect, Cotton was saying that
the Lord's Supper was a communal seal, so that sacramental celebration presupposed the existence of a faithful covenanted community,
which was an old Separatist doctrine. He denied later that New Englanders expressly barred members of English parish churches from
the sacrament, but he added that candidates were ineligible for communion if guilty of "publick offence," and then he designated membership in a "Nationall Church" as publicly offensive. [85] Such logic
failed to satisfy the English critics of the New England way, and even
in the colonies some ministers admitted to communion all English
Christians who carried letters of recommendation from their parish
ministers. [86]

Cotton's logic also left unanswered a variety of more immediately
pressing problems. Suppose that a stranger were to turn up claiming
to possess all of Cotton's requirements for communion, though as a
member of a distant Congregational church. Suppose the candidate
for communion were no stranger but a well-known member of a neighboring church. What would be the appropriate response? Could the
unregenerate even watch the celebration of the sacrament in their own
churches? Could they remain in the meetinghouse during the prayer
preceding the consecration? Should a blessing be pronounced upon
the unregenerate who were dismissed before the sacrament? And just
who should resolve conflicts over admission to the Lord's Supper? The
questions indicated a basic indecision about sacramental worship in
New England.

The uncertainty was reflected in the diversity of their solutions to
such problems. Chelmsford and Wenham decided to open the Lord's
Supper both to strangers and to members of neighboring churches who
could present convincing letters of recommendation; Salem, however,
feared that "letters recommendatory" could be "counterfeited" and
wanted to require oral testimony to the candidate's fitness from a
member of the church where the sacrament was administered. Anyone could watch the communion service in Boston; the Wenham
church debated at length before deciding to allow the unregenerate

84. John Cotton, *A Sermon Preached by the Reverend Mr. John Cotton To which
is Prefixed, A Retraction of his former Opinion concerning Baptism, uttered by him
immediately Preceeding the Sermon here Emitted* (Boston, 1713), pp. 1–6.

85. Cotton, *Way of the Churches of Christ*, pp. 76–80.

86. See Thomas Welde, *An Answer to W. R. His Narration of the Opinions and
Practices of the Churches lately erected in New England* (London, 1644), p. 19; and
Thomas Shepard, *A Defence of the Answer made unto the 9 questions* (London,
1645), p. 70.

even to remain for the prayer before the sacrament or to receive a blessing as they departed after the prayer. Salem thought that the elders should decide such questions; Wenham wanted the entire church to make the decisions, as apparently was the practice in Boston.[87]

There was a further question about New England church members' receiving communion in parish churches during visits to England, a sensitive issue since they denied that they had separated from the Church of England. Cotton decided shortly after his arrival in the colony that he could not receive the sacraments with his old congregation in England, or, by implication, in any parish church within the Anglican establishment, because "scandalous persons" continued to commune there. His friends in England also criticized him for allegedly saying that it was unlawful to "receive the sacrament where a stinted liturgy is used." [88] Other New England ministers, however, shared Cotton's opinion. Shepard decided before he left England that he could no longer receive the sacraments with scandalous and faithless persons, though he "ever judged it Lawfull to join with them in preaching." [89] Theoretically the colonial ministers did not join the Separatists in denying the English parish churches to be true churches, but despite their repudiation of Separatist theory, they adopted in practice a form of semi-Separatism. In the fashion of the Plymouth congregation, they acknowledged "the lawfulness of communicating with the Church of England, in the Word and Prayer: but not in the Sacraments and Discipline." [90] When accused of Separatism, Thomas Welde, the minister at Roxbury, defended himself and his fellow ministers by describing the New England practice in semi-Separatist terms:

We much differ from [Separatists], so in severall particulars of moment, we practise what the Separatists (properly so called) will not doe, as hearing, preaching, praying in the Assemblies in England, and also in private communion with them.[91]

87. Fiske, "Church Records," pp. 38–44, 55; Lechford, *Plain Dealing* p. 17; Cotton, *The Way of Congregational Churches Cleared*, (London, 1648), p. 29.

88. Cotton, *Way of Congregational Churches Cleared*, p. 29; John Dod, et. al., "Letter to John Cotton," Prince Collection, Cotton Papers, 2. 9, n.d., Boston Public Library.

89. Thomas Shepard, "The Autobiography of Thomas Shepard," *PCSM* 27 (1927–30) : 375.

90. Cotton, *Way of Congregational Churches Cleared*, p. 8, quoting a description of John Robinson's "semi-separatism" given by the Scottish Presbyterian, Robert Baillie in his *A Dissuasive from the Errours of the Time* (London, 1645), p. 17.

91. Welde, *Answer to W. R.*, p. 10. Private communion did not refer to the Lord's Supper but other forms of private meditation and prayer. See also Shepard, *Defence*, pp. 69–70.

English Puritans occasionally charged that the New England policy was implicitly Separatist. New Englanders denied the charge, and by 1648 some were condoning sacramental communion in churches where the scandalous were allowed to participate, but their concern for the sanctity of the Lord's Supper—which concern was itself a kind of sacramental piety—did cause some ministers to accept for a time semi-Separatist practice while rejecting Separatist theory.

As for the sacrament itself, the ministers never doubted that it was a meal for the holy rather than a means to produce holiness. Communion was therefore beneficial only to the faithful who prepared themselves by repentance and self-examination. Even before he arrived in New England, Hooker was informing prospective communicants of their responsibility to search their souls and find a "work of grace." Without the "graces" of faith, repentance, knowledge, and love, no man could "receive good from the sacrament." Hooker recognized that saints were prone to be skeptical about their gracious state, so he also suggested that each communicant lay open his inward estate to a judicious minister, but he still warned that the faithless ate and drank to damnation.[92]

Throughout his ministry, Hooker assumed that no sacrament could be "savoury and seasonable" without arduous meditation.[93] Such an assumption was pervasive in New England. Thomas Shepard spent the entire day before the celebration of the Lord's Supper—and sometimes longer—sequestered from all trivial distractions, preparing for communion.[94] This sacramental piety reflected an introspective mood characteristic of early New England devotion. While Puritan ministers were by no means averse to reflection on the visible creatures, the architecture of the outer world was never so alluring to them as the mansions of the spirit. When Hooker outlined the way of meditation, he taught the saint to pry into the crevices and corners of his soul, mapping out the course of his daily conversation and disposition, recalling the sins of the past and uncovering the corrupt thoughts of the present. The purpose of meditation was self-knowledge.[95] There was therefore little interest in "spiritualizing the creatures," and New Englanders had few kind words for other sensible aids to devotion. They were fearful of "debasing the infinite majesty" of God through image worship.[96] The starkness of New England's introspective spiri-

92. Thomas Hooker, *A Preparative to the Lords Supper,* in *The Paterne of Perfection,* pp. 350, 369–72.
93. Hooker, *Application of Redemption,* p. 247.
94. See for example Shepard's *Meditations,* pp. 49, 58, and his "Diary," August 24, November 13, February 12, April 23, 1643.
95. Hooker, *Application of Redemption,* 2nd ed. (London, 1659), pp. 210–49.
96. Shepard, *Theses Sabbaticae, Works,* 3 : 68.

tuality diluted the possibility of sensuous participation that had marked traditional Roman and Lutheran eucharistic devotion.

Even the logical presuppositions of the New England theologians comported poorly with a sacramental sensibility. They admired the new logic of Petrus Ramus, which had been introduced in the sixteenth century as a modification, though not a repudiation, of Aristotelianism. Characteristic of Ramism, however, was the subordination of "rhetoric" to dialectic; as a result, tropes, types, and figures technically constituted a distinct order of discourse. The implication was that figurative language could not actually convey truth until being reduced to purely logical expression. But what then was the status of sacramental language, which was primarily figurative and typical? The Puritans neither asked nor answered the question; one assumes that they were conscious of no problem. They simply continued to translate sacramental symbolism into doctrinal propositions, a procedure consistent both with Ramist logic and with traditional Reformed practice.[97] So long as they remained within the boundaries of Ramism, they had no alternative.

The major intellectual premises of the antisacramental mood among New England Puritans appeared not in treatises on logic, however, but in theological discourses, including sacramental sermons. The book that most fully clarifies early colonial eucharistic thought is Thomas Hooker's *Comment Upon Christ's Last Prayer in the Seventeenth of John*, which contains almost no explicit references to the Lord's Supper itself, even though it was composed of sermons delivered at the sacrament. Hooker developed a fitting sacramental theme: the union of God with Christ, and of Christ with the faithful saint. He defended the ancient Christian notion that salvation rested on the Incarnation; had not the second person of the Trinity assumed human nature, no man could have been saved. Yet Hooker was careful, as his seventeenth-century editors observed, to "keep the true distance" between the Creator and the creatures.[98] First, he described the union between the divine and human natures in Christ as "personal," an allusion to the conventional Reformed doctrine that both natures, though united in Christ's Person, yet retained their own properties after the Incarnation. This meant that the human nature of Christ could attain only the "fulness" that was "compatible to any creature." Even within Christ,

97. On Ramism, see Wilbur Samuel Howell, *Logic and Rhetoric in England 1500–1700* (Princeton, 1956); Charles Feidelson, Jr., *Symbolism and American Literature* (Chicago, 1953), pp. 77–118; Perry Miller, *The New England Mind: The Seventeenth Century* (Boston, 1961), pp. 111–53.

98. Thomas Goodwin and Philip Nye, "To the Reader," in Thomas Hooker, *A Comment Upon Christ's Last Prayer in the Seventeenth of John* (London, 1656), n.p.

the finite humanity was "inferiour" to the divine nature and was incapable of assuming such divine attributes as omnipresence. The sacramental implication was clear: the "flesh" of Christ could not "be in al places or in many places, according to the administrations of the ordinances, which signify or represent the same." Second, Hooker continued to interpret the Johannine claim that "flesh profiteth nothing" in terms of an ontological distinction between spirit and corporeality. There was therefore no reason even to desire a physical sacramental presence: "Nor yet can the very flesh of our Savior in it self considered be truly available to purchase any spiritual good or communicate any spiritual vertue." [99]

Hooker's sermons suggest also that the intense mood of eschatological expectation in New England could serve to diminish a sacramental consciousness. The colonial ministers expected to experience the final days: they envisaged their churches as gathered communities of visible saints awaiting the imminent return of Christ. In itself, their expectation did not preclude sacramental devotion. John Cotton defined the Lord's Supper as a type that prefigured the Last Judgment.[100] But it was also possible to take special delight in comparing the future glory with the burdens and limitations of the present. And Hooker included among the limiting "impediments" of this life the relative impotence of the "means of grace." Even though Christ did shine forth in them, much like a daystar rising, his presence in the Word and sacraments could not be compared to the radiance of his return to earth. Hooker's vision of the future made him impatient with the "narrowness of means" and the "weakness of instruments." [101]

In the rarified spiritual atmosphere of New England, therefore, one could discover an occasional sense of uncertainty about the Lord's Supper, and doubts could rise visibly to the surface. Shepard, for example, believed not only that the elements were assuring seals but "also that Christ by sacramental union was given" to the faithful in the Lord's Supper. The Supper was an effective seal, in fact, because Christ was "faithful to make his Body and Blood present there." [102] Shepard also believed, however, that Christ had ascended to heaven, and this belief gave him "much trouble of spirit" whenever he received the sacrament. How could Christ be in the Lord's Supper and yet still remain in heaven? Shepard conceded in his dairy that there were

99. Hooker, *Comment Upon Christ's Last Prayer*, pp. 83, 113, 218.
100. John Cotton, *Spiritual Milk for Boston Babes in either England Drawn out of the breasts of both Testaments for their souls nourishment* (Cambridge, 1656), pp. 12–14.
101. Hooker, *Comment Upon Christ's Last Prayer*, pp. 371–73.
102. Shepard, *Meditations*, p. 50.

periods when he was "unable to see Christ" in the sacrament. He agonized over the question through the winter of 1643 until finally, in the spring, he saw how "Christ in heaven might and did unite himself, by his Spirit so unto these seals as that thereby he did come to the sacrament and so come into the souls and so convey himself." In the following weeks, Shepard experienced "the Lord coming to me himselfe in a sacrament." [103]

If the other ministers harbored similar doubts, they managed to overcome them. John Norton, who preached at both Ipswich and Boston during his New England ministry, expressed the common belief that the worthy communicant experienced a genuine spiritual union with Christ, whose body and blood were actually "united to the Elements." This union was virtual rather than local, occurring "by vertue of Divine institution" and not through any transmutation of the bread and wine. That is, the elements were seals confirming a divine promise of spiritual oneness with Christ, so that to receive the seal was to experience the union.[104] Cotton thought also that the elements held forth "the body and blood of Christ," and like most earlier Reformed ministers, he assumed that sacramental communion with Christ could not be reduced to the communication of his "mercies." The Eucharist conveyed more than merits and benefits; Cotton insisted that the Lord's Supper was of "infinite mercy" precisely because Christ's body was both "united with God" and spiritually present to the faithful communicant.[105]

In a sacramental sermon delivered before his arrival in New England, Hooker assured his congregation that Christ was "exhibited . . . under the Elements of Bread and Wine." He continued in New England to affirm an "exhibition" of the body and blood, as did his fellow ministers.[106] In the seventeenth century, the word "exhibition" denoted a spiritual reception by the faithful alone, as opposed to the word "distribution," which implied a corporeal presence available to every communicant. The ministers were intent on possessing the middle ground between Zwinglian and Lutheran extremes. In a series of

103. Shepard, "Diary," January 23, 1642/43; April 10, 1643; April 23, 1643.
104. John Norton, *The Orthodox Evangelist* (London, 1654), p. 292.
105. John Cotton, *A Brief Exposition with Practical Observations Upon the whole Book of Canticles* (London, 1655), p. 197. This was Cotton's second book on Canticles, written after his arrival in New England. See also Cotton, *Spiritual Milk*, p. 12; idem, *Grounds*, p. 191.
106. Hooker, *Preparative*, pp. 374–75; idem, *Saints Dignitie and Dutie*, p. 161. Hooker's *Preparative*, pp. 362–64, reflects an English setting: he advises his readers, for instance, that they need not feel obliged to attend sacramental administrations three or four times each week, which is not advice he would have had to offer at Hartford.

sermons preached in 1647 and 1648, Shepard described "the great end" of the Lord's Supper as a remembrance of Jesus, thus suggesting a memorialist doctrine. But he added that Christ was "held forth" in the sacrament, so that faithful communicants could truly eat his flesh and drink his blood.[107] Shepard and his New England colleagues remained within the Reformed consensus that had been codified in the Zurich formula of 1549.

The ministers never fully escaped their sense of ambivalence about the sacraments. Many of them could recall dramatic experiences of conversion—and the memory suggested that the essence of religion consisted in inwardness. Some had subsequently undergone a wrenching "crisis of conscience" in England because of their distaste for outward ceremonies associated with sacramental devotion.[108] And they ministered within a society that was uneasy about the symbolic in religion. The New England Puritans constructed meetinghouses devoid of suggestive ornamentation; they worshipped largely without visual aids to devotion; their ministers discarded symbolic vestments. The churches deprecated the quasi-sacramental rite of ordination, defining it merely as an adjunct to election by a particular church.[109] Throughout the first generation, New Englanders even buried their dead under flat, plain tombstones, totally lacking in symbolism.[110] In other words, the absence of a pervasive sacramental piety was a consequence not simply of New England ecclesiology, or of theological predispositions, but also of a distrustful posture toward visible symbols of any kind. Doctrinally, however, the ministers preserved the potential for a vigorous sacramental life. However ambivalent they may have been, the articulate clergy refused to reduce baptism to a sign of obedience, or the Lord's Supper to a memorial of the past. Their ambivalence did contain an affirmation, which created the possibility of a sacramental renaissance even on this colonial frontier.

107. Thomas Shepard, "Sacramental Sermons, 1648," March 19, 1648, American Antiquarian Society, Worcester Massachusetts. Shepard's sermons dealt more with the state of the soul than the substance of the Lord's Supper.

108. David D. Hall, *The Faithful Shepherd: A History of the New England Ministry in the Seventeenth Century* (Chapel Hill, 1972), pp. 72–92, 156–175.

109. Hooker, *Survey of the Summe*, 2. 2. 75; and Thomas Welde, *A Brief Narration of the Practices of the Churches in New England* (London, 1645), p. 6.

110. Allan I. Ludwig, *Graven Images: New England Stonecarving and its Symbols, 1650–1815* (Middletown, Ct., 1966), p. 18.

6

THE NEW BAPTISMAL PIETY

In 1662 the churchmen of New England laid the foundation for a restructuring of baptismal theology and an expansion of sacramental piety, though few of them foresaw the eventual transformations. They met in a synod intended only to adjudicate differences over sacramental practice by determining whether baptized Church members who had never experienced regeneration could offer their children for baptism. The long-range consequences of the synod, however, far exceeded the original intentions. Within little more than a decade, theologians probing the implications of the 1662 decisions redefined the nature of the sacrament. During the same period, local ministers exerted unprecedented effort to stimulate baptismal devotion in the colonies. Preachers recalled baptismal promises and congregations covenanted to observe baptismal vows. It was as if a host of zealous Puritans had suddenly discovered the usefulness of the visible rites and tangible sacraments that so frequently had aroused their suspicions.

Discomfort over baptismal practice had been manifest in New England as early as 1634, when John Cotton sanctioned the baptism of an infant whose immediate parents had never experienced the conversion that entitled them to Church membership. Cotton and his clerical colleagues quickly discovered that unconverted parents were not invariably indifferent to the spiritual welfare of their children, and that some of those parents considered infant baptism as a desirable confirmation of spiritual potential. This was especially true of unconverted parents who had themselves received infant baptism in New England congregations. The question of admission therefore continued to create unrest until finally the Court of Massachusetts convened the elders. Meeting in Boston in June, 1657, the ministerial delegates affirmed the permanent and personal membership of the children baptized in New England churches and their right, upon reaching maturity, to offer their own offspring for baptism.[1] The decision so disturbed New England traditionalists, however, that the Court called an official synod in 1662 to determine a final solution. This gathering reaffirmed the earlier decision.

> Churchmembers, who were admitted in minority, understanding the Doctrine of Faith, and publicly professing their assent thereto; not scandalous in life, and solemnly owning the Covenant before the Church, wherein they give themselves and their Children to the Lord, and subject themselves to the Government of Christ in the Church, their Children are to be Baptized.[2]

The synod reserved the privileges of voting and receiving the Lord's Supper to the regenerate. Later generations dubbed this solution a "Half-Way Covenant."

The purposes of the synodical decision were varied. For one thing, its proponents wanted to prevent a decline in Church membership. "The Lord hath not set up churches," said Jonathan Mitchell (1624–1688), the pastor at Cambridge, "onely that a few old Christians may keep one another warm while they live, and then carry away the Church into the cold grave with them when they dye."[3] But the synod's defenders also viewed their policy as the only way to maintain a commitment to both infant baptism and the principle of regenerate membership, which protected the Lord's Supper from the profane.[4] And for many, the synod offered a program for maintaining control over unregenerate members: the third proposition of the synod's "Result" stated that the infants of "confederate visible Believers" were, as they grew to maturity, "personally under the Watch, Discipline, and Government" of the Church, and were thus liable to excommunication. One critic charged that this disciplinary concern was the only motivation for the synod's decision. In order that the third proposition "might the better pass," he said, "all the other propositions are formed as they are."[5]

1. [Nathanael Mather], *A Disputation Concerning Church-Members and their Children*, in *Answer to XXI Questions* (London, 1659), p. 21.
2. Walker, *Creeds and Platforms*, p. 328.
3. Jonathan Mitchell, "An Answer to the Apologetical Preface," in [Richard Mather], *A Defence of the Answer and Arguments of the Synod Met at Boston in the year 1662 Concerning the Subject of Baptism, and Consociation of Churches* (Cambridge, 1664), p. 45.
4. Morgan, *Visible Saints*, pp. 113 ff.
5. Walker, *Creeds and Platforms*, p. 325; John Davenport, "The Third Essay containing a Reply to the Answer unto the other Essay printed in Defense of the

The synodical delegates wanted not merely to discipline the unregenerate, however, but also to save them. At issue in 1662 was the nature of the Church and its contribution to the order of salvation. In effect, the synod's majority was arguing for a broad view of the Church as an institution that not only nourished the regenerate but also dispensed grace to the unsaved. Therefore baptized children, though barred from the Lord's Supper, were accepted as personal and plenary Church members who might receive through the external ordinances sufficient grace to make conversion probable. The dissenters, on the other hand, believed the Church to be an institution for the regenerate, or presumably regenerate, with their baptized children possessing only a provisional quasi-membership.

The Synod and Sacramental Thought

Within the Puritan tradition, debates over the nature of the Church inevitably involved baptismal theology, though the specific sacramental issues were constantly shifting. Some New England ministers, accustomed to thinking of baptismal doctrine in terms of the sealing of covenants or the conveying of sacramental grace, denied that the synod had tampered with theology. John Allin (1596–1671), the minister at Dedham, who approved the synodical decisions, insisted that "the Question is not, what state or right the Baptized are partakers of, as a consequent fruit of Baptism received? but, what is it that constitutes a person to be a fit subject to be Baptized?" [6] And insofar as the synod's defenders developed an explicit theological rationale, they turned first to the covenant motif. Church members could transmit the right of baptism to their children, according to Mitchell, the main architect of the "Result," even if they had not been baptized. The covenant conveyed the privilege, and the Church members were in that covenant before their baptism.[7]

Baptismal doctrine, then, did not determine the outcome of the 1662 synod, but the synod did influence sacramental thought. Despite Allin's disclaimers, the debates produced two important claims about the

Synods Booke," 1665, MSS, American Antiquarian Society, Worcester, Mass. There was some irony in Davenport's statement, since Chauncy was rumored to have written the third proposition. Chauncy probably interpreted it simply to mean that children were subject to Church discipline even though they were not actual, personal members. The synod decided that only Church members could be placed under the discipline of the Church.

6. John Allin, *Animadversions Upon the Antisynodalia Americana* (Cambridge, 1664), p. 21.

7. Mitchell, "Answer," in [Mather], *Defence* p. 39.

"fruit" of baptism which eventually figured in the redefinition of the relationship between baptism and particular visible churches and the flowering of a distinctive baptismal piety. Proponents of the "Result" argued, first, that baptism was a seal, proof, and guarantee of permanent, personal, and plenary membership in the visible Church; their critics denied this. And second, the proponents placed the baptismal promise at the center of their sacramental doctrine, while their antagonists pointed to baptismal obligations, which, they said, the unregenerate children of New England had failed to perform. In addition, the debate determined the extent to which typological arguments would continue to support sacramental doctrine; the dissenters undermined the typological foundations of Puritan thought, while the synodical theologians reaffirmed the sacramental import of the typological hermeneutic.

A Personal Seal

Were unregenerate adults, who had entered the Church as infants, permanent and personal members, even in the absence of a conversion experience? If so, claimed the synod's defenders, then they had every right to offer their own children for baptism. So crucial was this notion of "personal" membership that the ministers protected it with a virtual barricade of arguments: the unregenerate parents were alleged to be personal members because they were personally under discipline, personally within the covenant of grace, and personally responsible if they broke the covenant. But in tracing the development of baptismal doctrine, it is necessary to note that the synod added one specifically sacramental argument:

> They are personally baptized, or have had Baptism, the seal of membership, applied to their own persons: which being regularly done, is a divine testimony that they are in their own persons members of the Church.[8]

The synodical theologians did not claim that baptism created personal membership, for they still believed that infants of Church members were born into the Church by virtue of the covenant. But they did insist that the sacrament sealed, established, and guaranteed a permanent, distinctive, and personal membership in the visible Church.

Jonathan Mitchell declared that the dignity of the sacrament was in question. The successor to Thomas Shepard at Cambridge, Mitchell had become something of an authority on baptism following a series of discussions with Henry Dunster, his former Harvard tutor, who had

8. Walker, *Creeds and Platforms*, p. 331.

been President of the college since 1640. When Dunster rejected infant baptism, the Cambridge church dispatched Mitchell, still a young and inexperienced minister, to reclaim the erring educator. It was an unnerving responsibility, and Mitchell failed miserably; he himself began to have doubts about infant baptism. But he subsequently immersed himself in the Scriptures and emerged as a zealous paedobaptist, even turning back skillfully a wave of Baptist sympathy within his own congregation.[9] It was therefore as one of the colony's recognized experts on sacramental doctrine that Mitchell accused the dissenters of being far too "easie in letting go the Benefit of Baptism (or the Membership thereby Sealed)."

> Consider whether it be not . . . detracting from the sacredness of Baptism, when we make but a light matter of that Membership and Covenant that was sealed therein. . . . But the Solemn Covenant and Engagement between God and the Baptized, that was ratified in holy Baptism, wears away, and is a kinde of forgotten thing by [the dissenters from the synod].

Did God "make so light a matter of his holy Covenant and seal" as to take children into the Church, "seal up their taking in before Men and Angels," and then permit their sealed membership simply to lapse? Mitchell was not prepared to say that baptism entitled a child to all the privileges of Church membership; he would exclude the baptized from the Lord's Supper until they exhibited faith and repentance. But he thought it absurd to claim that "they who were Baptized in minority" became true and continuing Church members only after they "approved their Faith" as adults.[10]

Richard Mather (1598–1669), who authored the major apologia for the synod, accepted Mitchell's sacramental argument. Since the parents in question were "regularly baptized in their own persons," he asked, how could it "be avoided but that they are Church members in their own persons"? Unless the baptized were expelled for notorious sin, they possessed at least some of the privileges normally accruing to Church membership.[11]

Although John Allin believed that theological issues were peripheral, he in fact supplemented Mitchell's argument by recalling the Pauline doctrine of baptism as incorporation into the Body of Christ. Baptized children were actual and continuing members, he said, because "they are actually Baptized into the Body of Christ."

9. Cotton Mather, *Magnalia*, 4 : 166-85.
10. Mitchell, "Answer," in [Mather], *Defence*, pp. 31; 17-19.
11. [Richard Mather], *Defence*, p. 62.

> By Baptism, the Seal of the Covenant, we are all Baptized into
> one Body; and so as that there might be no schism in the Body:
> But how shall the Body be one, if some be Baptized into this
> Body, as actual and personal Members, some not actual nor per-
> sonal, some into a parental covenant, some personal? What a
> schism might this make? Some saying, I am not actually of the
> Body, though Baptized with the same Baptism, (and there is but
> one Baptism); others may say, I am of the Body personally, You
> are no actual Members of it? It seemeth the Apostle knew not
> these Distinctions: So Gal. 3. 27, 28. All are Baptized into Christ,
> and all are one in Christ.

To deny that baptized children were actual members would nullify
the covenant and rend the body of Christ.[12]

The most prolific of the dissenting brethren, however, John Davenport (1597–1670) of New Haven, was unimpressed by the sacramental
argument. A veteran of sacramental battles, he was as familiar as any
Puritan with the nuances of baptismal doctrine. After fleeing from
England to Amsterdam in 1633, Davenport had been compelled to defend himself against John Paget, the minister of the English church in
the city, who wanted him to baptize all infants offered to him. Davenport was willing only to accept infants whose parents would profess
their faith or demonstrate their membership in a respectable church,
though in 1633 respectability for Davenport encompassed even the lax
Church of England. After coming to New England in 1637, he adopted
a stricter practice; by 1662 he was adamant against any relaxation of
New England's standards.[13] In Davenport's view, a child's membership differed in "Essence" from that of his parents, despite the baptismal seal. Adults who took hold of the covenant through "personall
faith made visible," he said, could be considered as immediate and
personal members. Infants, however, and "children in Minority," were
only "mediate" members, whose standing in the Church was incomplete, temporary, and provisional until they experienced conversion.
Having never been complete members, the unregenerate parents possessed none of the privileges of Church membership. Their baptism
was no seal of personal membership, for they had been baptized only

12. Allin, *Animadversions*, pp. 30, 44.
13. Davenport's troubles at Amsterdam are recounted in John Davenport, *A Just
Complaint Against an Unjust Doer* (1634), to which I had access in a copy of the
original made in 1876 by H. M. Dexter. See also John Davenport, *An Apologeticall
Reply to a Booke Called An Answer to the unjust complaint of W. B.* (Rotterdam,
1636).

"by and for their parents covenanting for them." [14] The sacrament was more a gesture of parental faith than a seal of Church membership in the traditional Puritan sense.

After reading Mitchell's treatises, Davenport would still make only terminological concessions. Infants might be "personal" members, he said finally, but their membership was still only mediate, and baptism had nothing to do with either category. They were "mediate-personal members" even before being baptized; the sacrament did not seal an immediate Church membership, for it was administered to infants on the basis of a parental covenant. Davenport claimed that Mitchell's sacramental argument for personal membership had driven President Dunster into antipaedobaptism. To avoid additional defections, he suggested, the churches must acknowledge that unregenerate adults were not "Actual and Regular" members "whether they were Baptized in Infancy, or not." [15]

One delegate to the synod from Cambridge shared Davenport's intransigent uneasiness, though he was not free to voice his objections so openly: Charles Chauncy (1592–1672) had been too outspoken in previous years. At Plymouth, his first church in New England, Chauncy startled the faithful by announcing that there was only one way to baptize: "by dipping and putting the whole body under water." After his fellow ministers concluded against him, he moved to Scituate, Massachusetts, in 1641, where he promptly split that church over the same issue. There were rumors that he was a crypto-Baptist, but he denied them, and in 1654, after promising to keep his opinions about baptism to himself, he assumed the presidency of Harvard College. Perhaps because of his promise of silence, Chauncy's only printed rebuttal of the synod's conclusions appeared anonymously. He did, however, sign his name to the manuscript that, in a revised form, eventually became his *Antisynodalia Scripta Americana*. His arguments, which resembled Davenport's, probed the implications of the synodical decision. Were the "children of papists" true and personal members, he asked, since they too had received baptism? [16]

14. John Davenport, *Another Essay for the Investigation of the Truth* (Cambridge, 1663), pp. 35, 42. See also John Davenport, *New Haven Catechism, Originally Prepared for That Church, by John Davenport, Pastor, and William Hooke, Teacher,* (1659), in John Davenport and William Hooke, *Ancient Waymarks* (1853 edition), p. 51.

15. Davenport, "Third Essay," pp. 111, 127; 139.

16. [Charles Chauncy], *Anti-Synodalia Scripta Americana,* bound with *Propositions Concerning the Subject of Baptism and Consociation of Churches* (London, 1662), p. 37.

Chauncy did not pursue the question; it was Increase Mather (1639–1723) who foresaw the revolutionary implications of the claim that baptism established and guaranteed personal membership. He had returned from Ireland in 1661, a refugee from the Restoration, to join his father in Dorchester. Despite Richard Mather's sympathies, however, both Increase and his brother Eleazar opposed the synod's decision, and in 1663 Increase published a preface to Davenport's polemic, *Another Essay for the Investigation of Truth.* His preface suggested that the New England ministers were unknowingly on the verge of transforming the traditional relationship between baptism and the visible Church. What if a Muslim "Turk" were "baptized a Member of some Parish Church"? Was he a member of the Church of Christ or not? [17] In other words, was not the synod veering dangerously toward the view that the formality of external baptism rather than heartfelt assent to the covenant constituted entrance into the Church?

The synod was actually affirming the original New England conception of baptism as a seal to Church membership, while the opponents of the synod, by formally distinguishing two classes of membership, essentially and generically distinct, were minimizing the effect of the sacrament. For the dissenters baptism was no longer a seal and guarantee of the kind of membership that mattered. Davenport, Chauncy, and Mather were further downgrading even the ambivalent baptismal doctrine of the first generation. But Increase Mather did correctly recognize the new direction implicit in the synod's decisions, for the language about personal and plenary sealing at least opened the door for further change. The irony is that Increase Mather himself would be the man to push through the open doorway, though no one could have imagined that in 1662.

Promise or Obligation?

One additional doctrinal disagreement divided the ministers at the synod, though at first it seemed to involve merely a difference in emphasis. In defending the membership of the unregenerate baptized parents, the synodical theologians appealed to the baptismal promise. Since covenanted, baptized children were recipients of a divine promise, sealed by the sacrament, they said, it was presumptuous to question their status as members in the visible Church.

Being in covenant and baptized, they have Faith and Repentance indefinitely given to them in the Promise, and sealed up in Bap-

17. Increase Mather, "An Apologetical Preface," to Davenport, *Another Essay,* n. p.

tism, Deut. 30 : 6. which continues valid, and so a valid testimony
for them, while they do not reject it.[18]

Calvin had spoken of baptismal promises, as had most Puritans, so
the synod's defenders undoubtedly anticipated little opposition to
their doctrine.

Davenport, however, recalled the ambivalence of the earlier Puritan
tradition, noting especially John Cotton's insistence that baptism
sealed the grace of the covenant only for the elect. The baptism of
reprobate children, said Davenport, sealed only a right to "externall
means of grace," which they would inevitably neglect.

> To these, Faith and Repentance are not indefinitely given in the
> Promise, and sealed by outward Baptism; as neither was it given
> in the Promise, and sealed by outward Circumcision indefinitely
> to those [Jews of the Old Testament] who, when they became
> adult, brake the Covenant.

The Spirit, he said, was a "voluntary Agent, and therefore likened to
the wind which bloweth where it listeth," impervious to coercion by
covenants and covenant seals. Davenport thought that Cotton's subordination of baptism and the covenant to the doctrine of election was
absolutely necessary, not only to avoid the blasphemous diminution of
God's freedom, but also "to prevent that Opinion of Universal Bap-
tism-Grace." [19]

Davenport implied that the majority party held such an opinion,
but his implication was inaccurate, even though his opponents did
accent the baptismal promise. Davenport, however, wanted to place
the emphasis on the obligation signified by baptism: it bound "the
infant-seed of Confederates to various Gospel duties." [20] Those who
shirked their obligations had no right to appeal for special privileges.
He and his fellow anti-synodists would simply have removed from
the Church all unregenerate adults, despite the promises sealed by
their baptism, on the grounds that they had not fulfilled their required duties.[21] Increase Mather warned that loose talk about the seal-

18. Walker, *Creeds and Platforms*, p. 330.
19. Davenport, *Another Essay*, pp. 29–30; 6, 29.
20. Ibid., p. 43.
21. Charles Chauncy, Increase Mather, et. alia., "The judgement of the dissenting
brethren of the Synode concerning the resolution of the Questions propounded by
the Generall Court to the Rev. Elders and messengers of the Churches in this
Jurisdiction assembled at Boston by their authority," in "Copies of Documents bear-
ing upon the Synod of 1662," copied by David Pulsifer (1833), pp. 43–44. This is a
prior draft of *Antisynodalia Scripta Americana*. See *Antisynodalia*, pp. 36–37.

ing of promises was unwise: "It hath in it a natural tendency to the hardening of unregenerate creatures in this sinful natural condition, when Life is not onely Promised, but Sealed to them by the precious Blood of Jesus Christ." [22]

Mitchell denied that he taught baptismal regeneration, and he asserted that the synod's supporters were properly cautious when talking about the covenant promise and its seal. How could baptism harden anyone in New England, he asked, "when as men are told over and over, that onely outward advantages and dispensations are sealed to them in Baptism more absolutely . . . but the saving benefits of the Covenant (or Life Eternal) conditionally?" In other words, baptism was a seal to an external, conditional covenant, and there was "no certain, but only a probable" connection between membership in that covenant and salvation.[23] But Mitchell did not want to undervalue that probable connection. He pointed out that the encouragements and obligations of "Covenant-interest" had a tendency to "draw" the heart to God. Whereas Davenport had quoted Cotton to prove the unreliability of covenants and their seals, Mitchell cited Cotton to demonstrate that "conversion is to the Children of the Covenant a fruit of the Covenant," noting also that the experiences of many converts in New England had illustrated the efficacy of "the Lord's preventing Grace in his sealed Covenant." Baptism sealed "unto the party baptized, all the good of the Covenant to be in season communicated and enjoyed, from step to step, through the whole progress of Christianity." It was therefore the seal of a "Converting Grace-giving Covenant." [24] At the very least, John Allin added, one had to assume that the promise was still extended to the unregenerate second generation: "Yea are they not Baptized into Christ? Are not the Blood and Benefits of Christ Sealed up to them in Baptism? But our Brethren seem wholly to forget that, or to make nothing of it." [25]

Davenport remained unconvinced. The churches had been patient, he said, with the baptized infants of New England, but their failure to exhibit faith and repentance demonstrated their "violation of the covenant sealed to them by Baptisme in theyre Infancy." He hinted that his opponents were unable to face the hard truth that some of the baptized children of New England were likely candidates for damnation.

22. Increase Mather, "Apologeticall Preface," to Davenport, *Another Essay*, n. p.
23. Mitchell, "Answer," in Mather, *Defence*, p. 43.
24. Ibid., pp. 44–45. The citation from Cotton was a summary of an argument in Cotton, *Grounds*, pp. 28–29.
25. Allin, *Animadversions*, p. 58.

Though it is no pleasure for me to speak Contrary to the Synod, yet for the trueths sake I must declare that Faith and Repentance is not indefinitely given to such, for the present, which the Synod affirmeth. I shall add, that if indefinitely given, be equipollent in theyre meaning, to universally given, as usually that phrase is taken, then it is to be denied. For all that are in Covenant and Baptised, have not the grace of faith and Repentance given them in the promise, and sealed up in Baptisme. Reprobates may be in the outward Covenant and Baptized, yet Have not those gifts of grace given to them in the promise Deut. 30.6. But onely the Elect to whom it is given in theyre Regeneration.

Under a strong "obligation" to perform their baptismal duties, the children of the second generation had failed.[26] Mitchell and Allin, however, thought that the judgment of failure was premature; there was good reason to assume that their effectual calling was imminent.

Mitchell was distraught when one of his own children died without baptism: "as it is appointed to be a Confirming Sign, and as it is an Ordinance of Grace, so to be Deprived of it, is a great Frown, and a sad Intimation of the Lord's Anger." [27] He worried about the child's eternal state despite his theological conviction that baptism was not necessary for salvation. Obviously, his feelings about the sacrament were stronger than his doctrinal assertions. Both his doctrine and his piety, however, foreshadowed an increasing emphasis on the baptismal seal in New England preaching.

Typology and the Church

Soon after the synodical debate began, Mitchell charged that the dissenters sounded suspiciously like Baptists, which was true at least of Davenport and Chauncy. He added diplomatically that he was "not now speaking to Intentions or Persons, but to Arguments and Distinctions in themselves considered," but other proponents of the synod spoke with less diplomacy. John Allin said that the dissenting ministers exhibited a "great tendency" to move in a Baptist direction, and he implied that the despised Baptists of the colony were greatly encouraged by the anti-synodical arguments.[28]

Particularly shocking were the dissenters' occasional aspersions upon typological exegesis, the hermeneutic with which paedobaptists had

26. Davenport, "Third Essay," pp. 76, 96; 52.
27. Cotton Mather, *Ecclesiastes. The Life of the Reverend and Excellent Jonathan Mitchell* (Boston, 1697), p. 103.
28. Mitchell, "Answer," in [Mather], *Defence,* p. 6; Allin, *Animadversions,* p. 4.

withstood Baptist assaults for more than a century. Davenport still used typology whenever it suited his purposes, but he also questioned the analogy between baptism and circumcision:

> Circumcision was extended to all that were born in the house and bought with money, Gen. 17. 12, 13. But Baptism is limited to believing Jews and their children, and to so many as the Lord our God shall call.[29]

Davenport held on to the covenant while distinguishing between various modes of covenantal administration: under Abraham the covenant was "administered by circumcision to all that were of his house, and to their seed," but under Christ the method of administration differed. Christian churches were "in a more spiritual and gracious frame and state" than the communities of Israel, so they were not to be "continued and propagated" in the same way.[30] But what then was the new Christian mode of propagation? If a conversion experience was prerequisite, then infants were obviously excluded from membership, and the rationale for infant baptism became problematic. Davenport was a paedobaptist, but he seemed willing to discard the traditional foundations of Puritan baptismal thought and to begin anew.

Where Davenport was suggestive and tentative, though, Chauncy was blunt and explicit: the covenant of grace, he said, was simply "not the main ground of Baptism, as is asserted." That covenant belonged to the elect, whom the Church could never identify. The local Church covenant, rather, was the "ground of the Dispensation of the Seals," and it required "mutual consent of them that are admitted into communion to walk with God according to the Gospel." Chauncy's distinctions seemed to leave no provision for infants incapable of consent, because he also disallowed the typological warrants that had traditionally justified their inclusion in the Church. To build upon "the largenesse of Jewish practice," he said, was sinful in a time of reformation and purity. When the synodical theologians claimed that baptism, like circumcision, must be "continued on through posterity," Chauncy replied that the "similitude" between the two rites was inexact and misleading. Even if the sacrament had been implicitly instituted in the rite of circumcision, he said, the typological analogy was worthless without an additional "explicit and plain" command for baptism.[31] Baptists had been saying the same things for decades.

29. Davenport, *Another Essay*, p. 4. See also Davenport, "Third Essay," p. 68.
30. Davenport, *Another Essay*, pp. 22–27; see also *Antisynodalia*, p. 10.
31. [Chauncy], *Antisynodlia*, pp. 14, 17, 32–34.

They must have rejoiced as sacramental typology crumbled away under the impact of Chauncy's hostile probing.

Only Increase Mather would oppose the synodical theologians on their own typological grounds. Mather believed that the Old Testament could be adduced as evidence against the Half-Way Covenant, because even the Jews had restricted circumcision to infants whose parents were qualified to receive the Passover. He felt that the types themselves condemned the synod.[32] Mather's peculiarity foreshadowed his eventual desertion from the ranks of the dissenters; his acceptance of typology, however, did not protect him in 1662 from whispered rumors and open charges of Baptist sympathies.

The dissenters were aware that their doctrine was "laden with reproaches of Antichristianism and Anabaptism," and though they denied the allegations, there was some substance to the charges about their Baptist propensities. Not only did they employ arguments used by Baptists, but their conclusions also moved them closer to Baptist theory and practice. The Half-Way Covenant permitted children of the unregenerate to be baptized; the Baptists baptized no children; the dissenting brethren stood somewhere between. They insisted that "where there is no federal holiness, there is no right to Baptism; but where neither parent is a believer, there is no covenant holiness." [33] They seemed to be saying that baptism was a sign of obligation rather than a seal to a divine promise, while advocating at the same time a crypto–Baptist view of the Church as a voluntary organization of faithful believers. Their acceptance of infant baptism ran counter to sectarian patterns, but as the debate demonstrated, the dissenters did not actually consider children to be "essential" members of the Church. They expected, rather, that baptized children would actually join the Church by a further act of faith and repentance. The only alternative, Davenport said, was for the Church "to be Transmitted from Generation to Generation," which would corrupt the houschold of faith.[34] Christian churches were "spiritual" bodies, not institutions designed to dispense grace to unregenerate members, as the synodical theologians were implying.[35] Davenport and Chauncy especially stood in 1662 on the brink of accepting Baptist ecclesiology, though without the consistency that would have eliminated infant baptism altogether.

32. Mather, "Apologeticall Preface," to Davenport, *Another Essay*, n. p. See Robert Middlekauff, *The Mathers: Three Generations of Puritan Intellectuals 1596–1728* (New York, 1971), p. 121.
33. [Chauncy], *Antisynodalia*, p. 28.
34. Davenport, "Third Essay," p. 327.
35. Davenport, *Another Essay*, pp. 22–27; *Antisynodalia*, p. 10.

Many opponents of the Half-Way Covenant did in fact display remarkable tolerance for Baptists in the years following the synod. In 1669 Davenport accepted an invitation to become the minister of the First Church in Boston, prompting the formation of the Third Church by laymen disgruntled with their new pastor. According to Cotton Mather, First Church then became a bastion of anti-synodical sentiment, while the new congregation came to symbolize acceptance of the Half-Way Covenant.[36] Even the civil magistrates and deputies took sides. It is therefore revealing that magistrates favoring Davenport's church, along with several prominent First Church laymen, became known for their refusal to join in any crusade against Boston's struggling Baptist fellowship. Baptists themselves reported that the "old church in Boston" offered them abundant support, "as if it had been for their best friends in the world." [37] Some anti-synodists, struggling to retain the ecclesiastical purity that they believed the synod had sacrificed, apparently tempered their hostility toward their traditional Baptist antagonists, who at least displayed a passion for purity, even if they were misguided about infant baptism.[38] The congregational traditionalists feared that the next logical steps for the synodical theologians would be to make baptism itself the entrance to the Church and eventually to baptize unregenerate adults in hopes that they, too, might receive divine grace. It was not long until those steps were taken.

Transformations

Baptism and Church Membership

In 1671 Increase Mather changed his mind about the synod and in the process decided that he and his brethren of "Antisynodalian persuasion" had indeed veered too far in a Baptist direction: "This I find that there is hardly an Argument produced against such Inlargement, as is by the Synod asserted, but what the Antipaedo-Baptists make use of to serve their turn." He found that John Norton had demonstrated the distinction between mediate and immediate members to be specious eight years before the Synod met.[39] Mather subse-

36. Cotton Mather, *Magnalia,* 5 : 82.
37. In Isaac Backus, *A History of New England with Particular Reference to the Denomination of Christians called Baptists,* ed. David Weston (Newton, Mass., 1871), 1 : 316.
38. E. Brooks Holifield, "On Toleration in Massachusetts," *Church History* 38 (June, 1969) : 188–200.
39. Increase Mather, *The First Principles of New England, Concerning the Sub-*

quently assumed a leading position in a collective reevaluation of the sacrament, redefining the relationships between baptism and the Church and vociferously supporting a movement to vitalize New England piety through exhortation and instruction focused on baptism. His efforts helped to make sacramental piety a prominent part of colonial religious life.

In a defense of the synod published in 1675, Mather completely revised the traditional New England conception of baptism by suggesting that the sacrament of initiation was logically prior to the Church covenant. He openly contradicted the conclusions of his father, who had argued in 1653 that converted Indians were to be formed into a particular covenanted church before being baptized. Disregarding the earlier consensus, Increase decided by 1675 that baptism was "precedanous to the Institution of particular Gospel Churches," and he criticized the venerable congregational precept that membership in a particular church had to precede the sacrament.

> Suppose a Company of Indians should be Converted to the Faith of Christ; according to this notion, they must first of all be formed into an Instituted Church and then baptized, so here is an Instituted Church, and not one baptized member in the Church. A thing never known in Apostolical dayes.

Mather now emphasized a distinction between "the Church visible" and any "particular Church strictly taken." [40] Christians willing to profess their faith and to pursue the conditions of the covenant of grace were members of the "visible church" and so possessed a right to baptism both for themselves and for their children, even before they became members of particular covenanted churches. That was an important reversal of previous New England doctrine and biblical interpretation. In 1648, John Norton had criticized exegetes who said that Cornelius, Lydia, and Paul's jailer were baptized before becoming members of particular churches (Acts 10 : 48; 16 : 15, 33); Increase Mather now criticized the suggestion that they were members before baptism.[41]

Though Mather was defending the synod, he was also moving beyond it. Although firmly committed to the synod's decisions, Jonathan

---

ject of Baptisme and the Communion of Churches (Cambridge, 1675), "To the Reader," pp. 4–20.

40. Increase Mather, *A Discourse Concerning the Subject of Baptism Wherein the present Controversies, that are agitated in the New English Churches are from Scripture and Reason modestly enquired into* (Cambridge, 1675), pp. 50; 47.

41. Norton, *Answer*, p. 59; Increase Mather, *Discourse Concerning Baptism*, pp. 48–49.

Mitchell was baffled by the speculation about baptism and the visible Church: "Whether the Persons described in the Fifth Proposition of the Synod should be Baptized as a Catholick, or in a Particular Church-State, is another Question. And I confess my self not altogether so peremptory in this latter as in" the conviction that they should be baptized.[42]

By 1692, though, Cotton Mather (1663–1728) was talking as though Increase's doctrine had always been conventional New England orthodoxy. Cotton had been with his father at North Church, first as assistant and than as pastor, since 1681, and he was never heard publicly opposing any doctrine that Increase Mather espoused. Accordingly he told John Richards, an influential merchant who resisted innovation in the church, that baptism was "an ordinance that belongs to Visible Christians, or those that are visibly of the Catholic Church, before and in order to, their joining to a particular." [43] This was one of the few controversial sacramental issues that did not divide the Mathers from their troublesome neighbor to the west, Solomon Stoddard of Northampton, who did as much as any man to propagate the new doctrine.[44]

The revamping of doctrine was accompanied, however, by a change in baptismal practice, which distressed Increase Mather. In Connecticut at least three ministers began even before 1671 to baptize unregenerate adults who had never been related to the Church through a parental covenant. That was not what Mather had in mind, for he believed in 1675 that the Old Testament types forbade the baptism of merely orthodox believers. A "justifying faith" was requisite for admission to baptism, he said, not a purely intellectual "historical faith." [45] But by 1677 at least one church in Massachusetts, at Charlestown, was baptizing unconverted adults with no prior church connection, and in subsequent years other churches followed Charlestown's lead.[46]

By 1691 even the Mathers, possessed by ecumenical enthusiasm, offered their support to a proposed union of English Presbyterians and Congregationalists that required a tolerant acquiescence in diverse

42. Quoted in Cotton Mather, *Magnalia*, 4 : 177.
43. Kenneth Silverman, ed., *Selected Letters of Cotton Mather* (Baton Rouge, 1971), pp. 46–50.
44. Solomon Stoddard, *The Doctrine of Instituted Churches Explained and Proved from the Word of God* (London, 1700), p. 18.
45. Increase Mather, *Discourse Concerning Baptism*, pp. 19–21. See Middlekauff, *The Mathers*, p. 124.
46. Robert Gardiner Pope, *The Half-Way Covenant: Church Membership in Puritan New England* (Princeton, 1969), pp. 96–128, 247–52.

standards of admission to baptism.[47] From Cotton Mather's viewpoint, the move toward a broader policy was timely, for when the witches invaded Boston in 1692, Mather told John Richards that an expanded application of Christian baptism was needful as a defense against the devils who had baptized so many miserable souls into witchcraft: "I would mark as many as I should, that the destroying angels may have less claim unto them." Mather wanted to offer the sacrament of initiation unto all orthodox and virtuous believers who would publicly covenant to surrender themselves to Christ and to seek the further grace that entitled them to the Lord's Supper. He intimated that North Church was losing scores of potential members by reason of its continued rigidity.[48] Within the next seven years other New England preachers came to share Cotton Mather's new openness. In 1699 a convocation of ministers at Cambridge sanctioned the comprehensive admission policy.

> That such as do profess the True Christian Religion, and do not by any Fundamental Error in Doctrine, or by a Scandalous Conversation contradict that Profession; They and their Children, do belong unto the Visible Church and have right unto Baptism; Whether they be Joyned in Fellowship, with a Particular Church, or not.[49]

Absent was any mention of the distinction between historical faith and justifying faith. The churches required of baptismal candidates nothing more than orthodox doctrine and pious behavior.

In 1699 a small group of Boston merchants and educators formed a new church on Brattle Street in Boston and advertised in a provocative manifesto their willingness to administer baptism to all who would "profess their Faith in Christ and Obedience to him, and to the children of such." [50] Increase Mather immediately denied that all professed Christians were entitled to baptism, but his rationale revealed the transition that had occurred. Taken literally, he said, the Brattle Street *Manifesto* might justify the baptism of heretics who professed a faith in Christ.[51] Instead of reviving the distinction between historical and justifying faith, Mather spoke of orthodox as opposed to heretical belief. He also deplored the absence of any provision for public cov-

---

47. Walker *Creeds and Platforms*, p. 457.
48. Silverman, *Selected Letters*, pp. 46–50.
49. Cotton Mather, *Thirty Important Cases Resolved* (Boston, 1699), p. 70.
50. *A Manifesto or Declaration, Set forth by the Undertakers of the New Church Now Erected in Boston in New England, November 17, 1699* (Boston, 1699), p. 2.
51. Increase Mather, *The Order of the Gospel, Professed and Practised by the Churches of Christ in New England* (Boston, 1700), p. 8.

enanting by Brattle Street baptismal candidates, as did other New England ministers, but apart from his fondness for covenants Increase Mather's admission requirements did not greatly differ from those of the new church, which presumably did not intend to baptize heretics. The Brattle Street minister, Benjamin Colman, simply replied that church covenants were without scriptural foundation, and that he would continue to baptize "any child" offered by "any professed Christian." [52] Solomon Stoddard of Northampton, responding to Mather's criticism of the Brattle Street church, subsequently proclaimed that he would baptize the children of wicked, excommunicated church members—a proclamation that indicated anew the broadening of New England standards for admission.[53]

By 1726 almost anyone could obtain baptism in New England. In that year Cotton Mather rebutted the insinuation that the streets of the colony were crowded with unbaptized victims of the churches' unrealistic and rigid requirements. It was, he said, "well known there is not one Person in all the country free from a scandalous and notorious disqualifying Ignorance and Impiety, but what may repair to some Hundred Ministers in these Colonies and be Baptised." [54]

Baptismal Piety

The widespread acceptance of the Half-Way Covenant by the end of the century, and the tendency for many churches to move even beyond the synod's recommendations, helped produce a change in New England piety. Faced with growing numbers of baptized but unregenerate "half-way" members, the ministers sensed the potential of a peculiarly Reformed sacramental evangelism. They came to believe that hortatory addresses on baptismal obligations and promises would maintain the vitality of their churches. There were still confrontations with Baptists, and after 1688 with the Quaker theologian George Keith, but baptism became for most ministers an object more of devotion than of disputation. In their pulpits, the careful technical distinctions of earlier controversies often evaporated, though the absence of precision did not impede, but probably facilitated, the spread of "baptismal meditation."

52. *Manifesto,* p. 2; [Benjamin Colman, et. al.], *Gospel Order Revived* ([New York], 1700); John Higginson and Nicholas Noyes, "Letter to the Undertakers of the Brattle Street Church," December 30, 1699, in Samuel Lothrop, *A History of the Church in Brattle Street* (Boston, 1851), pp. 30–31.
53. Stoddard, *Doctrine of Instituted Churches,* p. 18.
54. Cotton Mather, *Ratio Disciplinae Fratrum Nov Anglorum. A Faithful Account of the Discipline Professed and Practised in the Churches of New-England* (Boston, 1726), p. 80.

Samuel Willard (1640–1707), the minister of the Old South Church in Boston from 1676 to 1707, perceived and stated the basic intellectual premise of the baptismal sermons: God, said Willard, had been "pleased to make use of sensible things, for the furtherance of Spiritual Good to the Children of Men." [55] Baptismal evangelism was a practical corollary of the doctrine of divine accommodation: God's essence was pure mystery but his purposes were discernible, if only in part, through the written Word and the visible sacraments. Hence a sacramental rite became one of the mainstays of New England piety, not because of any innovative doctrines of baptismal grace but rather through sermonic reflection on the symbolic meaning of the "visible gospel."

The new emphasis was embodied in two distinct but overlapping motifs, the first being a demand for sacramental obedience. In 1675 James Fitch, citing earlier precedents, demanded from the children of his Norwich congregation a pledge to fulfill their baptismal duties by "owning the covenant," or pledging themselves to strive after faithfulness.[56] The practice of mass covenant renewal, which received official sanction in a 1679 Reforming Synod in Boston, fostered baptismal piety, though some congregational covenants made no specific mention of baptismal obligations. More directly sacramental were the appeals directed to the baptized as individuals. "And as to the Young generation," intoned Samuel Danforth of Taunton, "Let us Encourage them to renew their Baptismal Covenant." [57] Most New England ministers took such advice to heart, proclaiming in the manner of Peter Thacher at Weymouth that "Baptized persons when grown to years, should know it to be their duty and interest to die to sin and to live to Righteousness." [58]

During the 1670's Increase Mather began to insert into his sermons at North Church numerous messages to the baptized, reminding them of their sacred obligations to renounce sin, Satan, and the world. To some children, he said, the sacrament would become a "Sign and Seal" of salvation, but to those who dared break their baptismal covenant, Mather predicted nothing but woe.[59] Similar exhortations pervaded

---

55. Samuel Willard, *A Compleat Body of Divinity in Two Hundred and Fifty Expository Lectures on the Assembly's Shorter Catechism* (Boston, 1726), p. 841.

56. Pope, *Half-Way Covenant*, p. 241. See also Perry Miller, *The New England Mind: From Colony to Province* (Boston, 1961), p. 116.

57. Samuel Danforth, *Piety Encouraged, Brief Notes of a Discourse Delivered unto the People of Taunton* (Boston, 1705), p. 17.

58. Peter Thacher, *Unbelief Detected and Condemned; and the Long Continuance of Many therein, in Immanuels Land, Lamented* (Boston, 1708), p. 35.

59. Increase Mather, *A Plain Discourse, Shewing who shall, and who shall not, Enter into the Kingdom of heaven, and How far Men may go and yet fall short of*

New England sermons, though not in sufficient quantity to satisfy Cotton Mather.[60] The dawning of the eighteenth century found him instructing and admonishing his colleagues lest they omit a properly timed word on the obligations of the baptized.

> By the too Epidemical Ignorance and Negligence of men, con-
> cerning their Baptismal Engagements, it is that Christianity is
> almost lost in the world. The Use that we should make of our
> Baptism, is a thing which if the Ministers of the Gospel would
> both Publickly and Privately, more insist upon it, it would be of
> marvellous Advantage unto Christianity.[61]

No one was quite so vivid as Cotton Mather, who delighted in elaborate comparisons between the "Waters of Baptism" and the "Rivers of
Brimstone" awaiting "Baptised Rebels." [62] Mather promoted the baptismal devotion in publications ranging from his *Work Upon the Ark*
(1689), which illustrated the continuing relationship between sacramental thought and typological exegesis, to *Baptismal Piety* (1727), in
which he related how baptism engaged men to live and act as though
they were united to Christ.[63] All baptized Christians, he said, were likewise obliged to resist temptations, repent of sin, believe in God, be-
have properly, and consent to the Lord.[64] Mather was not demanding
that the children of New England create their own experiences of
conversion; he was, rather, asking them to live as though God had
converted them, in hopes that the regenerate might thereby be granted
an awareness of their gracious state.[65] Though his colleagues lacked

---

Heaven, After their seeming to be Converted and Religious (Boston, 1713), pp. 45–46;
Increase Mather, *Pray for the Rising Generation* (Boston, 1679), p. 22.

60. See, as several examples among many, *Records of the First Church at Dorchester in New England, 1636–74*, transcribed by C. H. Pope (Boston, 1891), pp. 17–18;
Joseph Belcher, *The Worst Enemy Conquered* (Boston, 1698), p. 22; Benjamin Colman, *Some of the Glories of our Lord and Saviour Jesus Christ, Exhibited in
Twenty Sacramental Discourses* (London, 1728), p. 262; Benjamin Colman, *Two Sermons Preached at Boston, March 5, 1723* (Boston, 1723), p. 15; William Cooper,
"God's Concern for a Godly Seed," in Colman, *Two Sermons Preached at Boston*,
p. 36; Cotton Mather, *A Family Well-Ordered* (Boston, 1699), p. 13; Cotton Mather,
Fair Weather (Boston, 1692), p. 3; Joseph Sewall, *Desires that Joshua's Resolutions
may be Revived* (Boston, 1716), p. 67; Benjamin Wadsworth, *The Bonds of Baptism*
(Boston, 1717); Benjamin Wadsworth, *A Course of Sermons on Early Piety* (Boston,
1721), pp. 23–24. The citations could be multiplied.

61. Cotton Mather, *Cares About the Nurseries* (Boston, 1702), p. 62.

62. Cotton Mather, *The Duty of Children, Whose Parents have Pray'd for them*
(Boston, 1703), pp. 29–30. See also Cotton Mather, *Work Upon the Ark. Meditations
upon the Ark as a Type of the Church* (Boston, 1689), pp. 43 ff.

63. Cotton Mather, *Baptismal Piety* (Boston, 1727), p. 6.

64. Cotton Mather, *Cares About the Nurseries*, pp. 63 ff. See also Cotton Mather,
Baptismal Piety, pp. 14 ff.

65. See the discussion of Mather's evangelistic rhetoric in Middlekauff, *The
Mathers*, pp. 231–46.

his penchant for rhetorical flamboyance, they conveyed the same message. By the early eighteenth century it was not considered at all unusual when a ministerial association in the neighborhood of Hatfield called a special meeting simply to consider means of bringing the unregenerate to a sense of their baptismal obligations, prompting the Hatfield minister, William Williams, to deliver a vivid sermon about the "binding force" of the sacrament.[66]

It seemed at times as if John Davenport had impressed upon the ministers of New England his conviction that obligation was the heart of baptismal doctrine, but the sermons also contained a second prominent motif: baptism was a promise. Though Cotton Mather urged his auditors to be sensible of baptismal duties, he also wanted them to rejoice at the favorable "obsignations" that the sacrament made to them.

> Reckon it as a sign of your Interest in, and Union with the Lord Christ. . . . We may lay hold on Heaven it *self* by the help of this Raising Ordinance, if with it we give the complying and conforming Answer of a good Conscience, to all the proposals of the Gospel.[67]

Baptism was only as effective as the covenant that it sealed, but any accent on the power of the covenant became an oblique affirmation of the potency of its seal, and by 1678, some ministers were prepared to place full confidence in the power of the covenant to produce godly saints. Increase Mather explained that God had "cast the line of Election" so that it ran for the most part "through the loyns of godly parents." [68] Both the metaphor and the idea behind it were enthusiastically appropriated for New England pulpit theology. The children of the covenant, said Increase Mather, had a promise that they would be "blessed above other children." There was a "promise of converting grace to be bestowed on such children," and the collective experience of the colony confirmed that grace indeed fell most often upon "the Children that are sprung from Godly Parents." [69] Mather did not intend to impinge upon the freedom of God to elect whomever he pleased, and he acknowledged that a reprobate child oc-

66. William Williams, *The Obligations of Baptism and the Duty of Young Persons to Recognize them; or to take their Parents Covenant Engagements for them upon Themselves, etc.* (Boston, 1721), pp. 3, 20.

67. Cotton Mather, *Work Upon the Ark,* pp. 45–46.

68. Increase Mather, *Pray for the Rising Generation,* p. 12.

69. Increase Mather, *A Call from Heaven to the Present and Succeeding Generations* (Boston, 1679), pp. 8–9; Increase Mather, *The Duty of Parents to Pray for their Children* (Boston, 1703), p. 19; see also Edmund Morgan, *The Puritan Family* (New York, 1966), pp. 161 ff.

casionally issued from the loins of the godly. Divine grace was "Sovereign" and therefore "not engaged to any Particular Family." [70] Clearly, however, Mather was not beleaguered with Davenport's doubts about the efficacy of covenants—or of covenant seals.

Increase Mather gladly accepted the sacramental implications of his confidence in the covenant, and he urged that the children of New England take full advantage of their baptismal sealing: "why should you let your Baptism lye by you, as if it were of no use?" Children who had received the covenant seal had a special right of appeal: "Go to God in secret, and say, Lord thou hast promised to give a new heart to the children of thy Servants, and thy Covenant hath been sealed to me in my Baptism." [71] Cotton Mather added that the sacrament guaranteed to its recipient not only an offer of the gospel, but also "some striving of the Spirit." [72]

> Accordingly, There are very few Children of Godly Ancestors, but what have had the Baptism of the Lord, in his Name, administered unto them: And God by this Baptism, has Prae-ingaged these children for Himself: He marks them for His own Propriety; He binds them closer to Himself than others; Yea, He Assures them, that if they grow up, they shall have an Opportunity under the means of Grace, to make choice of Him for their God, and that His Holy Spirit shall Strive with them, till they impenitently and incurably Resist the Strivings. [73]

Baptism was a testimony of divine favor and for that reason a means of grace. If the baptized died as infants, they would be blessed: "They shall be none of them lost, as minute as they are." If they lived to adulthood, they would receive the tidings of Christ and the strivings of the Spirit, through which the elect among them would be saved. Thus would the "water of baptism" lift the serious Christian to such a fellowship with God "that one step more carries him into Heaven it self." The younger Mather denied that baptism was necessary for salvation, or that it effected regeneration, but he described it as an important step toward salvation. Like other New England ministers, he suggested that the sacrament sealed a conditional covenant, but also that it ratified a covenantal promise to send the Spirit, thereby establishing a probability that the conditions would be fulfilled. [74]

70. Increase Mather, "Advice to the Children of Godly Ancestors," in *A Course of Sermons on Early Piety* (Boston, 1721), p. 6.

71. Increase Mather, *Call from Heaven*, p. 31.

72. Cotton Mather, *Baptistes, Or a Conference About the Subject and Manner of Baptism* (Boston, 1705), p. 6.

73. Cotton Mather, *Duty of Children*, p. 28.

74. Cotton Mather, *Baptismal Piety*, pp. 36–37; idem, *Duty of Children*, p. 28; idem, *Work Upon the Ark*, pp. 43–44.

The covenantal terminology easily merged with traditional Reformed definitions of baptism as an "instrument." By virtue of the promise and the operation of the Spirit, baptism, according to Samuel Willard, was an "instrument of Conveyance." The instrumental efficacy was not physical, for there was no "natural Vertue" in the water itself, but rather moral, which meant that supernatural virtue accompanied the sacrament. Like earlier Reformed theologians, the ministers were actually utilizing a notion developed by the medieval theologian Duns Scotus: that the sacrament, by sealing a divine *pactio*, in some sense compelled the accompanying presence of grace, even though the symbols did not contain the grace. Willard believed that baptism "sacramentally" expunged the guilt and domination of sin by confirming God's promise to release the faithful from the sway of sin.[75]

But how was one to overcome the gap between corporeal symbols and spiritual grace? Samuel Willard knew that until that question received an answer the colony's baptismal piety would remain open to criticism from the "despisers" of the sacraments. He himself acknowledged that the physical elements, being "Corporeal things," had no power to confer grace, which was of a purely "spiritual nature." Yet he wanted to assert the instrumental efficacy of the "carnal Elements." Willard faced the issue openly, and his solution was perfectly consistent with Reformed theology: the arbitrary Divine Will could overcome the dichotomy. Sacraments were "arbitrary" signs, constituted solely by divine appointment. The mind could not construct a bridge between spirit and corporeality, but the "Sovereign Pleasure" of Christ could transform water into a medium for spirit. Willard finally embraced mystery, which was in fact the precondition of vital sacramental piety. The dualism remained, as Willard said, but the mystery of divine volition confounded "the Enthusiasts," who discarded the sacraments in order to serve God "in Spirit and in Truth." [76]

If God could arbitrarily establish sacraments, however, he could also impose limits to their efficacy, as every Puritan minister acknowledged. Therefore the Puritans never claimed that baptism conferred an ability to compel, or even to receive, the Spirit, but rather that it denoted God's intention normally to convey his Spirit upon the baptized. Sacramental language provided intimations of divine predictability, but Puritans always warned against presumption. The baptized reprobate received only the external washing, not the internal cleans-

75. Willard, *Compleat Body*, pp. 835, 850. See Reinhold Seeberg, *Textbook of the History of Doctrines*, trans. Charles Hay (Grand Rapids, Michigan, 1964). pp. 126–61.
76. Willard, *Compleat Body*, pp. 843–48.

ing from the guilt of sin. Puritans occasionally sounded Arminian, as when Cotton Mather alluded to the possibility of resisting the Spirit, but neither he nor any other significant New England theologian ever forgot that the means of grace were "effectual to Salvation" only for the elect.[77] The baptismal devotion remained securely within the boundaries of Reformed orthodoxy.

The Brattle Street Church, however, did propose one astounding innovation. Its minister supported a practice that supposedly had been banned forever in the orthodox churches of New England: private baptism. Without advancing any notions about the necessity of baptism for salvation, Benjamin Colman nevertheless decided that private baptism might be of some comfort to the dying.[78] Increase Mather was convinced that the practice would lead inevitably to the erroneous conclusion that baptism was necessary for salvation. The sacrament, he protested, was part of a public ministry, and it represented a public profession of discipleship.[79] But Solomon Stoddard, who seemed to take delight in hounding Mather at every step, announced promptly that there was nothing in the nature of the ordinance necessitating its public performance.[80] By 1718 words were translated into action, and New England actually witnessed a private baptism.

> A child, being at the point of death, the pastor [at Plymouth] was requested to call at the house and baptize it. This made some stir, as the first instance of this kind. He said, "I could never find in Scripture that baptism was limited to the Sabbath or public assembly." [81]

Apparently some New England Christians were willing to acknowledge that in some circumstances a sacrament need not be a visible gospel addressed to a faithful congregation, a notion which marked a drastic break with Puritan tradition.

As Increase Mather suspected, permissiveness about private baptism could indeed reflect unfamiliar doctrines of sacramental efficacy. Solomon Stoddard (1643–1729) is remembered mainly for his views on admission to the Lord's Supper, but his baptismal doctrine also disturbed some of his clerical neighbors, especially when he called baptism a "converting ordinance," through which God gave saving grace to some children "in their infancy." [82] When Stoddard summarized for

77. Ibid., p. 809.
78. *Gospel Order Revived*, pp. 17–18.
79. Increase Mather, *Order of the Gospel*, pp. 62–65.
80. Stoddard, *Instituted Churches*, p. 18.
81. Morton, *New England's Memorial*, p. 434.
82. Solomon Stoddard, *An Appeal to the Learned. Being a Vindication of the*

public appraisal the views of Cornelius Burges and Samuel Ward, Increase Mather envisioned a repetition of the English sacramentalist conflicts. Mather's alarm was unnecessary, for Stoddard did not accept Burges's idea that infant baptism conveyed a regenerating "seminal grace" conducive to eventual conversion. If this were true, Stoddard suggested, then the "actual conversion" of baptized infants should occur "in early days," and his Northampton church had never been blessed with a wave of juvenile conversions.[83] And whereas Ward had said that all baptized infants were justified, Stoddard wrote that only some infants received the grace of conversion through the sacrament. Stoddard's rhetoric was startling, however, since nobody in New England had ever called baptism a "Converting Ordinance," and it seemed to the Mathers' followers that Stoddard was promising too much: "We cannot understand the insinuation," they said, "That Baptism is a Converting Ordinance." [84]

Social Experience and Sensory Piety

Despite their doctrinal differences, however, both Stoddard's treatises and the Mathers' sermons exhibited one common characteristic: both were suited to a Church filled with birthright members rather than to a voluntary community of converted visible saints. The new baptismal piety was implicit in the decision of the 1662 synod to grant a continuing membership to baptized but unregenerate believers and their children. Even before 1662, New England ministers had responded to a disappointing rate of conversions by gradually accenting pastoral duties, especially the catechetical instruction of children. As churches accepted the synodical "Result," there was an increasing need for a type of discourse that could appeal directly to baptized halfway members, and the ministers naturally had recourse to traditional Reformed baptismal theology, with its language of promise and obligation. The Church became a locus of sacramental and pastoral nurture. In fact, some ministers repudiated traditional New England ecclesiology and

Right of Visible Saints to the Lords Supper, Though they be destitute of a Saving Work of God's Spirit on their Hearts (Boston, 1709), p. 48.

83. Solomon Stoddard, *The Inexcuseableness of Neglecting The Worship of God Under a Pretence of being in an Unconverted Condition* (Boston, 1708), p. 25; idem, *Appeal,* pp. 34 ff.; Increase Mather, *A Dissertation, Wherein the Strange Doctrine Lately Published in a Sermon, the Tendency of which, is, to Encourage Unsanctified Persons (while such) to Approach the Holy Table of the Lord, is Examined and Confuted* (Boston, 1708), p. 68. For Burges and Ward, see chapter three.

84. Anon., *An Appeal, of some of the Unlearned, both to the Learned and Un-Learned; Containing Some Queries on a Discourse Entitled, An Appeal to the Learned* (Boston, 1709), p. 6.

reaffirmed the unity and catholicity of the visible Church, of which a particular congregation now became simply one branch.[85] The broadening conception of the Church facilitated the growth of sacramental devotion.

The transition reflected a changing social order in the colonies. A growing cleavage between church and state in Massachusetts during the seventies created the need for renewed evangelical effort to ensure the continued authority of the churches in New England society. Sacramental evangelism was one means of perpetuating orderly ecclesiastical growth and vitality. At the same time, increasing contention within the churches produced disturbing challenges to ministerial prerogatives. Among the disaffected were pietistic laymen, distrustful of the Harvard educated ministers who seemed so attuned to the colonial social establishment. Some laymen preferred to hear the fervent sermons of lay exhorters, who advanced claims to charismatic inspiration. The clergy responded by redefining ordination as admission to an historical order that transcended the local church. A visible rite with quasi-sacramental associations thus became the basis of their authority. The ministers, in other words, began to value symbols of order that magnified their status. Since only ministers could dispense baptism and the Lord's Supper, sacramental worship became a silent indicator of clerical distinctiveness.[86]

Yet one cannot understand the surge of ministerial interest in baptismal devotion without also noting one additional intellectual development: the practice of spiritualizing the creatures. In imitation of their English counterparts, the colonial ministers transformed natural theology into a distinctive and popular technique of meditation. This piety of sensation assumed more or less explicit forms, ranging from Increase Mather's catalogues of illustrious providences and his inquiries into the hidden meaning of comets to Cotton Mather's detailed handbooks on "spiritualizing the most earthly objects." Cotton Mather believed that a fruitful heart could "make the whole Creation Fruitful, and fetch fine Lectures and Lessons from all the Creatures of God." [87] He had the support of his fellow ministers; in 1727 eleven prominent Boston divines recommended that every colonial Christian be taught to "spiritualize the common actions of life." [88]

85. Hall, The Faithful Shepherd, pp. 168, 225.
86. I am especially indebted to the interpretation of the changing social order by Hall, Faithful Shepherd, pp. 156–246.
87. Cotton Mather, Christianus Per Ignem (Boston, 1702), pp. 12, 146: Increase Mather, Kometographia, Or a Discourse Concerning Comets (Boston, 1683); idem, An Essay for the Recording of Illustrious Providences (Boston, 1684).
88. Cotton Mather, Agricola (Boston, 1727), "Preface." See the essays by Mason I.

The new meditation was of course no innovation of the colonial theologians, who were indebted not only to such English Puritans as John Flavel but also to older medieval and Reformed handbooks. Yet recent scientific thought seemed to arouse renewed interest in these older forms of piety. Increase Mather appealed to the authority of "mathematical instruments" and of learned men who had recently discovered new light on "things natural as well as divine," while Cotton gratefully acknowledged his debt to the fathers of English science, especially to Robert Boyle, who himself had written that the study of chemistry would yield a Christian "a whole book of meditations." [89] The scientists confirmed the ministers in the confidence that the visible and concrete material order was transparent to an invisible, spiritual realm. The ministers then assumed responsibility for teaching their parishioners how to incorporate visible objects into the activity of prayer and reflection.

The New Englanders perceived the relationship between spiritualizing the creatures and baptismal piety. In this connection, the form of their baptismal devotion was as revealing as its doctrinal content. As described from the New England pulpit, the sacrament was one visible spectacle among others capable of nourishing the meditative life. Cotton Mather taught that the practice of meditation encompassed "all the Ordinances, and all the Providences of God," which meant that the proper "Methods of Piety" could transform either baptism or a natural object into a "profitable Spectacle."

> To Piety, everything that we behold, may be and should be, a profitable Spectacle. But the Holy Baptism of our Lord, being His own institution, how hopefully may we endeavour to make that a very singularly profitable Spectacle and serviceable to the Ends of Piety.[90]

Just as the natural objects and the activities of daily life suggested "Numberless Lessons," so also the "Improvement of our Baptism" through pious meditation conveyed knowledge of the glorious Trinity, the wickedness of man, the mystery of rebirth, and the second coming of Christ.[91] Mather's *Christianus Per Ignem* (1702), a series of godly reflections on fire, was identical in form and method with sections of

Lowance, Jr., and Karl Keller in Sacvan Bercovitch, ed., *Typology and Early American Literature* (Amherst, Mass., 1972).

89. Increase Mather, *Kometographia,* p. 3; Cotton Mather, *Christianus Per Ignem,* p. 13. See Middlekauff, *The Mathers,* pp. 279–304, 399 n. 37.

90. Cotton Mather, *Baptismal Piety,* pp. 3, 5.

91. Cotton Mather, *Christianus Per Ignem,* p. 11; Cotton Mather, *Baptismal Piety,* pp. 7, 15–16.

his *Baptismal Piety,* which contained similar reflections on water.
He originally intended that his *Agricola,* a handbook of sensory piety,
be bound and sold with a sacramental meditation, though the project
was abandoned as impractical.[92] The Puritans did not believe that
nature was sacramental, for they understood a sacrament as an arbitrary divine institution, different from all other signs by virtue of
divine appointment. Not every sign was a sacrament, but every sacrament was a seal and sign. Any widespread religious interest in visible
signification therefore had sacramental implications.

There are hints that the laymen of New England were increasingly
receptive to the use of visible symbols in a religious context. Evidence
can still be found on the colony's tombstones, which after 1668 almost
invariably displayed a rich cluster of Christian symbols in vivid
contrast to the plain simplicity of earlier markers.[93] Certainly many
colonists were still uncomfortable with the symbolic; even Cotton
Mather had second thoughts about the piety of sensation.[94] But by the
early eighteenth century, New England religion was infused with a
new symbolic consciousness. A visible sacrament was the acknowledged
entrance to the local church; baptismal devotion, with its symbolic
associations, was a prominent mode of piety; the visible ceremony of
ordination established ministerial authority; and the spiritualizing of
the creatures transformed all of nature into an instrument of the
meditative life. In that intellectual atmosphere, sacramental piety
could and did flourish. New England was undergoing a sacramental
renaissance.

92. Cotton Mather, *Agricola,* "Appendix."
93. See discussion of New England symbolism in Ludwig, *Graven Images,* pp. 18–
52, 176–424.
94. Middlekauff, *The Mathers,* pp. 312–19.

7

THE SACRAMENTAL RENAISSANCE

In 1690 Cotton Mather, disturbed by the "Paucity" of sacramental manuals in New England, published a *Companion for Communicants,* a series of discourses on the nature and purpose of the Lord's Supper with instructions on preparing for "that Holy Ordinance." [1] The publication was a notable event, for it marked the first time that any sacramental meditation, in the true sense of the term, was printed on New England presses, which had been pouring forth religious treatises continuously since 1639. The book also portended a transition in the development of New England piety; it was one of many sacramental manuals to be printed in the colonies.

Sacramental meditations provide a singular insight into the changes in the New England religious sensibility during the late seventeenth and early eighteenth centuries. They reflect the emergence of an evangelistic sacramental piety, oriented around practical and pastoral concerns, intended to evoke conversions and to fill the churches with regenerate visible saints. They also reveal a remarkable preoccupation with the dilemmas of scrupulous Christians who failed to come to the sacrament for fear that they were unworthy. In fact, the meditations suggest that concern for the scrupulous as well as dismay over the indifferent established the immediate context of the celebrated Stoddardean controversy. Furthermore, the sacramental handbooks clarify the rational presuppositions of Puritan reflection on the problem of finitude and infinity, while also demonstrating that by the early eighteenth century sacramental piety was becoming a highly visible and significant part of New England religious life.

1. Cotton Mather, *A Companion for Communicants: Discourses on the Nature, the Design, and the Subject of the Lords Supper; with Devout Methods of Preparing for, And Approaching to that Blessed Ordinance* (Boston, 1690), n.p.

For over two decades Cotton Mather was the sole New England minister to publish a sacramental manual. In 1711, however, Ebenezer Pemberton, pastor of the Old South Church in Boston, arranged for the posthumous publication of Samuel Willard's *Some Brief Sacramental Meditations,* which Willard had written for his own edification while he was the teacher at Old South. Three years later, Cotton Mather published *A Monitor for Communicants,* which was eventually reprinted four times. In 1724 Benjamin Wadsworth, the new president of Harvard College, published *A Dialogue Between a Minister and his Neighbour, About the Lord's Supper,* and in 1728 Benjamin Colman, minister at the Brattle Street Church, published twenty of his sacramental discourses in London.[2]

The New England ministers were unable to satisfy the demand for meditations by themselves. In 1700 Bartholomew Green, the Boston printer, published *The Young Mans claim unto the Sacrament of the Lords Supper,* a popular manual on preparation by the English Presbyterian John Quick, and the work went through two editions. In the same year, Green printed a *Treatise Concerning the Lord's Supper,* written by another English Presbyterian, Thomas Doolittle. This work underwent three reprintings in New England within three decades. The Mathers reported that "Many Hundreds" of Doolittle's manuals were sold in the colonies.[3] Eight years later Green's press produced an edition of John Flavel's *Sacramental Meditations Upon divers Select Verses of Scripture.* Within four years this Presbyterian manual was also reprinted. In 1715 the Boston printers Fleet and Crump reissued the *Sacramental Exercises* of Jabez Earle, another English Presbyterian, who lived to see his book reprinted twice in New England. Then in 1716 and again in 1723, Fleet and Crump reprinted *The Communicants Companion* by Matthew Henry, and in 1718 James Franklin printed *A Familiar Guide to the Right and Profitable Receiving of the Lord's Supper,* by still another English nonconformist minister, Theophilus Dorrington.[4] During the same period books of sacramental meditations printed outside the colonies were also selling in New England bookstores. According to Increase Mather in 1708, "Many of the Lords People in New England" were reading treatises on the sacrament by Richard Vines, Jeremiah Dyke, Stephen Charnock, and

2. Benjamin Colman, *Some of the Glories of Our Lord and Saviour Jesus Christ, Exhibited in Twenty Sacramental Discourses* (London, 1728).
3. Increase and Cotton Mather, "A Defence of the Evangelical Churches," in Quick, *Young Mans claim,* p. 62.
4. For a discussion of the English manuals, see chapter four.

Daniel Rogers, all English Puritan divines, while the Mathers also possessed copies of meditations by the Englishmen John Reynolds and William Pemble.[5]

This was the milieu in which Edward Taylor, New England's finest Puritan poet, wrote his poetic meditations on the Lord's Supper in connection with sermons delivered in his Westfield parish.[6] This was also the setting in which the Boston layman Samuel Sewall tried to arrange for the sacrament to be so scheduled in the four Boston churches that the city could enjoy the "Great Priviledge and Honor" of having "the Lord's Supper administered in it every Lord's Day." [7] Neither the lay nor the clerical enthusiasm for the sacrament represented any marked change in New England's reverence for the Lord's Supper. Earlier in the seventeenth century, Thomas Shepard and Michael Wigglesworth had given evidence in their diaries of an intense sacramental devotion, as had the merchant Robert Keayne, who in 1653 bequeathed to his son as a "special gift" a manual that he esteemed "more precious than gold," having read through it, by his own testimony, hundreds of times.[8] As a young minister, Increase Mather had administered and received the sacrament with tears of joy and gratitude.[9] Never before, however, had the religious leaders of New England cultivated sacramental piety as in the waning years of the seventeenth century and the early decades of the eighteenth. The transition was reflected most clearly in the volumes printed on New England presses: in the first fifty-one years of printing, not one sacramental meditation issued forth; in the subsequent thirty-eight, New England printers produced twenty-one separate editions of manuals. Though partly a response to controversies over admission to the Lord's Supper, most of the manuals were products of piety, not of

5. Increase Mather, "An advertisement, Directed to the Communicants in the Churches of New England," in Doolittle, *Treatise Concerning the Lord's Supper*, n.p. Also see Julius H. Tuttle, "The Libraries of the Mathers" *Proceedings of the American Antiquarian Society*, n.s. 20 (1911) : 269–356.

6. Edward Taylor, *The Poems of Edward Taylor*, ed. Donald E. Stanford (New Haven, 1960); Edward Taylor, *Christographia*, ed. Norman Grabo (New Haven, 1962).

7. Samuel Sewall, *Diary of Samuel Sewall, MHSC*, 5th ser. 5–7 (Boston, 1878–1882) 6 : 138.

8. Bernard Bailyn, ed., *The Apologia of Robert Keayne: . . . The Self-Portrait of a Puritan Merchant* (New York, 1965), p. 28: Edmund S. Morgan, ed., *The Diary of Michael Wigglesworth, 1653–1657: The Conscience of a Puritan* (New York, 1965); Thomas Shepard, "Diary," New York Public Library, New York.

9. Michael G. Hall, ed., "The Autobiography of Increase Mather," *Proceedings of the American Antiquarian Society* 71 (Worcester, 1961) : 318.

polemic, and continued to appear long after controversy had diminished.[10]

Sacramental Evangelism

The sudden preoccupation with the Lord's Supper was prompted in part by the change in baptismal practice brought about by the synod of 1662. With their increasing acceptance of the Half-Way Covenant, the New England churches acquired a multitude of baptized members who were unable to testify to the experience of grace that would admit them to the Lord's Table. Because of their confidence in the baptismal promise and the efficacy of the covenant, most ministers assumed that an ever–broadening host of regenerate communicants would emerge from the ranks of these baptized halfway members and their children: "The Continuation of Churches," said Cotton Mather, "is ordinarily to depend on the Addition of Members out of the Families already incorporated thereinto." [11]

To the profound disappointment of the godly, however, the baptized seemed to be surprisingly resistant to the promise of grace sealed by their baptism, and being unregenerate, they failed to seek access to the Lord's Supper. Increase Mather complained in 1711 that there were "many thousands of Children born in New-England" who had never sought to receive the Lord's Supper.[12] His son Cotton lamented over the "Multitudes, and Quantities" of New Englanders who did "daily turn their Backs upon the Table of the Lord Jesus."

[When I see] whole Scores of People going away from the Table that has the Bread of Life upon it; then, The Fire Burns, my Heart is hot within me, and I cannot Suppress the just indication of my Sorrowes at so Unchristian a practice in those that will yet be called Christians. . . .[13]

In some towns, according to Solomon Stoddard, there were "scarce five or six" young people who would "attend the Lords Supper." [14]

The ministers reacted with an evangelistic sacramental piety. If the hearts of the baptized were unmoved by the benefits promised by

10. For example, John Quick's sacramental manual was still being reprinted in New England in 1728, without the polemical introduction by the Mathers that had accompanied its first colonial publication during days of controversy.
11. Cotton Mather, *Companion*, p. 79.
12. Increase Mather, *An Earnest Exhortation to the Children of New England, To Exalt the God of their Fathers* (Boston, 1711), p. 32.
13. Cotton Mather, *Companion*, p. 62.
14. Solomon Stoddard, *Three Sermons Lately Preached in Boston* (Boston, 1717), p. 107.

baptism, they could yet be broken and humbled with an appropriately ominous reminder about baptismal obligations and eucharistic duties. So the ministers began to publish and import sacramental manuals addressed to two different audiences: "Mainly to Communicants" already qualified for communion, but "not only to them." [15] Cotton Mather, for example, wrote his *Companion for Communicants* partly to assist faithful visible saints to prepare themselves for the Lord's Supper, but he was equally concerned to instruct, admonish, and exhort unregenerate baptized Christians in the hope that they might find the grace to approach the Lord's Table. "Every Christian," he said, had "the Duty of Self–Examination incumbent on him," and he advised the unregenerate as well as the converted to "set apart a time for due and deep thoughts" on their readiness for the sacrament.[16]

For those who were already communicants, the instructions of the manuals were precise, detailed, and rigorous. Cotton Mather told them that "there should be a Time, with us, which we may call, A Preparation for the Sacrament. And We should oftentimes count a Whole Day, but enough to be so laid out." During this period of introspection, the communicant was to examine the condition of his soul, the rectitude of his beliefs, and the quality of his relation to God and man. Mather's manual was primarily an exercise in spiritual cartography, guiding the communicant into the difficult terrain of the soul and describing the landmarks he should expect to find there. Was his knowledge of Christian doctrine competent and his belief orthodox? Did he yield a full intellectual assent and a cordial consent to the whole Word of God? Did he rely on Christ alone? Did he exalt Christ above all creatures? Did he desire above all things to be conformed to Christ and to look upon sin as the worst of all evils? Had he placed his chief happiness in acquaintance and fellowship with God? Did he desire the prosperity of his neighbors and endeavor to return good for evil? Was he convinced of his own sinfulness? Did his conviction produce contrition and did that in turn issue in confession? Did he possess a "sense of Truth," so that he could "Tast and See, that the Lord is Good?" Page after page, by the sheer force of repetition and the thoroughness of their demands, the meditations compelled the sincere communicant to purge himself of impurity and to approach the sacrament with humility and sanctity. In Mather's words:

15. Cotton Mather, *Companion*, p. 101. See also pp. 3–4, 62–80.
16. Ibid, pp. 78, 84. See also Cotton Mather, *An Essay to Excite and Assist Religious Approaches to the Table of the Lord Offered by an Assembly of New-English Pastors, unto their owne Flocke and unto all the Churches, in these American Colonies: A Monitor for Communicants*, 3rd ed. (Boston, 1715), pp. 9–11.

There ought to be a very Industrious and Conscientious Preparation in us, for that Fellowship with the Lord Jesus, which the Holy Spirit will then afford. . . . Thus would I say, You are to Sanctify yourselves, that you may come to the Sacrament. If Joseph judg'd it proper for him to cleanse and change himself, before his going in before the King of Egypt, how much more ought we to get our selves well fitted when we are going in unto the King of Heaven! [17]

The sacramental meditations differed in tone and emphasis. Cotton Mather's were intensely subjective and preoccupied with analyzing the dispositions of the soul, though also exploring the symbolic meaning of the eucharistic elements and ministerial gestures visible to the communicant. Samuel Willard displayed greater interest in the objective data of the Christian tradition, devoting most of his manual to reflections on such matters as the sufferings and obedience of Christ, the necessity of vicarious satisfaction for sin, the holiness and righteousness of God and his redeeming love, and the concurrence of the Persons of the Trinity in the work of salvation.[18] Willard, however, shared with Mather a zealous concern for worthy communion: "If I have obstructed my Spiritual frame, by carnal and vain thoughts or actions, and come rushing to this Ordinance without any fore-preparation for it, how shall I shew that due respect to Christ that I ought?" [19]

To the second audience that the manuals addressed—unregenerate absentees from the Lord's Table—the ministers posed a difficult dilemma. They directed the unregenerate to consider, first, that absence from the Lord's Supper was a positive sin. Baptism obliged a man to procure the grace sufficient for communion at the Lord's Supper. Cotton Mather reminded the absentees:

The baptised are under bonds, to do all things whatsoever the Lord Jesus has Commanded. And is not This one of Those Things? Do not think now to mock the God of Heaven, by something that Looks like a Renewal of your baptismal Covenant, without seeking the Supper of the Lord.[20]

Neglect of the Lord's Supper by the baptized was decried as a "continual breach of the vow made to God in Baptism." [21] Furthermore,

17. Cotton Mather, *Companion*, pp. 95; 95–123; 95–96.
18. Samuel Willard, *Several Brief Sacramental Meditations Preparatory for Communion at the Great Ordinance of the Supper* (Boston, 1711), pp. 90–169.
19. Ibid., p. 51. See also Benjamin Wadsworth, *A Dialogue Between a Minister and his Neighbour, About the Lord's Supper* (Boston, 1724), p. 46.
20. Cotton Mather, *Companion*, p. 68.
21. Wadsworth, *Dialogue*, p. 61.

those who absented themselves from the sacrament were guilty of more than breaking their baptismal covenant, however serious that might be. To abstain was blatantly to dishonor God, it was a "Scarlet, and a Crimson Sin." The ministers accused the absent of disobedience to the commands of Christ, disrespect toward the remembrance of a dying Friend and Savior, and disdain for the welfare of their neighbors, whom they were leading astray into a life of neglect and indifference. "In a word, Look and see, whether you can find any thing among the worst of men to Equalize, and so to Justify, the Iniquity of this Omission." [22]

At the same time that they decried abstention from the Lord's Supper, the ministers insisted that saving faith was a prerequisite for worthy communion. Unworthy, faithless communion was a dangerous presumption, Samuel Willard warned; it created "the risque . . . of Damnation."

> If I do not partake in this Ordinance, according to the nature, worth, dignity, and excellency of it, I shall so far bring myself under this guilt: and how many ways may I thus do? What watchfulness then, and what care had I need to use in this regard? If I am not in Christ by a true and living Faith, I must inevitably partake unworthily. This Ordinance is a Seal of the Covenant, and if I am not in Covenant with God, what right have I to the seal of it?

"There are those," he said, "to whom this Ordinance may become a Seal of their Damnation." [23] Willard's warning echoed through all the sacramental manuals read in New England. Cotton Mather insisted that only a man who possessed "the Graces of a Regenerate Christian" could partake without danger,[24] and he said in 1700 that he wrote his *Companion for Communicants* mainly to show "the Importance of probable Regeneration, as a Qualification for the Subjects of Sacraments." [25]

The ministers recognized that the repetition of such warnings created a dilemma.

> In fine, There is no escaping or avoiding of Great Sin without coming to the Table of the Lord. It is a sin to come unworthily to, but it is also a sin to stay unworthily from, that Blessed Ordinance. Neither of these things must be done; to choose either of

22. Cotton Mather, *Companion*, pp. 63–69.
23. Willard, *Meditations*, pp. 49–50; 41.
24. Cotton Mather, *Monitor*, pp. 17–18.
25. Cotton and Increase Mather, "A Defence of the Evangelical Churches," in ·Quick, *Young Man's Claim*, p. 55.

them, is, As if a Man should flee from a Lion, and a Bear should meet him.[26]

Precisely such a dilemma, they thought, was the perfect "inducement . . . to constrain sinners to conversion." The "main design" of the invitation to the Lord's Supper, said Edward Taylor, was to bring men "out of a state of sin and into a state of grace." [27]

The proliferation of manuals with such warnings after 1690 might seem to indicate a declining religion in late seventeenth-century New England. Certainly the colonies had their share of obtuse and indifferent sinners. Cotton Mather complained that absentees from the Lord's Table were often simply "not willing to be at the pains of Getting and Keeping good Terms between God and their own Souls." [28] Therefore it might appear that the manuals were essays in spiritual rehabilitation, attempts to attract and discipline the indifferent with the promise of a sacramental feast and to terrify the recalcitrant with reminders of the ominous consequences of shunning communion.

Though partly true, such an explanation for the sudden appearance and continued popularity of the manuals is insufficient, for the ministers made it quite clear that they wished to comfort and assure the scrupulously pious as much as to scold and threaten the impious. In fact, Cotton Mather acknowledged in his *Companion for Communicants* that "the most common and usual objection with which men Apologize for their not coming to the Lords Supper" was their fear that they were "not fit for the Supper of the Lord" and their belief that it was "a dangerous thing to come unworthily thereunto." [29] Fourteen years later, when he wrote his *Monitor for Communicants,* the situation was unchanged: "The common Apology made for this Omission is: I am afraid; I shall come unworthily; and by doing so, I shall Eat and Drink Judgment unto my self." The year Mather published his *Monitor,* an entire association of ministers meeting at Dedham unanimously endorsed the manual, precisely because they found it well adapted to bring to the Lord's Supper those "children of the Covenant" who were convinced of "their Unfitness and Unpreparedness for it." [30] Benjamin Wadsworth directed his *Dialogue Between a Minister and his Neighbour, About the Lord's Supper* to a similarly

26. Cotton Mather, *Companion* p. 78. See also Wadsworth, *Dialogue,* p. 57.
27. Edward Taylor, *Edward Taylor's Treatise Concerning the Lord's Supper,* ed. Norman Grabo (East Lansing, Michigan, 1966), p. 21.
28. Cotton Mather, *Companion,* p. 78.
29. Ibid., p. 76.
30. Cotton Mather, *Monitor,* pp. 5, 23.

conscientious audience. In his preface, Wadsworth observed that "one particular Objection often insisted on" by non-communicants in New England was "the danger of unworthy receiving, in not discerning the Lord's Body." Consequently, he had the "neighbour" of his dialogue express at the outset a fearfulness of unworthy communion: "because those who in this Ordinance eat and drink unworthily do eat and drink Damnation to themselves, I'm so startled and frighted thereby, that I dare not come." [31] A large part of the dialogue was devoted to assuaging such anxieties.

Having set out to purify sacramental communion, the Puritan ministers had succeeded almost too well. Cotton Mather told John Richards that many baptized, presumably sincere potential communicants in Boston's Second Church were inhibited by their "Doubts and Fears," [32] and in an appeal for closer relations with English Presbyterians in 1726, Mather acknowledged that such scrupulosity was common in the colony.

> According to this, that many of those who in their Adult Age are admitted unto Baptism, do not presently also come unto the Lord's Supper, it seems owing rather to their own chusing to stay till they are more satisfied in their Qualifications, than from the Churches refusing to admit them, should they desire it.[33]

Ministers who otherwise disagreed violently about sacramental issues testified with one voice to the prevalence of an extreme conscientiousness about the sacrament. Solomon Stoddard complained about men neglecting the Lord's Supper from "meekness of Conscience, fearing whether they have liberty to come." [34] Edward Taylor agreed that some persons abstained because of fear and doubt. While recognizing that other sinners lived in "total neglect" of the sacrament, he devoted his longest description of the New England absentee to the earnest Christian who was guilty of the sin of abstention.

> What a lamentation is this! Persons professing the gospel, religious in their lives, knowing in the concerns of religion and the things of God, orderly walkers in their conversation, attending God's worship public in assemblies, private in their families, secret in their closets, and filled with experiences of God treating of them in His Word, yet miserably neglecting this wedden supper.

31. Wadsworth, *Dialogue*, pp. ii, 2, 68.
32. Cotton Mather to John Richards, Dec. 14, 1692, in *MHSC*, 4th ser., 8 (1868) : 399 See also Silverman, ed., *Selected Letters of Cotton Mather*, pp. 46–50.
33. Cotton Mather, *Ratio Disciplinae*, p. 86.
34. Stoddard, *Three Sermons*, p. 108. See also Stoddard, *Inexcusableness*, p. 19.

Oh! what a lamentation is this! Certainly they fall under rebuke from our doctrine for their neglect.

Taylor testified that "several Congregational churches" had "admitted persons into a full state, that have desired the church's forbearance with them, as to the Lord's Supper till they have had more light as to their own fitness for it; and it hath been granted." [35]

The fearful introspection of the New England communicant emerged clearly in Samuel Sewall's diary. Sewall joined the church in 1677 with hopes that God would "communicate himself" in the sacrament, but he was "afraid that because I came to the ordinance without belief, that for the abuse of Christ, I might be stricken dead." Sewall considered fleeing from the meetinghouse. But he feared that such a course would leave him unfit for the next sacrament, and he "thought that it would be strange for me who was just then joined to the Church, to withdraw, wherefore I stayed." Even then, however, Sewall could "hardly sit down to the Lord's Table," so terror-stricken was he. The entire experience was painful; after Sewall convinced himself to receive the sacrament, his hopes that Christ would proffer "some glimpse of himself" were disappointed, and although he was not "stricken dead," he did not record his first communion with any sense of joy.[36] One purpose of the sacramental manuals was to comfort the Samuel Sewalls of New England.

The Problem of Admission and the Stoddardean Controversy

As a consequence of the mixture of indifference and extreme scrupulosity among potential New England communicants, the problem of admission became extremely complex, particularly in view of New England's traditional restriction of the Lord's Supper to converted visible saints. The complexity appeared most prominently in Cotton Mather's sacramental meditations, since he was more concerned to preserve the New England tradition than were Willard, Wadsworth, or Colman. Mather required of communicants a credible expression of saving faith, but for a defender of a rigorous tradition he also exhibited remarkable generosity to potential communicants whenever their search for grace seemed to prove disappointing. He told them, first, that a little earnest effort would probably bring them safely to the table: "Immediately set upon doing your parts for the preparing of your selves: Who knows, what God may work in you, both to Will

35. Taylor, *Treatise,* pp. 20, 24; 122, 186.
36. Sewall, *Diary,* 5 : 46–47.

and to Do?" Second, he suggested that anyone sufficiently motivated to follow his program of preparation possessed enough faith to benefit from communion. Any man who truly desired grace, he said, was qualified to receive the Lord's Supper, since "the Desires of Grace are Grace." Any man who sincerely grieved at his lack of faith could experience the benefits of communion: "You have what you Groan to have." And the sacrament, he said, required only a modicum of grace: "If there is but the least Grain of Grace in your Souls, God has made a glorious provision for it and the Holy Supper is part of that provision." [37] Mather's doctrine was not revolutionary. The celebrated ministers of New England's first generation—Thomas Hooker, John Cotton, Thomas Shepard—had never required perfect assurance of salvation from communicants. Those ministers, however, had not pleaded with the doubtful to advance a claim for the sacrament. Mather was pleading.

To judge that a minimum of grace was sufficient to ensure beneficial communion was not to address directly the question of admission. On that matter, the authors of the meditations appealed again to the scrupulous. Not only was the barest minimum of grace sufficient, but also the most ambiguous perception of that grace entitled a claimant to approach the Lord's Table. The Mathers believed that grace was discernible, but they required of communicants no infallible assurance of saving grace. Indeed, they required no assurance at all.[38] It was enough merely to hope: "If you have any preponderating Hopes that you have these Things, or cannot fairly and justly pronounce the Sentence, that you have them not; you may and ought to come." [39] There was no need to be "fully Sure of Sincerity." [40] In fact, a suitable communicant might entertain "many Fears" about the genuineness of his faith; Cotton Mather urged the doubtful and wary to "Run some Hazard and Venture, out of Obedience to the Lord Jesus Christ." At Second Church in Boston, Mather required of communicants only a profession of faith, showing their knowledge and belief, and a statement of "hope," oral or written, that the "Grace of God" had quickened their souls.[41]

While holding to the formal requirements established by the first generation, Mather tried to relax them just enough to attract poten-

37. Cotton Mather, *Companion*, pp. 29; 78, 130–1.
38. Ibid., p. 31. See also Increase and Cotton Mather, "A Defence of the Evangelical Churches," in Quick, *Young Man's Claim*, p. 53.
39. Cotton Mather, *Monitor*, p. 17. See also Increase Mather, *Dissertation*, p. 84; and Taylor, *Treatise*, p. 121.
40. Cotton Mather, *Monitor*, p. 6.
41. Cotton Mather, *Companion*, pp. 132; 76.

tial communicants who feared the consequences of unworthy reception. He noted with approval the generosity with which the New England churches evaluated communicants:

> Whatever might seem too strict and hard in the demands of these Churches formerly, is now generally Relaxed and Abated; the Churches generally require no more at the Admission of any to their communion, than any Godly Man would be willing to come up unto.[42]

For Mather, the sacrament was a promise and a demand directed to all baptized adults, an occasion to convert the sinful and to convince the wavering souls that their rightful place was within the community of the redeemed.

This attempt to combine rigor and generosity in a rejuvenated sacramental piety formed the immediate background of the celebrated controversy that erupted following a 1677 sermon by Solomon Stoddard in Northampton. In that year, Stoddard issued from his pulpit a decree against the prevailing sacramental piety; he denied that the churches should—or even that they could—limit admission to the regenerate. Some of his fellow ministers decided immediately that Stoddard was an apostle of laxity. Increase Mather protested against the "teachers found in our Israel, that have espoused loose, large Principles here, deigning to bring all persons to the Lords Supper," and in 1679 Stoddard had to sit quietly while Edward Taylor attacked his ideas during the organizing ceremony at Taylor's Westfield church.[43] There was a measure of vindication for Stoddard at a 1679 reforming synod in Boston, when he convinced the delegates to omit from the Confession of Faith any requirement that candidates for communion offer a "relation" of the experience of saving grace.[44] Despite Increase Mather's objections, the synod decided that communicants were to make only a personal and public profession of faith and repentance. The ambiguity of the phrase permitted Mather to claim a victory, but Stoddard professed himself satisfied, suggested that Mather was knowingly misrepresenting the synod's actions, and went on "strenuously promoting" his views at Northampton.[45] Though he swayed the synod-

42. Ibid., p. 75.

43. Increase Mather, *A Discourse Concerning the Danger of Apostasy* (Boston, 1679), p. 84; Edward Taylor, "A Particular Church is God's House," MSS, Boston Public Library, pp. 158, 38–39. See the discussion in Norman Grabo, "Edward Taylor on the Lord's Supper," *Boston Public Library Quarterly* 12 (1960) : 22–36.

44. Stoddard, *Appeal*, pp. 93–94. See also Walker, *Creeds and Platforms*, p. 280.

45. John Russell to Increase Mather, March 28, 1681, *MHSC*, 4th ser., 8 (1868) : 83–84.

ical delegates, however, Stoddard could not escape his reputation as an apologist for lukewarm religion. In 1688 Taylor warned him in a brotherly letter that God's faithful would in subsequent years "date the beginning of New Englands Apostasy in Mr. Stoddards motions." [46]

By 1690, Taylor was complaining that Stoddard had convinced "a major part" of his congregation to open the Lord's Supper to the unregenerate.[47] Cotton Mather decided in that year that the situation was sufficiently serious to warrant publication of his *Companion for Communicants,* which was a defense of New England tradition as well as an aid to eucharistic devotion. In 1693 Taylor added to the anti-Stoddardean movement eight long sermons containing an overwhelming variety of logical refutations and scriptural interpretations, all aimed directly or indirectly at Stoddard. But the Mathers emerged as the leaders of the crusade. Cotton used his 1697 biography of Jonathan Mitchell to demonstrate Stoddard's apostasy from revered ideals. In 1700 Increase published *The Order of the Gospel,* a paean to the New England Way that appeared immediately before Stoddard's first extended defense of his practice, *The Doctrine of Instituted Churches,* and, as the Mathers saw it, "anticipated" Stoddard's book "with an Answer." The same year, the Mathers arranged for the publication in New England of John Quick's popular sacramental meditation, *The Young Mans claim unto the Sacrament of the Lord's Supper,* and lest anyone overlook Quick's agreement with their own position, they added a fifty-nine page preface, which revealed, among other things, that Stoddard had dared to publish his doctrine in the face of their warning "that if it came abroad we would as Publicly Animadvert it." [48]

The Mathers carried out the threat. Increase denounced Stoddard; Cotton challenged him to public debate and traveled to Salem and Ipswich to procure the aid of some of the "many elderly" patriarchs of New England's intensely patriarchal society.[49] Stoddard was not intimidated. In 1708 he published another provocative sermon: *The Inexcusableness of Neglecting the Worship of God, under a Pretence of being in an Unconverted Condition.* This was too much for Increase Mather, who promptly attacked the "Strange Doctrine" of Northampton in a point by point rebuttal, which he then supple-

46. See Norman Grabo, "The Poet to the Pope: Edward Taylor to Solomon Stoddard," *American Literature* 32 (1960) : 197–201.

47. Citation in Grabo's introduction to Taylor's *Treatise,* p. xxiii.

48. Increase and Cotton Mather, "A Defence of the Evangelical Churches," in Quick, *Young Man's Claim,* p. 22.

49. Cotton Mather, *Diary of Cotton Mather, MHSC,* 7th ser., 7 (1911) : 364, 387.

mented with a polemical appendix to yet another English sacramental meditation.[50] Mather succeeded in provoking Stoddard to a reply— *An Appeal of the Learned*—to which some of the Mathers' supporters responded in *An Appeal, of some of the Unlearned,* but it soon became clear that Stoddard had converted to his viewpoint a number of ministers in western Massachusetts and the Connecticut Valley.[51] The Mathers never openly surrendered, though by 1714 they could accept the diversity of New England sacramental practice with considerable equanimity. In that year Increase even wrote a complimentary preface for Stoddard's *Guide to Christ:*

> It is known, that in some Points (not Fundamentals of Religion) I differ from this beloved Author; Nevertheless (as when there was a difference of Opinion between Jerom and Austin) Jerom said for all that, I cannot but love Christ in Austin; so do I say concerning my Brother Stoddard.[52]

Throughout the controversy, Stoddard's opponents pictured him as an advocate of disorder within an undisciplined Church. Stoddard was indeed attempting to remove existing barriers to membership, but he was also criticizing the laxity, as well as the rigor, of prevailing New England practices. He believed that the Mathers were too rigorous when they excluded moral and orthodox but unconverted Christians from the sacrament, but too generous when they encouraged men to receive communion and thus to think of themselves as regenerate on the basis of a mere "probable hope."

Stoddard did not think it wise to encourage conscientious absentees from the Lord's Supper to enter the circle of the presumably regenerate on the basis of an ambiguous perception or an anxious hope of saving grace. Such laxity was no real solution to the problem of the scrupulous, which worried Stoddard as much as it did the Mathers. Almost all his comments on the Lord's Supper in his first major work, *The Safety of Appearing at the Day of Judgment,* were directed to conscientious absentees.

> Attend the Sacrament of the Lord's Supper: the great design of this Ordinance is for the strengthening of Faith . . . herein the hearts of Gods people have had peculiar establishment, some

50. Increase Mather, *Dissertation.* See also Increase Mather, "An Advertisement," in Doolittle, *A Treatise Concerning the Lord's Supper.*

51. Walker, *Creeds and Platforms,* p. 282.

52. Increase Mather, "Preface" to Solomon Stoddard's *Guide to Christ* (Boston, 1714), p. xii.

when in a discouraged condition are backward to come to this
Ordinance, the Devil has a great hand in it, to keep them from
that which is the means of help: they are afraid that they shall
eat and drink judgment to themselves: but God no where requires a faith of assurance in those that partake of that Ordinance. . . .[53]

He said later that his 1707 sermon on *The Inexcusableness of Neglecting the Worship of God* was written "to answer a case of Conscience,
and direct those that might have Scruples about Participation in the
Lords Supper, because they had not a work of Saving conversion." To
advise such doubting Christians to approach the Lord's table was
simply to compound their sense of anxiety, for their tender consciences would usually rebel: "they will say, We may have such hopes
and yet not be Converted." [54] To tell the merely hopeful that they
should venture and dare to present themselves for communion was
still to turn "Sacrament days which should be days of Comfort" into
"Days of Torment." [55]

Stoddard believed that the generosity of the Mathers stood in the
way of conversion. By encouraging men to think of themselves as
sanctified on the basis of a vague perception or a mere hope of grace,
charged Stoddard, the Mathers were actually inhibiting the conversion
process.

Many that judge that Persons should be Converted before they
come to the Sacrament, do run unto a great fault, viz. they per-
swade Persons that they are Converted before they are: they are
zealous against mens coming to the Lords-Supper in an Unconverted condition, yet advise and incourage such persons to come
under a notion that they are Converted. . . .

Any advice that encouraged men to reach premature conclusions
about their own godliness was a likely impediment to genuine conversion.[56] In reply, the Mathers insisted that Stoddard was too demanding, and that there was too great an "Exactness, in his Thoughts
about a Work of Regeneration." If the ministers were compelled to
apply "the Judgement of Severity" proposed by Stoddard, they said,
then no town in New England could provide enough regenerate saints

53. Solomon Stoddard, *The Safety of Appearing at the Day of Judgment* (Boston,
1687), p. 338.
54. Stoddard, *Appeal*, pp. 2; 88.
55. Stoddard, *Doctrine of Instituted Churches*, p. 22.
56. Stoddard, *Inexcusableness*, pp. 20–21.

to produce a church, whereas the Mathers' own "Judgment of Charity would find a considerable number." [57] But Stoddard thought that their charity would produce complacent communicants, blind to the danger of their own unregenerate state and satisfied with a mere hope of conversion.

At the same time, Stoddard also insisted that the rigor of the Mathers was as misguided and uninformed as their generosity. He argued that the attempt to restrict the Lord's Supper to the converted was based on the entirely false presupposition that the Church could distinguish them from the unconverted. In fact, he said, the absence of a "certain rule given in Scripture" ensured that the guides of the Church would always lack "certain knowledge who have Sanctifying Grace." It was occasionally impossible for the converted to recognize their own gracious state; the godly could harbour anxious fears. And hypocrites were even more susceptible to error in evaluating their piety. Though Stoddard insisted that the saints should be able to "discover their Sincerity," and were even duty-bound to do so, he acknowledged that "particular persons" might find it impossible to detect the signs of grace within themselves.[58] Their dilemma underlined the utter presumptuousness of any man who claimed the ability to identify with certainty the presence of sanctifying grace in other men.

To fence the Lord's Table, moreover, was to erect still another barrier to conversion. Stoddard believed that New England admission policies excluded many who might benefit from the sacrament, which he defined as a converting ordinance able to transform moral and orthodox visible saints into regenerate servants of God. Conversion, in Stoddard's view, was the climax of three spiritual experiences: conviction of sin, humiliation, and saving faith. The Lord's Supper was designed to evoke each of these dispositions. In receiving the elements signifying Christ's body broken and his blood shed, the communicant learned of God's anger against sin and his determination to destroy it. As tokens of Christ's sacrifice, the elements taught, in addition, the need for depending solely on Christ's righteousness. And then by presenting an affecting representation of the love and death of Christ, the sacrament convinced the sinner that a Savior had atoned for his

57. Increase and Cotton Mather, "Defence of the Evangelical Churches," in Quick, *Young Man's Claim,* p. 47.

58. Stoddard, *Inexcusableness,* p. 14; idem, *Appeal,* p. 9; idem, *The Defects of Preachers Reproved* (New London, Ct., 1724), p. 10; idem, "All such as do make a Solemn Profession of their Repentance. . . ." MSS, bound with Taylor MSS, Boston Public Library.

sin. Only a hardened reprobate could resist such a compelling demonstration of human sinfulness and divine mercy.

> This Ordinance has a proper tendency in its own nature to Convert men. Herein men may learn the necessity and sufficiency of the Death of Christ in order to Pardon. Here is an affecting order of Christ crucified: here is a Sealing of the covenant, that if men come to Christ, they shall be saved, which is a great means to convince of safety in coming to Christ.

Stoddard obviously did not hesitate to offer a purely psychological interpretation of sacramental efficacy. The Lord's Supper was a mnemonic ceremony that converted men by teaching them and stirring their emotions, thereby evoking internal assent to doctrines that they had known before only as cold, lifeless propositions. Stoddard liked to talk of the "preaching of the word" in the sacrament, which was a converting ordinance simply because it published the Gospel that Christ was "the bread of life." [59]

All that Stoddard said about sacramental efficacy, however, apart from his rhetorical flourishes, was taken from the earlier English debates. Taylor labeled him an Erastian, which was correct only in the sense that Stoddard was using sacramental motifs that Thomas Erastus had developed on a rudimentary level.[60] Increase Mather's supporters, though, recognized that John Humfrey and John Timson were Stoddard's "Authors." [61] Stoddard read a summary of the English sacramental debates that Humfrey had published in 1656, *A Second Vindication of a Disciplinarian, Anti-Erastian, Orthodox Free-Admission to the Lords-Supper*. In what was clearly a reference to the preface of that book, he described Timson as having been "bred up" under Robert Bolton.[62] Stoddard was selective in his appropriation of ideas from the English debates. He never adopted Timson's notion that all Church members were recipients of an absolute promise, and as Increase Mather observed, he never used the popular argument that the presence of Judas at the Last Supper justified the admission of the unconverted. The major outlines of Stoddard's sacramental doctrine, however, emerged out of the Erastian controversies in seventeenth-century England.

Stoddard's opponents also drew on the English debates, which had

59. Stoddard, *Appeal*, pp. 72; 25; 43, 49.
60. Taylor, *Treatise*, p. 68.
61. Anon., *An Appeal, Of some of the Unlearned*, p. 7.
62. Stoddard, *Appeal*, p. 39; Humfrey, *Second Vindication*, n.p.

attracted their attention, as well as Stoddard's, long before the controversy divided the colony.[63] Increase Mather transformed English Presbyterians into apologists for the New England tradition. George Gillespie, Richard Vines, Stephen Charnock, and Richard Baxter suddenly became sacramental authorities for Congregational ministers. The Stoddardean debate was therefore no isolated event on the colonial frontier, and neither Stoddard nor his opponents contributed any genuinely original ideas to the continuing discussions over the nature of the sacrament.

Increase Mather believed that the earlier disputes had demonstrated the illogical and unscriptural character of Stoddard's proposals. If the Lord's Supper were a converting ordinance, he asked, why exclude the scandalous and profane? [64] Stoddard replied that the sacrament was a converting ordinance only for adult Church members, whom he presumed to be capable of understanding and affirming sacramental symbolism. He pointed to the familiar distinction between two kinds of conversion, the first a merely formal assent to the truth of Christian doctrine, the second an inward consent to the gospel.[65] The Lord's Supper presupposed the first and produced the second. In answer to Stoddard, Edward Taylor carefully assembled biblical references in order to prove that conversion was nothing more, or less, than a transformation from sinfulness to a state of grace.[66] Taylor's exegesis stood unchallenged, however, for Stoddard never responded to his arguments.

The criticism of Stoddard rested ultimately on an alternative view of the sacrament itself. His critics first argued that the Lord's Supper was an ordinance designed to strengthen rather than to produce grace in the soul. According to Taylor, even the elements of bread and wine suggested that the sacrament nourished an existing principle of spiritual life. Faithful communion therefore required the existence of a vital faculty that could educe spiritual benefit from the rite and "minister it to the spiritual man." [67] The critics then added, as a second point, that the Lord's Supper was by definition a "eucharistical" ordinance, a rite of thanksgiving for the gift of redeeming grace. Only the regenerate, who had received the saving gift, could truly

63. Tuttle, "The Libraries of the Mathers," pp. 269–356; and Norman S. Fiering, "Solomon Stoddard's Library in 1664," *Harvard Library Bulletin* 20 (1972): 255–269. By 1664, both Stoddard and the Mathers owned relevant books by Samuel Rutherford, George Gillespie, or John Beverley.

64. Increase Mather, *Dissertation*, pp. 33, 65.

65. Stoddard, *Appeal*, p. 26; Stoddard, *Inexcusableness*, pp. 27–28.

66. Taylor, *Treatise*, pp. 77–80.

67. Ibid., p. 76.

feel and express gratitude. Consequently, they alone possessed the right to receive a sacrament of thanksgiving.[68]

In other words, Stoddard's critics asserted the uniqueness of the Lord's Supper, while Stoddard himself affirmed the conventional Reformed doctrine that the sacrament was simply a visible Word. In fact, he believed that the rite was merely one sermonic exhortation among others, on exactly the same level as preaching and prayer. He concluded that the unregenerate, assisted by the Holy Spirit, possessed the capacity to understand the sacrament's doctrinal symbolism and thus to derive benefit from it, as often happened when the Word was proclaimed. Both Taylor and the Mathers agreed that the Lord's Supper was a visible Word, and that sacramental devotion might occasionally produce a conversion. The communion prayer and the words of institution were "suitable instruments" for conveying redemptive grace to the soul. Yet this converting efficacy was only "accidental" and not essential to the sacrament, which according to Taylor was more than simply a sermon. While he defined the Lord's Supper as a visible Word, Taylor also distinguished Word and sacrament: it was the function of the Word, not the sacramental ceremony, to enlighten the understanding, and hence to convict and convert the soul. Taylor outlined in conventional fashion the doctrinal message implicit in the elements and gestures of the rite, but he also argued that the Lord's Supper was not, in essence, an appeal to the mind through the senses. With that argument he minimized the psychological interpretation of sacramental efficacy that was so characteristic of early Puritan thought. The unique essence of eucharistic worship, he said—echoing the English anti-Erastian theologians—was the act of eating and drinking, a symbolic involvement in a mysterious ritual.[69] He never pretended to know precisely how these essential eucharistic activities confirmed and strengthened the grace of the faithful. One historian has argued that during the seventeenth century the Puritans gradually abandoned their confidence in the priority of the intellect in religion and accorded increasing attention to the emotions.[70] Certainly Taylor's sacramental piety was consistent with such a transition.

Though Taylor could not explain the dynamics of sacramental efficacy, he was of course convinced, as were the Mathers, that the primary function of the Lord's Supper was to seal the covenant. In fact, the anti-Stoddardean theologians felt that the definition of a

68. Ibid., pp. 41, 76, 88–89; Increase Mather, *Dissertation*, p. 62.
69. Taylor, *Treatise*, pp. 70–72; 87, 94–96, 138, 214.
70. Eugene E. White, *Puritan Rhetoric: The Issue of Emotion in Religion* (Carbondale, Ill., 1972), pp. 6–40.

sacrament as a covenant seal precluded the admission of the unregenerate.

> But that we may Cutt Home, we need only say; Is the Lords
> Supper a Seal of the New Covenant, or no? . . . That a man who
> knows himself to be an Unbeliever, may not come unto the Holy
> Table, is thus Evinced. A man may not Receive the Seal of the
> Covenant, while he does reject the Covenant it self. But an Un-
> regenerate and an Unbeliever does Reject the Covenant of God,
> and of Life.[71]

The sacrament, said Increase, sealed to the worthy partaker all of the
blessings promised in the New Covenant, and particularly the remission of sins, but to administer the elements to the unregenerate was to
"set the Lords Seal to a Blank." [72] Both Mathers assumed that the
Lord's Supper was a seal to faith as well as to the covenant; that it
sealed to the faithful the benefits of the internal and absolute as well
as the external covenants; and that it was not a merely conditional or
external seal. Taylor shared these assumptions.[73]

According to Stoddard, however, the definition of sacraments as
covenant seals justified a policy of open admission. Stoddard's assumptions differed radically from those of the Mathers. He denied that the
Lord's Supper was a seal to faith; it was rather a seal to the truth of
the covenant promise that faith was efficacious to salvation. There was
therefore no need to restrict communion to the truly faithful in heart.
He denied also that the sacrament sealed an absolute covenant; instead, it confirmed and attested the spiritual and eternal blessings of
the covenant, though "not absolutely but conditionally." Consequently
there was no necessity of reserving the sacrament for the presumably
elect recipients of absolute promises.[74]

By the early eighteenth century, Stoddard had drastically modified
the current New England understanding of sacramental sealing. The
Lord's Supper, he said, sealed not only the spiritual promises offered
to individual believers but also promises of "outward Prosperity" to
the visible Church.[75] The sixteenth-century Separatists had also said
that sacraments were communal seals that obligated the Church to
offer obedient worship and promised blessings to the faithful community. No Separatist, however, could have tolerated Stoddard's

71. Increase and Cotton Mather, "A Defence of the Evangelical Churches," in
Quick, *Young Man's Claim*, pp. 48–50.
72. Increase Mather, *Dissertation*, pp. 28–30.
73. See also Taylor, *Treatise*, pp. 85, 105.
74. Stoddard, *Appeal*, pp. 22, 47.
75. Ibid., p. 22.

claims, for he had begun by 1700 to make the visible Church coextensive with the state. For Stoddard, the sacraments attested the temporal prosperity of a national Church rather than merely the spiritual blessings of a select community of regenerate saints. Of course, the sealed promises extended only to the Church, and not to the state, though most New England ministers felt that Stoddard blurred the lines between the two realms, thus making it seem as if the sacrament sealed a social contract rather than a spiritual covenant.[76]

Increase Mather believed, moreover, that Scripture prohibited the comprehensive parish system that Stoddard proposed. Mather discovered through typological exegesis of the Old Testament that the perquisites of Church membership belonged solely to the regenerate. It seemed obvious to him that the ceremonial holiness demanded of the Jews typified the inward holiness required of New England Christians. The ceremonial restrictions that limited access to the Jewish temple therefore justified the exclusion of the impure in heart from the inner sacramental sanctum of the Church.

The Mathers struggled to maintain the traditionally intimate connection between typology and sacramental thought because they both believed that typological exegesis demonstrated Stoddard's fallacies. Increase insisted, along with Edward Taylor, that the Jewish Passover was a type of the Lord's Supper. The moral and ceremonial cleanliness required for the Passover therefore typified the real holiness found in proper Christian communicants.[77] Stoddard, however, denied that the ordinances of the Old Testament were "Types of the Ordinances of the New Testament." Old Testament ordinances, rather, signified evangelical doctrines: the command that unclean persons abstain from the Passover meal meant that the spiritually unclean would be excluded from the Kingdom of God.[78]

Stoddard did on occasion draw subtle distinctions that permitted him to establish analogies between Jewish and Christian sacraments. Since the Passover was a type foreshadowing the advent of Christ, he said, and the Lord's Supper was a subsequent representation of Christ crucified, the two rites were indeed sufficiently analogous to justify similarities in the policy of admission. Accordingly, Stoddard pointed out that the tribes of Israel had been instructed to observe the Passover even when God looked upon them as "an evil Generation." [79] Increase Mather described this as Stoddard's "Cardinal Argument"

76. See Middlekauff, *The Mathers*, pp. 135–8.
77. Increase Mather, *Dissertation*, p. 16; Taylor, *Treatise*, p. 128.
78. Stoddard, *Inexcusableness*, p. 28; idem, *Appeal*, p. 13.
79. Stoddard, *Inexcusableness*, p. 8; idem, *Appeal*, p. 50.

and replied that the Jewish Passover was appointed for a national Church, not for the voluntary covenanting churches of the Gospel dispensation.[80] But Stoddard of course had argued as early as 1700 that New England churches should also be "national." [81] Despite Stoddard's frequent allusions to the Passover, though, he subtly undermined the conventional relationship between typology and sacramental thought in the Puritan tradition. Increase Mather claimed to have discovered a distinct anti-sacramental implication in Stoddard's exegesis; carried to its logical conclusion, he said, Stoddard's treatment of typology would threaten the justification even for infant baptism, which rested in part on the supposition that Jewish circumcision typified the sacrament.

Stoddard also disliked the sacramental allusions that his critics discovered in the New Testament, especially in the narrative of the wedding feast in the twenty-second chapter of Matthew. Increase Mather began his *Dissertation* with an exegesis of the passage, interpreting the feast as a prototype of the Lord's Supper and observing that the invitation specified the need for a wedding garment, which Mather equated with true sanctity. Edward Taylor's eight anti-Stoddardean sacramental sermons were essentially an extended interpretation of the same passage, consuming one hundred ninety manuscript pages.[82] The wedding feast, he said, was a parabolical emblem of the sacrament, and the garment signified "a sanctifying work of the spirit." [83] Stoddard argued, against Mather, that the feast was really "Christ Jesus, and Pardon, and Salvation," and not the Lord's Supper.[84] Taylor, however, said that this was impossible: the Matthean banquet could not be faith, or repentance, or salvation, since "whosoever attains to them shall never be without the wedden robe nor cast into outer darkness," and some wedding guests in Matthew's narrative were in fact cast out from the feast.[85] To Taylor's detailed argumentation Stoddard never replied.

Stoddard's exegesis reflected a pattern that consistently characterized his sacramental thought and piety: he translated into abstract doctrinal precepts the biblical references that had usually been understood to typify and signify the sacraments. In a similar manner, he also interpreted sacramental efficacy as the visual presentation of

80. Increase Mather, *Dissertation*, p. 73.
81. Stoddard, *Doctrine of Instituted Churches*, pp. 7–8.
82. The manuscript is described in detail by Grabo, "A Note on the Text," in Taylor, *Treatise*, pp. liii-lvi.
83. Taylor, *Treatise*, pp. 9, 29.
84. Stoddard, *Appeal*, p. 3.
85. Taylor, *Treatise*, pp. 9–10.

an affecting doctrinal message. Despite his claims for the sacrament's efficacy, Stoddard viewed the Lord's Supper as one sermon among others, and he criticized the implied "sacramentalism" of ministers who disagreed with him. In one sense, then, Stoddard held a lower estimation of the sacrament than most other New England ministers. Yet for more than a century Puritan theologians had spoken of sacramental grace in terms of the dynamics of psychological interiority and the enrichment of the understanding. The Mathers believed that the Lord's Supper was a visible Gospel, and Taylor usually agreed. Impressed by Humfrey and Timson, Stoddard pondered the implications of this traditional Puritan sacramental language and concluded that the prevailing regard for the sanctity of the sacrament had blinded New England divines to the potential power of the rite. Stoddard's doctrine was entirely consistent with the perennial Reformed contention that the sacrament was a visible Word. He not only compelled the ministers to take seriously a debate that they had managed to avoid for decades, and therefore stimulated interest in eucharistic doctrine, but he also proposed an alternative mode of sacramental piety, which had firm grounding in earlier Puritan theory.

Open admission attracted support from ministers who did not accept Stoddard's doctrines. At least one clergyman concluded that New England's admission policies—as modified by the Mathers and their followers—were fundamentally inhumane. Benjamin Wadsworth (1670–1737) became president of Harvard in 1724; in the same year, he also became a self-appointed protector of the conscientious.

> To say, 'tis itself sinful for an unregenerate Person to come, and yet that Assurance is not necessary in order to a right coming, I say these Assertions seem to me very Inconsistent, tending very much to perplex and distract the Consciences of the Weak.

Wadsworth proposed to admit to the sacrament all moral and orthodox Christians who were capable of self-examination, but not because he believed that the Lord's Supper would convert them. He assumed that the unworthy would eat and drink to damnation, but that unregenerate communicants might well be worthy, since the benefits of the Lord's Supper could be appropriated through faith long after any administration of the elements. An unregenerate communicant was potentially faithful: "God may afterwards give saving Faith to such an one." [86] Samuel Willard also believed that it was presumptuous to describe the Lord's Supper as a converting ordinance, yet he, too, opened the table to all adult Christians of sound belief and behavior.

86. Wadsworth, *Dialogue*, pp. 66; 46, 56, 68.

He simply doubted, as did Stoddard, that the Church could discern
the faithful. Inevitably there would be communicants who had no
spiritual right to the sacrament, he acknowledged, but that was a
matter "between God and their own Souls." [87] The Mathers disagreed
with Willard, though from the perspective of the history of Puritan
piety, they shared at least one common goal: to expand the circle of
sacramental devotion. The Lord's Supper was no longer the exclusive
property of a spiritual aristocracy.

Sacramental Presence

In the realm of piety, the sacramental devotionalism was a step toward bridging the gap between corporeality and spirit within the Puritan tradition. Whether in Northampton or Boston, the resurgent interest in eucharistic worship demonstrated that New England could
fully appreciate external visual aids to spiritual growth. Through sacramental piety the churches not only issued a vivid evangelistic appeal
but also responded to the popular desire for a symbolic confrontation
with spiritual reality—the same desire that was reflected on New
England tombstones and in Cotton Mather's program for spiritualizing
the creatures. Eucharistic piety was a means of incorporating graphic
symbols into New England worship, though in a manner consistent
with accepted modes of corporate devotion and with traditional doctrinal safeguards against confusing the symbol with that which it
symbolized.

As in the past, the theoretical basis for this piety was found in the
principle of accommodation. The New England theologians assumed
an "infinitely vast distance between God and the creature." Between
the finite and the infinite, said Samuel Willard, there is "no proportion," the two realms being utterly incomparable. Even before the fall
of man, therefore, an immediate revelation of God to the finite understanding would have resulted in the obliteration of the creature. Consequently, God mercifully decided "to accommodate this revelation to
our capacities," and to speak only through his Word, his created
works, and his instituted means of grace. The trees of life and knowledge were divine accommodations to Adamic finitude, sealing a promise of happiness on condition of obedience. The Jewish types and
Christian sacraments were further means of grace by which God accommodated himself to human fallenness. To enhance the spiritual
growth of his children, he arbitrarily appointed sensible signs, which
were analogous to the refracted beams of light visible to men unable

87. Willard, *Mediations*, p. 234; idem, *Compleat Body*, p. 863.

to gaze directly into the blinding sun.[88] Thus did visible symbols acquire legitimacy.

The ministers considered it crucial, however, that there be no confusion between the sign and the reality that it signified. Therefore they insisted, like earlier Reformed theologians, that sacramental language—particularly the phrase "This is my body"—was "plainly Metonymical" or tropical, a metonymy in this instance being simply a figure of speech in which the name of the signified object was predicated of the sign itself. Roman Catholics found no trope in the sacramental words; Lutherans acknowledged an unusual predicate in the words of institution, but nevertheless affirmed a corporeal presence. Both positions, according to the Puritans, undercut the very notion of a sacramental "sign," which by definition pointed beyond itself to a transcendent reality.[89]

Puritans attributed the confusion of their Lutheran and Roman opponents primarily to a faulty understanding of the relationship between the divine and human natures in Christ. *Finitum non capax infiniti:* by the late seventeenth century the principle had become a rational axiom governing Reformed sacramental and Christological doctrine. As a consequence, no Puritan theologian believed in a genuine communication of properties between the infinite divine nature of Christ and his finite humanity. Samuel Willard expressed this fundamental postulate of Reformed Christology:

> My Reason assures me, that though his Divinity is Omnipresent, being infinite, yet his Humanity being a Creature, is finite, and cannot be divers places at once.[90]

Willard added that this rational deduction was consonant with faith, which affirmed that Christ's glorified humanity, having ascended to the right hand of God, remained in heaven, theoretically distinct from the infinite divine nature. A corporeal sacramental presence was therefore both impious and impossible.[91]

New England Puritans did accept a qualified, Reformed version of the doctrine of the communication of properties. Edward Taylor acknowledged that the properties of the Godhead were "Communicated unto the humanity," though only "in and by the Person" of Christ, in the sense that there was a mutual concurrence of both natures in all of Christ's personal activities. The divine properties,

88. Willard, *Compleat Body,* pp. 41–42; 42–46, 806–810, 842–44.
89. Ibid., p. 865; Cotton Mather, *Companion,* p. 7.
90. Willard, *Meditations,* p. 19; idem, *Compleat Body,* p. 865.
91. Willard, *Meditations,* p. 19; Cotton Mather, *Companion,* p. 7.

however, were never inherent in the human nature considered in ab-
straction from the union of the two natures in the Person.[92] The
human nature, Taylor concluded, did not share the divine property
of ubiquity; it possessed "a Certain place." This fact, he added, "confounded" the Lutherans and fatally "wounded" the Roman Catholics.[93]

The Puritan doctrine of Christ therefore precluded any affirmation
of a corporeal presence, as did the common Reformed assumption that
the Christian benefitted only from a spiritual, not a fleshly, feast.[94]
But was there nothing then in the elements, asked Samuel Willard,
except a similitude representing Christ? On occasion, New England
sermons and sacramental devotions seemed to suggest that the Lord's
Supper was indeed little more than a token of remembrance. Cotton
Mather often spoke of the sacrament as a "Memorial of a Dying
Saviour," and his language could sound flatly Zwinglian:

> Our Lord is gone from us, and as we do by some Token keep
> up the Remembrance of an Absent Friend; so do we in this
> Ordinance Retain and Revive the Remembrance of an Absent
> Lord. We do therein, as it were, behold the Death of our Lord
> Jesus acted over again to the Life; and we Remember what he
> was, we Remember what he did, we Remember what He said,
> when He was Incarnate here.[95]

Mather valued the sacrament primarily for the subjective dispositions
it evoked in the worshipper. He considered a "Rationall" and Christian "Exercise of our Understandings" to be prerequisite for beneficial
communion, and in his manuals he outlined a series of appropriate
"thoughts" that should pass through the minds of communicants.[96]
Mather's sacramental piety was vivid and heartfelt, but it derived
more from the symbolic character of the eucharistic service than from
any strong sense of Christ's presence in the rite.[97] Even Cotton
Mather, though, was able to agree that Christ dispensed himself in
"Spiritual communion" to the worthy worshipper. Mather was no
Zwinglian: he believed that "the King of Heaven" was "peculiarly
and eminently present" at the Lord's Supper, even though he rarely
found occasion to emphasize that presence in his writings.[98]

92. Taylor, *Christographia*, pp. 148–49.
93. Ibid.; Taylor, "Meditation 108," *Poems*, p. 244; Cotton Mather, *Companion*,
p. 7.
94. Willard, *Meditations*, pp. 19–20; idem, *Compleat Body*, p. 865.
95. Cotton Mather, *Companion*, p. 60.
96. Ibid., p. 113; Cotton Mather, *Monitor*, pp. 19–20.
97. See also Wadsworth, *Dialogue*, pp. 7–10.
98. Cotton Mather, *Companion*, p. 141.

Other New England Puritans maintained a firmer grasp on Calvinist sacramental doctrine. Edward Taylor's allegiance to Calvin permeated the series of personal poetic sacramental meditations that he wrote between 1682 and 1725. In the Lord's Supper, Taylor wrote, Christ feasted the souls of the faithful disciples upon "His own flesh and blood most royally served up." Samuel Willard also affirmed a "Real Presence of the Man Christ, in and with" the sacrament. Willard spoke of an "exhibition" of the body and blood, rather than a "distribution," thereby distinguishing himself from Lutheran theologians. He denied, through his choice of nouns, that Christ was "materially present" in or with the physical elements; the communicant therefore did not receive him through the "Bodily Organs." [99] Yet there was a genuine spiritual presence: "Surely there is something else here to be met with than the naked Elements; and what is that but Christ Himself?" [100]

New England theologians rarely described the Lord's Supper in terms of its benefits alone. Samuel Willard, for one, assumed that the presence was the precondition of sacramental efficacy. Only through receiving the body and blood did the communicant partake of the benefits of Christ. Thus Willard designated the spiritual presence as an instrument "whereby" the virtue and merits of Christ were conveyed.[101] Colonial ministers regularly spoke of both "Christ and His benefits" in the Lord's Supper. A few placed notable emphasis on the availability of Christ's humanity in the sacrament. Edward Taylor wrote that the communicant received the "Theandrick Blood, and Body"; the sacrament conveyed both the divine and the human natures of Christ.[102] Taylor often defined the meaning of the Lord's Supper specifically in terms of the Incarnation. Jesus himself, he said, took up bread and wine at the Passover "to shew that he our nature took." [103] Every Puritan, of course, also believed that the glorified humanity of Christ remained in heaven. How then could the "Theandrick" body and blood, in Taylor's terms, be "Disht" on the sacramental table? Calvin had solved the problem by means of his doctrine of the Holy Spirit. Strangely, however, New England ministers never joined Calvin in combining pneumatology and the liturgical *sursum corda*. Willard merely took for granted that Christ must be "in some sort here according to his Human Nature, else he would not have said, 'This is my Body, and this is my Blood.' " [104] In one sense, however,

99. Willard, *Compleat Body*, p. 867.
100. Willard, *Meditations*, p. 18.
101. Willard, *Compleat Body*, pp. 866–67.
102. Taylor, *Treatise*, pp. 76; 136, 170; idem, "Meditation 111," *Poems*, p. 251.
103. Taylor, "Meditation 105," *Poems*, p. 238.
104. Willard, *Meditations*, p. 18.

this recourse to mystery was itself fully reminiscent of Calvin's own sacramental piety.

New Englanders were not troubled by the issues that had divided Calvin and Zwingli. Like the English preachers of the early seventeenth century, they were interested in the practical and pastoral application of sacramental doctrine, in piety rather than doctrinal precision. The frequent appearance of distinctively Calvinist doctrinal motifs, however, is striking. Viewed from the perspective of a century of Reformed eucharistic theology, the New England Puritans appear to have retained a remarkable sacramental consciousness. It is difficult to sustain the image of Puritanism as a consistently anti-sacramental movement. Edward Taylor wrote that the love of Christ was uniquely manifest in the eucharistic feast. He was not alone in his conviction that the Lord's Supper was the "most honorable" of all Christian rites: many of his ministerial colleagues fully agreed.[105]

New England's agony over admission to the Lord's Supper must therefore be seen in the light of a burgeoning interest in a sacramental piety that promised to comfort the faithful, disturb the faithless, and lure the hesitant into the fold. The Mathers and their followers wanted to bar the sacrament to the unregenerate for a variety of reasons: they were afraid of dishonoring the Lord's Supper, reluctant to break with tradition, and solicitous for the purity of their churches. But they were also convinced that the dilemma posed by the sacrament to the unconverted would help bring "half-way" members into full communion. Consequently, they preached that abstention, as well as faithless communion, was sinful; but at the same time, they tempered their rigor with a generous interpretation of the signs of regeneration in an effort to induce the hesitant to approach the sacrament.

Stoddard rebelled against that program. He thought it presumptuous to try to identify the regenerate and inadvisable to encourage the merely hopeful to think of themselves as converted. Having been convinced by the earlier English controversy that the Lord's Supper itself was one solution to the problem of conversion, he expounded that view in New England. Though he did not share his opponents' exalted view of the sacrament, Stoddard, too, helped to ensure that New England's concern for sacramental matters would be intense and widespread as the eighteenth century began.

105. Taylor, *Treatise*, pp. 40–41, 170.

EPILOGUE

In 1688 the Quaker George Keith entered Boston to inform the colonial Christians that they should seek the baptism of the Holy Spirit and spiritually feed on Christ daily through the experience of faith. They would be well-served, he added, to abandon the idolatrous practice of sacramental worship. The Boston ministers responded by warning the saints against the temptation to "unchurch themselves by parting with all the meanes of Communion between them and their God." Spiritual feeding and inward baptism were indispensable, but so also were the external institutions divinely appointed to assist faith. Internal spiritual efficacy, therefore, could not be opposed to the external corporeality of the sacrament: "these are two, but not contraries, but concomitants, as being indeed two parts of the same sacrament." [1] Keith embodied a tendency ever-present within Puritanism—the impulse to discard externals and to dwell within the internal realm of the Spirit. His Boston antagonists espoused a different Puritan precept: that finite, fallen, embodied men needed visible and audible means of grace. Within the broad mainstream of Puritanism —which produced the Westminster and Savoy Confessions and dominated the four commonwealths in Massachusetts and Connecticut— this sensitivity to sinfulness and finitude inhibited the movement toward spiritual immediacy and provided a justification for sacramental piety.

Despite continuing ambivalence about baptism and the Lord's Supper, therefore, a notable Reformed sacramentalism, assuming varied forms and provoking intense debate, could and did emerge within the Puritan tradition during the seventeenth century. Covenantal doc-

1. James Allen, Joshua Moody, Samuel Willard, Cotton Mather, *The Principles of the Protestant Religion Maintained* (Boston, 1690), "Preface," pp. 140–45.

trines provided most Puritan theologians with a rationale for infant baptism and a clarification of the meaning of eucharistic communion. But a small minority wanted a stronger doctrine than the covenant motif, as generally interpreted, would permit. During the seventeenth century in both England and New England, the Puritan tradition produced intricate reflections on baptismal regeneration and the converting efficacy of the Lord's Supper. While some ministers proposed revisions—both moderate and radical—in accepted sacramental doctrine and practice, others sought to recover the Calvinist themes that their predecessors had minimized or ignored. Throughout the latter half of the century, moreover, sermons on baptism and manuals for communion marked a significant effort on both sides of the Atlantic to propagate a sacramental piety in Puritan churches.

No single explanation can account for this complex sacramental renaissance. In part, it was simply an expression of resistance to the antisacramental mood of Baptists, Quakers, and other spiritualistic radicals. Political considerations and fears of social and ecclesiastical disorder also intruded into sacramental discussions, as did changing attitudes about the visible created world and the meditative life. The various manifestations of Puritan sacramentalism, however, reflected primarily a change in the doctrine of the Church and its ministry. Many early Puritans had been tempted by the vision of churches as voluntary communities of faithful believers, free from external forms and ceremonies, led by a charismatic ministry. New Englanders attempted for a time to institutionalize that vision in pure churches of converted visible saints and their children, though they also maintained some ecclesiastical control over the unregenerate citizenry. But when the children of the saints, among others, often proved to be among the unregenerate, the ideal required adjustment. New England churches underwent a gradual transition: the regenerate communities of a pilgrim plantation became the ordered ecclesiastical institutions of provincial society. The transition by no means obliterated experiential piety; even some of the unregenerate were scrupulously pious. Both scrupulosity and indifference, however, required new patterns of ministry—gradual nurture and evangelistic outreach—that were compatible with a renewed sacramental piety. And after 1645 English Puritans also were faced with the responsibilities of administering an ecclesiastical establishment, erecting presbyteries, maintaining the institutional life of Independent churches, and ensuring the orderly continuation of worship and piety. In the light of this transition, Puritans in both England and the colonies reasserted the importance of exter-

nal means of grace. Without abandoning earlier concerns about conversion and purity, they exhibited a growing receptivity to sacramental
and sacerdotal patterns of worship and ministry.

One historian has argued that baptismal and eucharistic thought in
New England represented a reshaping of "downright Calvinism" in
response to peculiar colonial problems.[2] The Stoddardean controversy,
however, cannot be interpreted as an isolated response to the problems
of a colonial frontier, and the conventional sacramental piety and
doctrine of the New England ministers cannot be viewed as a transformation of Calvinism. Both Stoddardeanism and the sacramental
renaissance reflected, rather, the cosmopolitan character of Puritan
concerns in the late seventeenth century. The communion meditations
and the treatises on baptism were the fruits of a Reformed tradition
that extended into the early sixteenth century, and Stoddard's doctrine
had roots both in continental and in the English Erastian controversies. Most of the sacramental manuals printed in New England had
been written by English dissenting ministers who also felt themselves
to be part of a continuing tradition with respected advocates throughout Europe.

Accordingly, Puritan sacramental reflection was guided more by
perennial Reformed assumptions than by cultural and social experience. For that very reason, the analysis of sacramental theology reveals and clarifies some of the basic and enduring presuppositions of
Puritan thought. First, the New England ministers continued to assume that the finite could not bear the infinite—as these terms were
understood in technical theological discourse. By the late seventeenth
century *finitum non capax infiniti* had become not simply an implicit
postulate of piety but also an explicit rational principle, especially informing Christology and sacramental doctrine. Yet Reformed theologians had never pushed the principle to extreme conclusions. They
always acknowledged a divine accommodation to finitude and sinfulness: the Creator revealed himself in and through the created world,
even though the sinful understanding distorted the revelation, and the
Spirit manifested itself through instituted means of grace capable of
attracting and moving the created, embodied faculties of men. Both
the piety of sensation and the sacramental devotion of seventeenth-
century Puritans were rooted in this doctrine of accommodation.

Second, the Puritans accepted the distinction between spirit and
flesh as it had been formulated in the sixteenth-century humanist tra-

2. Miller, "The Puritan Theory of the Sacraments in Seventeenth Century New
England," *The Catholic Historical Review* 22 (January, 1937) : 409–25.

dition.[3] Historians have observed how often the term "spiritual" in Puritan thought denoted a relationship to God rather than an incorporeal order of being.[4] Still, their sacramental writings demonstrate a continuing suspicion of corporeality among the Puritan ministers. They could not tolerate the notion of a physical presence of Christ in the Eucharist, partly because of their interpretation of the Johannine claim that the flesh profited nothing. Yet again, Reformed theologians had never been proponents of a thoroughly spiritualized religion. When Puritans began to insist on the consecration of material elements in the Lord's Supper, or to attribute regeneration to tangible sacraments, or even to defend infant baptism against "spiritualizers," it was clear that the ontological chasm between spirit and matter did not for all of them entail the elimination of the tangible from the religious life. Indeed, Puritan sacramental writings can be read as a series of attempts to reduce the distance between the finite and the infinite, while still affirming their ultimate incompatibility, and to grasp spiritual realities through physical means without confusing matter and spirit.

By 1718 sacramental controversy almost ceased in New England. The Mathers even joined in the ordination service of a Baptist minister.[5] But in that year Stoddard experienced the fifth of his evangelistic "harvests" at Northampton, foreshadowing the widespread revivalistic fervor of the Great Awakening. In 1734, the sermons of Stoddard's grandson, Jonathan Edwards, sparked an outburst of religious excitement at Northampton, and for a decade New England was shaken by religious revivals. Edwards and his fellow revivalists were unhappy with the new sacramental practices. They rejected Stoddard's admission policies; they demanded of communicants a credible profession of saving faith; and they denied that the Lord's Supper was in any sense a converting ordinance. At the same time, Edwards was clearly no proponent of the evangelistic sacramental piety espoused by Cotton Mather. He believed with Mather that communion was a religious duty, but he would not plead with the scrupulous to apply for admission on the basis of a mere "hope." He wanted candidates who could "judge themselves truly and cordially" to be pious disciples of

3. On the humanist background of Puritan thought, see Leonard Trinterud, ed., *Elizabethan Puritanism* (New York, 1971).

4. John E. Smith, ed., *A Treatise Concerning Religious Affections,* by Jonathan Edwards (New Haven 1969), pp. 24–25.

5. Isaac Backus, *A History of New England With Particular Reference to the Denomination of Christians Called Baptists,* 2nd ed. (Newton, Mass., 1871), 1 : 484–85.

Christ by their possession of genuine saving faith, and he thought it far more important to exclude hypocrites than to lure conscientious saints or merely orthodox believers into Church membership with sacramental evangelism.[6]

The Great Awakening and its aftermath severely inhibited the expansion of sacramental piety. New England printers, who had produced twenty-one editions of communion manuals between 1690 and 1738, printed only eight between 1739 and 1790.[7] Baptismal doctrine and practice once more divided the New England churches. John Cotton of Plymouth, the great grandson of the famous teacher at Boston, joined other ministers in defending the claim that baptism was administered for the "begetting of life" in elect infants, and that God gave to the baptized "the striving of his Spirit; which if not resisted will prove effectual to their conversion." [8] But prominent Edwardsean theologians repudiated such baptismal doctrine, as did hundreds of New England Congregational laymen, many of whom left their churches and became Baptists.[9] Whatever else it may have been, the Awakening was also a repudiation of the sacramental renaissance.

This antisacramental mood became characteristic of American revivalism. By the mid-nineteenth century, John Williamson Nevin, a German Reformed theologian at Mercersburg Seminary, complained that American Protestants generally shared an "unsacramental feeling" and looked upon baptism and the Lord's Supper as "mere outward signs." But as Nevin recognized, that nineteenth-century, "modern Puritan" view was by no means characteristic of all earlier, seventeenth-century Puritans.[10] The Puritan tradition may have engendered hostility toward baptism and the Lord's Supper, but it also produced serious sacramental discussions, widespread concern about sacramental prac-

6. See Jonathan Edwards, *An Humble Inquiry into the Rules of the Word of God, Concerning the Qualifications Requisite to a Complete Standing and Full Communion in the Visible Christian Church,* in *The Works of President Edwards,* ed. Sereno Dwight (New York, 1830), 4 : 293, 341, 348, 369, 416–17.

7. See Charles Evans, *American Bibliography: A Chronological Dictionary of all Books, Pamphlets, and Periodical Publications Printed in the United States of America from the Genesis of Printing in 1639 Down to and Including the Year 1820* (New York, 1941), vols. 2–8.

8. John Cotton, *The general practice of the churches of New-England, relating to baptism, vindicated* (Boston, 1772), pp. 16–17.

9. For a typical Edwardsean treatment, see Joseph Bellamy, *That There is But One Covenant, Whereof Baptism and the Lord's Supper are Seals, viz. The Covenant of Grace* (New Haven, 1769). See C. C. Goen, *Revivalism and Separatism in New England* (New Haven, 1962), for a description of eighteenth-century Separatism and its Baptist tendencies.

10. John Williamson Nevin, *The Mystical Presence* (Philadelphia, 1846), p. 107.

tice, and a strong Reformed sacramental piety and doctrine. An understanding of the convictions that underlay that concern is essential to a comprehensive grasp of Puritanism in its greatest age of vigor and power.

APPENDIX

The treatise, *A Moderate Answer to these Two Questions 1) Whether ther be sufficient Ground in Scripture to Warrant the Conscience of a Christian to present his infants to the sacrament of Baptism 2) Whether it be not sinfull for a Christian to receiv the sacrament in a mixt Assembly . . . .* was signed simply T. B. Its authorship has traditionally been assigned to Blake. See Alexander Gordon, "Thomas Blake," *DNB* 2 (1949–50) : 642, and Donald Wing, *Short-Title Catalogue of Books Printed in England, Scotland, Ireland, Wales, and British America and of English Books Printed in other Countries, 1640–1700* (1945) 1 : 159. I am convinced that it was written by Thomas Bedford:

1. *A Moderate Answer*, pp. 8–10, argued that baptism of infants could be justified on the basis of tradition. This was Bedford's view in his 1638 *Treatise of the Sacraments*, p. 92: "Traditions Apostolicall are authenticall, and not to be refused (because not written) if found to be Apostolicall." Baxter, *Appendix*, p. 305, and Tombes, *Praecursor*, p. 4, referred critically to Bedford's acceptance of tradition. In *Vindiciae Foederis*, p. 420, Blake explicitly refused to defend infant baptism on that basis: "Infant Baptism is not bestowed on unwritten tradition."

2. *A Moderate Answer*, p. 4, distinguished between initial or seminal grace, given to infants in baptism, and the grace of regeneration given to adults. The distinction was crucial in Bedford's 1638 *Treatise*, p. 192, and in his *Vindiciae Gratiae Sacramentalis*, n. p. Blake never mentioned the distinction.

3. *A Moderate Answer*, pp. 11, 15, also distinguished between a "virtuall" or "implicit" pattern or Scriptural precedent and a "formall" or "explicite" pattern. This was Bedford's language, developed at length in his *Treatise*, pp. 184 ff. Again, Blake never made such a distinction.

4. Bedford made a great deal of the notion that the Spirit was a hyperphysical or metaphysical or supernatural agent in baptism. See his *Treatise,* p. 192, and *Vindiciae,* p. 50. This language was also prominent in *A Moderate Answer,* p. 4. Therefore I have felt free to use quotations from *A Moderate Answer* to illustrate Bedford's doctrine, though in almost every instance I also add references to his other works.

BIBLIOGRAPHICAL ESSAY

Although Puritan sacramental doctrine has been virtually ignored, there are several studies that help to illuminate it. The indispensable study of continental Reformed sacramental doctrine is Walter Koehler, *Zwingli und Luther: Ihr Streit über das Abendmahl nach seinen politischen und religiösen Beziehungen,* 2 vols. (Leipzig: M. Heinsius Nachfolger, 1924–53). Wilhelm Niesel, *Calvin's Lehre vom Abendmahl* (München: Chr. Kaiser Verlag, 1935), emphasizes Calvin's stronger statements about the Lord's Supper. Hans Grass, *Die Abendmahlslehre bei Luther und Calvin* (Gütersloh: C. Bertelsmann Verlag, 1954), isolates some important ambiguities in Calvin's doctrine. Ronald S. Wallace, *Calvin's Doctrine of the Word and Sacrament* (Edinburgh: Oliver and Boyd, 1953), is the best study in English.

Alting von Geusau, *Die Lehre von der Kindertaufe bei Calvin* (Bilthoven: H. Nelissen, 1963), is a lucid exposition of the tensions in Calvin's baptismal doctrine. Shorter studies that reach similar conclusions are: Egil Grislis, "Calvin's Doctrine of Baptism," *Church History* 31 (1962) : 46–65, and Jean D. Benoit, "Calvin et le Baptême des Enfants," *Revue d' Histoire et de Philosophie religieuses* (Strassbourg: Bureau de la Revue, 1937). Francois Wendel, *Calvin: The Origins and Development of his Religious Thought,* trans. Philip Mairet (New York: Harper and Row, 1963) treats sacramental doctrine in the wider context of Calvin's theology. E. David Willis, *Calvin's Catholic Christology* (Leiden: E. J. Brill, 1966) clarifies the debate over the *finitum non capax infiniti* in Reformed historiography.

To supplement Koehler's description of Zwingli's views, one should see especially Jacques Courvoisier, *Zwingli: A Reformed Theologian* (Richmond: John Knox Press, 1963), and Julius Schweizer, *Reformierte Abendmahlsgestaltung in der Schau Zwingli's* (Basel: Verlag Friedrick Reinhardt, 1953), who both emphasize the corporate character of

Zwinglian sacramental doctrine and worship. Helmut Gollwitzer offers a discerning interpretation of Zwingli's presuppositions in "Zur Auslegung von Joh. 6 Bei Luther and Zwingli," *In Memoriam Ernst Lohmeyer*, ed. Walter Schmauch (Stuttgart: Evangelisches Verlagswerk, 1951). For continental Anabaptist sacramental doctrine, see Rollin Stely Armour, *Anabaptist Baptism: A Representative Study* (Scottdale, Pa.: Herald Press, 1966). B. A. Gerrish, "The Lord's Supper in the Reformed Confessions," *Theology Today* 23 (April, 1966) : 224–243, studies the notion of instrumentality in sacramental doctrine.

William A. Clebsch, *England's Earliest Protestants 1520–1535* (New Haven: Yale University Press, 1964), stresses the influence of Protestant theological and sacramental ideas in England prior to Henry's break with Rome. C. W. Dugmore, *The Mass and the English Reformers* (London: Macmillan and Co., 1958), minimizes that influence and emphasizes the Augustinian and medieval background of English sacramental theology. August Lang, *Puritanismus and Pietismus: Studien zu ihrer Entwicklung von M. Butzer bis zum Methodismus* (Buchhandlung des Erziehungsvereins Neukirchen Kreis Moers, 1941) clarifies some relationships between English Puritanism and continental Reformed theologians.

Much of the literature on the sacramental doctrine of the English Reformation has focused on Thomas Cranmer, because of his influence on the Anglican liturgical and doctrinal standards. Gregory Dix, *The Shape of the Liturgy* (London: Adam and Charles Black, 1945), maintained that Cranmer was a Zwinglian. He was challenged by G. B. Timms, "Cranmer Dixit," *Church Quarterly Review* (January–April, 1947), pp. 214 ff., 33 ff. C. C. Richardson, *Zwingli and Cranmer on the Eucharist* (Evanston: Seabury Western Theological Seminary, 1949), modified and refined, but nevertheless accepted, the general view of Dix. But more recently, Joseph C. McLelland, *The Visible Words of God: An Exposition of the Sacramental Theology of Peter Martyr Vermigli* (Edinburgh: Oliver and Boyd, 1957), has demonstrated that by 1549, Martyr, Calvin, Bullinger, and Bucer shared sacramental views that were "practically identical," and that Cranmer was influenced by this Reformed consensus. Peter Brooks wrote *Thomas Cranmer's Doctrine of the Eucharist: An Essay in Historical Development* (New York: Seabury Press, 1965), to document Cranmer's alleged "Lutheran period," but he also emphasized the broadly Reformed tenor of his mature thought and claimed that Zwinglianism was an "outmoded and unhistorical term" by the middle of the sixteenth century. The debate is summarized in detail in J. I. Packer's introduction to *The Work of Thomas Cranmer* (Appleford, Berkshire: G. E. Duffield, 1964). He notes the Reformed heritage of Cranmer's thought, while at the same time emphasizing his individuality.

The best introductions to early English Puritanism are Patrick Collinson, *The Elizabethan Puritan Movement* (Berkeley: University of California Press, 1967), and M. M. Knappen, *Tudor Puritanism: A Chapter in the History of Idealism* (Chicago: University of Chicago Press, 1939). Knappen notes the Reformed influence on early Puritan sacramental doctrine. Charles and Katherine George, *The Protestant Mind of the English Reformation 1570–1640* (Princeton: Princeton University Press, 1961) deny that there was a distinctive Puritan movement. John F. H. New, *Anglican and Puritan: the Basis of their Opposition, 1558–1640* (Stanford: Stanford University Press, 1964), disagrees, distinguishing "Puritans" from "Anglicans" on doctrinal and other grounds, but suggesting that their sacramental views differed more in emphasis than in substance. G. W. Bromiley, *Baptism and the Anglican Reformers* (London: Lutterworth Press, 1953), reinforces my belief that differences between the Puritans and their opponents over baptismal efficacy were largely differences of emphasis, though I have not in my study attempted to make systematic comparisons. David Little, *Religion, Order, and Law: A Study in Pre-Revolutionary England* (New York: Harper and Row, 1969), argues that Puritans and their opponents held differing conceptions of ecclesiastical order and, implicitly, of social order. Alan Simpson, *Puritanism in Old and New England* (Chicago: University of Chicago Press, 1955), has influenced my emphasis on conversion in defining Puritanism. William Haller, *The Rise of Puritanism* (New York: Columbia University Press, 1938), examines the preachers of the "spiritual brotherhood," though without discussing sacramental doctrine. Leonard Trinterud, ed., *Elizabethan Puritanism: A Library of Protestant Thought* (New York: Oxford University Press, 1971), examines the humanist antecedents of Puritan thought.

Geoffrey Nuttall, *The Holy Spirit in Puritan Faith and Experience* (Oxford: Basil Blackwell, 1946), finds the seeds of Quakerism in early Puritan doctrine and traces a growing indifference to sacraments within one stream of Puritanism. James Fulton Maclear, " 'The Heart of New England Rent': The Mystical Element in Early Puritan History," *Mississippi Valley Historical Review* 42 (March, 1956) : 621–652, finds similar tendencies among the early New England Puritans. Those tendencies were pronounced among the early Separatists: see Stephen Mayor, "The Lord's Supper in the Teaching of the Separatists," *CHST* 19 (1963) : 212–221. Especially illuminating is B. R. White, *The English Separatist Tradition From the Marian Martyrs to the*

Pilgrim Fathers (Oxford: Oxford University Press, 1971). Also important is Leland H. Carlson's introduction to *The Writings of Henry Barrow 1587–1590* (London: Allen and Unwin, 1962), and sections of Geoffrey F. Nuttall, *Visible Saints: The Congregational Way* (Oxford: Basil Blackwell, 1957). Donald J. McGinn, *John Penry and the Marprelate Controversy* (New Brunswick: Rutgers University Press, 1966), shows the importance of baptismal issues in the Separatist break with the Church of England. Frederick J. Powicke, *Henry Barrow, Separatist (1550?–1593) and the Exiled Church of Amsterdam (1593–1622)* (London: J. Clarke and Co., 1900), stresses Separatist confusion about baptism, but argues that Barrow held a Calvinist doctrine of the Lord's Supper.

Leonard Trinterud, "The Origins of Puritanism," *Church History* 20 (1951) : 37–57, and Jens G. Moeller, "The Beginnings of Puritan Covenant Theology," *The Journal of Ecclesiastical History* 19 (April, 1963) : 46–67, describe the early development of covenant doctrine in England. C. J. Sommerville, "Conversion *Versus* the Early Puritan Covenant of Grace," *The Journal of Presbyterian History* 44 (June 1965) : 178–97, notes the sacramental significance of the development. John von Rohr, "Covenant and Assurance in Early English Puritanism," *Church History* 34 (June, 1965) : 195–203, describes Puritan speculation on the absolute and conditional dimensions of the covenant. Champlin Burrage, *The Church Covenant Idea: Its Origin and its Development* (Philadelphia: American Baptist Publication Society, 1904), examines the relationships between covenantal thinking and church polity. Burrage's, *The Early English Dissenters in the Light of Recent Research 1550–1640*, 2 vols. (Cambridge: Cambridge University Press, 1912), contains valuable information about the early Separatists and non-separating Congregationalists.

Until recently there has been little effort to describe the sacramental doctrine of the Puritan "spiritual preachers" of the seventeenth century. Horton Davies, *The Worship of the English Puritans* (London: Dacre Press, 1948), describes Puritan attitudes toward liturgy and ceremony. Perkins is discussed by Louis B. Wright, "William Perkins: Elizabethan Apostle of 'Practical Divinity,'" *The Huntington Library Quarterly* 3 (1939–40): 171–97. Norman Pettit, *The Heart Prepared* (New Haven: Yale University Press, 1966), was one of the first scholars to stress the importance of sacramental theology for the Puritans, though I disagree with his interpretations. Stephen Mayor's, *The Lord's Supper in Early English Dissent* (London: Epworth Press, 1972) offers precise and accurate textual analysis of sacramental material.

The baptismal doctrine of Burges, Ward, and Bedford—and its significance—has been ignored. William Goode, *The Doctrine of the Church of England as to the Effects of Baptism in the Case of Infants* (New York: Stanford and Swords, 1850), briefly mentioned Ward's ideas. Morris Fuller, *The Life Letters and Writings of John Davenant, D. D.* (London: Methuen and Co., 1897), reprinted correspondence between Ward and Davenant. Baxter's doctrine is discussed in Geoffrey Nuttall, *Richard Baxter* (London: Thomas Nelson and Sons, 1965); F. J. Powicke, *A Life of the Reverend Richard Baxter 1615–1691* (New York: Houghton Mifflin Co., 1924); and Irwonwy Morgan, *The Nonconformity of Richard Baxter* (London: Epworth Press, 1946).

The English Puritan debate over the Lord's Supper has also received insufficient attention. Wilfred W. Biggs, "The Controversy concerning Free Admission to the Lord's Supper, 1652–1660," *CHST* 16 (July, 1951) : 178–189, perceptively discussed the debates subsequent to 1652. William A. Lamont, *Marginal Prynne 1600–1669* (London: Routledge and Kegan Paul, 1963) offers a persuasive interpretation of Prynne's sacramental writings. One should also consult Lamont, *Godly Rule: Politics and Religion, 1603–1660* (London: Macmillan and Co., 1969). Stephen Mayor, "The Teaching of John Owen Concerning the Lord's Supper," *The Scottish Journal of Theology* 18 (June, 1965) : 170–81, accurately describes Owen's thought, but tends to evaluate him from the point of view of the " 'Catholic' tradition." John Williamson Nevin, *The Mystical Presence* (Philadelphia: P. P. Lippincott and Co., 1846), recognized the forceful character of Owen's doctrine. Relevant material on Puritan piety can be found in Gordon Stevens Wakefield, *Puritan Devotion* (London: Epworth Press, 1957), while J. Paul Hunter, *The Reluctant Pilgrim* (Baltimore: Johns Hopkins Press, 1966), illuminates the English Puritan practice of "spiritualizing the creatures," as does Louis L. Martz, *The Poetry of Meditation: A Study in English Religious Literature of the Seventeenth Century* (New Haven: Yale University Press, 1954).

For Puritan theology in England and New England, Perry Miller, *The New England Mind: The Seventeenth Century* (Cambridge: Harvard University Press, 1939), is still the one indispensable study, despite subsequent reevaluations of many of Miller's conclusions. Miller, *Orthodoxy in Massachusetts 1630–1650* (Cambridge: Harvard University Press, 1933), reaffirmed the distinction, made earlier by such scholars as Champlin Burrage, between the non-separating Congregationalism of Massachusetts Bay and the Separatist tradition. The sharpness of the distinction has been challenged by Larzer Ziff, "The Salem Puritans in the 'Free Aire of a New World,' " *Huntington Library Quarterly* 20 (1956–57) : 373–83, and by Darrett B. Rutman, *Winthrop's*

Boston: Portrait of a Puritan Town 1630–1649 (Chapel Hill: University of North Carolina Press, 1965). Some of Ziff's evidence has been evaluated more fully by David Hall, "John Cotton's Letter to Samuel Skelton," *William and Mary Quarterly,* 3rd ser., 22 (July, 1965) : 478–85. See also Ziff's biography of Cotton, *The Career of John Cotton: Puritanism and the American Experience* (Princeton: Princeton University Press, 1962), and especially David D. Hall, *The Faithful Shepherd: A History of the New England Ministry in the Seventeenth Century* (Chapel Hill, N.C.: University of North Carolina Press, 1972), which contains a brilliant description and interpretation of early Puritan development in New England.

In "The Puritan Theory of the Sacraments in Seventeenth Century New England," *The Catholic Historical Review* 22 (January, 1937) : 409–25, Miller suggested, wrongly I think, that that the New England Puritans implicitly affirmed a doctrine of baptismal efficacy without intending to do so. Pettit, *The Heart Prepared,* discussed baptismal doctrine in New England, although I also disagree with his interpretations. There are some helpful insights in David Lewis Beebe, "The Seals of the Covenant: The Doctrine and Place of the Sacraments and Censures in the New England Puritan Theology Underlying the Cambridge Platform of 1648" (Th.D. diss., Pacific School of Theology, 1966). Everett H. Emerson, *John Cotton* (New York: Twayne Publishers, 1965), incorrectly assumed that Cotton believed baptism to be the "means by which children come to be admitted to fellowship in the Covenant of Grace"; Cotton actually believed that the sacrament simply sealed a pre-existing covenant relationship. Emerson did observe the ambivalence in Cotton's discussion of baptism and the covenant, though he described it as a flat "inconsistency." William K. B. Stoever, "The Covenant of Works in Puritan Theology: The Antinomian Crisis in New England" (Ph.D. diss., Yale University, 1970), offered a careful and discerning analysis of technical Puritan theology. Edmund Morgan, *Visible Saints: The History of a Puritan Idea* (Ithaca: Cornell University Press, 1963), clarified an ecclesiastical issue with important sacramental implications and also reinterpreted the Half-Way Synod of 1662.

In "The Half-Way Covenant," *New England Quarterly* 6 (1933) : 675–715, Perry Miller described the 1662 synod as a sign that the Puritans had failed to achieve an impossible ideal. In *The New England Mind: From Colony to Province* (Cambridge: Harvard University Press, 1953), he interpreted the synod in the setting of Puritan perceptions of their religious declension, though Miller did not accept at face value all the protestations of failure in the Puritan jeremiads.

Miller also described the baptismal piety of the second generation of ministers. E. S. Morgan called for a thorough reevaluation of the notion of religious decline in "New England Puritanism: Another Approach," *William and Mary Quarterly*, 3rd ser., 18 (April, 1961) : 237–42. He was challenged by Darrett B. Rutman, "God's Bridge Falling Down: 'Another Approach to New England Puritanism' Assayed," *William and Mary Quarterly*, 3rd scr., 19 (1962) : 408–21. But Robert G. Pope, *The Half-Way Covenant: Church Membership in Puritan New England* (Princeton: Princeton University Press, 1969), has offered some evidence for Morgan's suggestion. My interpretation of the communion manuals in New England coincides with Pope's institutional analysis. Bernard Bailyn, *The New England Merchants in the Seventeenth Century* (New York: Harper and Row, 1955), is also relevant to the discussion of ecclesiastical declension, as is William McLoughlin, *New England Dissent 1630–1833*, 2 vols. (Cambridge: Harvard University Press, 1971).

The leader of the opposition to the Synod can be studied in Isabel Calder, ed., *Letters of John Davenport: Puritan Divine* (New Haven, Yale University Press, 1937). Kenneth B. Murdock studied another opponent of the Synod: *Increase Mather: The Foremost American Puritan* (Cambridge: Harvard University Press, 1925). Murdock did not analyze Mather's theology in any detail. There are no modern published monographs on Charles Chauncy. A. H. Newman, *A History of the Baptist Churches in the United States* (New York: The Christian Literature Co., 1894), argued that Chauncy became a Baptist at Scituate. Chauncy's letter to Davenport (see chapter five) provides substantial evidence against that supposition. The documents reprinted by Samuel Deane, *History of Scituate, Massachusetts* (Boston: James Loring, 1831), also contain no references to Chauncy's alleged Anabaptism, even though they are filled with charges against Chauncy. S. E. Morison, *Harvard College in the Seventeenth Century* (Cambridge: Harvard University Press, 1936), pp. 320 ff., has further information on Chauncy's career. The synodical documents are reprinted, with valuable commentary, in Williston Walker, *Creeds and Platforms of Congregationalism*, with an Introduction by Douglas Horton (Boston: Pilgrim Press, 1960).

Two exceptional studies have clarified the nature of social and intellectual change in late seventeenth-century New England: David Hall, *The Faithful Shepherd: A History of the New England Ministry in the Seventeenth Century*, and Robert Middlekauff, *The Mathers: Three Generations of Puritan Intellectuals 1596–1728* (New York: Oxford University Press, 1971). E. S. Morgan, *The Puritan Family*, 2nd rev. ed. (New York: Harper and Row, 1966), described the Puritan confidence in the salvific efficacy of the covenant in late seventeenth century New England. Ernest B. Lowrie, "A Compleat Body of Puritan Divinity: An Exposition of Samuel Willard's Systematic Theology (Ph.D. diss., Yale University, 1971), is the best analysis of Willard's theology. Institutional and social changes receive attention in Richard L. Bushman, *From Puritan to Yankee* (Cambridge: Harvard University Press, 1967), and Richard S. Dunn, *Puritans and Yankees: The Winthrop Dynasty of New England 1630–1717* (Princeton: Princeton University Press, 1962). On changing Puritan attitudes toward visible symbols, see Allan I. Ludwig, *Graven Images: New England Stonecarving and its Symbols, 1650–1815* (Middletown, Ct.: Wesleyan University Press, 1966). For changing conceptions of typology, one should consult the essays in Sacvan Bercovitch, ed., *Typology and Early American Literature* (Amherst: University of Massachusetts Press, 1972), especially the pieces by Mason Lowance, Jr. and Karl Keller. Eugene E. White, *Puritan Rhetoric: The Issue of Emotion in Religion* (Carbondale: Southern Illinois University Press, 1972), examines Puritan reflection on reason and emotions.

Perry Miller wrote a study of "Solomon Stoddard, 1643–1729," *Harvard Theological Review* 34 (October, 1941) : 277–320. He asked the question: "What intellectual sources contributed to Stoddard's thinking, or did he evolve his ideas merely out of the New England background?" Miller tended to interpret Stoddardeanism as a response to the colonial frontier. He also discussed Stoddard in *From Colony to Province*. Miller's interpretation was challenged by James P. Walsh, "Solomon Stoddard's Open Communion: A Reexamination," *New England Quarterly* 43 (March, 1970) : 97–114. But neither Miller nor Walsh examined the intellectual sources of Stoddard's doctrine. Frank H. Foster, *A Genetic History of the New England Theology* (Chicago: University of Chicago Press, 1907), argued that Stoddard held a low view of the sacrament. Stoddard's view of conversion was treated by Thomas A. Schafer, "Solomon Stoddard and the Theology of the Revival," *A Miscellany of American Christianity: Essays in Honor of H. Shelton Smith*, edited by Stuard C. Henry (Durham: Duke University Press, 1963). See also Paul Lucas, " 'An Appeal to the Learned': The Mind of Solomon Stoddard," *William and Mary Quarterly*, 3rd, ser. 30 (April, 1973) : 257–92.

There has been a tendency to interpret Edward Taylor's theology as somehow standing outside the Reformed consensus. Willie T. Weathers found Taylor to be more Platonic than Calvinist at important points in "Edward Taylor and the Cambridge Platonists," *American Litera-*

ture 26 (March, 1954) : 1–31. Sidney Lind, "Edward Taylor: A Revaluation," *New England Quarterly* 21 (December, 1948) : 518–30, reached similar conclusions. Mindele Black, "Edward Taylor: Heavens Sugar Cake," *New England Quarterly* 24 (1956) : 159–81, said that his writings on the Lord's Supper were far more Catholic in tone than Willard's "sensuous but still scriptural prose." Herbert Blau, "Heaven's Sugar Cake: Theology and Imagery in the Poetry of Edward Taylor," *New England Quarterly* 26 (1953) : 337–60, on the other hand, thought that Taylor did not even "believe that Christ was present at the communion in his spiritual nature," and that his "celebration of the sacrament" was "motivated by nothing except an intense feeling for the ritual."

Taylor's orthodoxy, sacramental and otherwise, is established in Donald E. Stanford, "Edward Taylor and the Lord's Supper," *American Literature* 27 (1955) : 172–78, Thomas H. Johnson, "Edward Taylor: A Puritan 'Sacred Poet,' " *New England Quarterly* 10 (1937) : 290–322, and Norman S. Grabo, "Edward Taylor on the Lord's Supper," *Boston Public Library Quarterly* 12 (1960) : 22–36. Grabo, however, argues that the structure of Taylor's meditations was influenced by an older tradition in "Catholic Tradition, Puritan Literature, and Edward Taylor," *Papers of the Michigan Academy of Science, Arts, and Letters* 45 (1960) : 395–402. The most recent biographies are: Norman S. Grabo, *Edward Taylor* (New York: Twayne Publishers, Inc., 1961), and Donald Stanford, *Edward Taylor* (Minneapolis: University of Minnesota Press, 1965). Kenneth B. Murdock, *Literature and Theology in Colonial New England* (New York: Harper and Row, 1949), also discusses Taylor's sacramental doctrine.

Unpublished Manuscripts

The American Antiquarian Society possesses the manuscripts of "Sacramental Sermons, 1648," written by Thomas Shepard, and also a sermon by Shepard entitled "Scripture Grounds Tending to Prove the Baptizing of the Seed of Believers." Shepard's "Diary" is in the New York Public Library. John Davenport began his polemic against innovation in "An Essay for the Investigation of the Truth," which I have not been able to locate, but to which he alluded in his printed criticism of the synod, as well as in "A Vindication of the Treatise Entituled Another Essay for the Investigation of the Truth, printed in the yeare 1663 it being a Reply to a Defence of the Answer and Arguments of the Synod met at Boston" and "The Third Essay in Defense of the Synods Booke." These manuscripts, written in 1664

and 1665, are also in the possession of the American Antiquarian Society, as is Davenport's "Answer to the 21 Questions" propounded by
the Connecticut General Court on the issue of baptism in 1656 and
his "Reply to the 7 Propositions Concluded by the Synod, Sitting at
Boston, June 10, 1662."

Correspondence between Davenport and Chauncy can be found in
the Prince Library, the Cotton Papers, Boston Public Library. That
library also provides access to positive microfilms of sermons and manuscripts written by Edward Taylor and pertaining to the Stoddardean
controversy. These are described by Norman Grabo, ed., *Edward Taylor's Treatise Concerning the Lord's Supper* (East Lansing, Michigan,
1966).

INDEX